In the Shadow of the Dragon

The Global Expansion of Chinese Companies—
How It Will Change Business Forever

WINTER NIE AND WILLIAM DOWELL
WITH ABRAHAM LU

AMACOM AMERICAN MANAGEMENT ASSOCIATION
New York ◆ Atlanta ◆ Brussels ◆ Chicago ◆ Mexico City
San Francisco ◆ Shanghai ◆ Tokyo ◆ Toronto ◆ Washington, D.C.

Library of Congress Cataloging-in-Publication Data

Nie, Winter.
In the shadow of the dragon : the global expansion of Chinese companies—and how it will change business forever / Winter Nie and William Dowell ; with Abraham Lu.
     p. cm.
Includes bibliographical references and index.
ISBN-13:978-0-8144-3170-2
ISBN-10: 0-8144-3170-4
1. Business enterprises—China. 2. Entrepreneurship—China. 3. Globalization—China. I. Dowell, William. II. Lu, Abraham. III. Title.
HD4318.N54 2012
338.60951—dc23

                                                                        2011046525

American Management Association (www.amanet.org) is a world leader in talent development, advancing the skills of individuals to drive business success. Our mission is to support the goals of individuals and organizations through a complete range of products and services, including classroom and virtual seminars, webcasts, webinars, podcasts, conferences, corporate and government solutions, business books and research. AMA's approach to improving performance combines experiential learning—learning through doing—with opportunities for ongoing professional growth at every step of one's career journey.

Printing number
10 9 8 7 6 5 4 3 2 1

To James and Aspen Wang
and
Toni and Charles Lubrecht

CONTENTS

PREFACE

Knowing others is intelligence; knowing oneself is true wisdom. Mastering others is strength; mastering oneself is true power. —Lao Tsu

Napoleon Bonaparte's famous prophecy that "When China awakens, the world will tremble" has not fully come to pass yet, but it is clearly on the horizon. *The Economist* recently noted that although China is now the world's second economy, its share in global business investment is still only around 6 percent, and most of that is in wealthy countries, and to a large extent in the United States. In contrast, Great Britain accounted for more than 50 percent of overseas investment in 1914, and the United States accounted for a larger share than that in 1967. Whether or not it eventually surpasses the United States as the world's next leading power, China is already having an important impact in the international world on everything from business to employment.

Anyone who doubts China's importance only has to look at the figures. China's population is more than four times the size of the population of the United States, and China has already absorbed a large share of the world's low-cost manufacturing, ranging from consumer electronics to textiles, plastics, shoes, clothing, and bicycles. The affordable prices of the goods that flood into the Walmarts, Costcos, and Best Buys of the world are made possible by the continuing willingness of Chinese workers to put in long hours at low pay. China's low-cost–high-productivity approach helped fuel a worldwide boom in consumerism without creating runaway inflation. The downside has been the loss of thousands of low-end manufacturing jobs in the United States and Europe. They are not likely to return.

Other countries have also provided cheap labor for routine manufacturing, but several important factors make China different. The enormous size of China's internal market and the density of the population in its cities make it possible for new business to obtain a critical mass much more quickly than in other countries. They also create fierce competition. Those companies that make it through the Darwinian struggle that is now taking place in China's private sector have streamlined themselves for maximum efficiency, and even more important, they've learned to respond to changing market conditions with impressive speed. The lesson emerging from China's turbulent marketplace is that profit margins are razor thin, competition is ruthless, and only the best and quickest can survive.

Cornering the lion's share of the world's basic manufacturing has given China an advantage when it comes to systems and infrastructure that makes it even harder for other countries to compete. Chinese ports can ship goods faster, cheaper, and more efficiently than any other emerging economy and more conveniently than many advanced economies. China's high-speed rail links and improvements in transportation and power generation mean that start-up companies can get support in China at a level that other countries have difficult matching.

The enormous scale of China as a manufacturing powerhouse has also given it considerable leverage when it comes to attaining access to new technologies developed by the leading industrialized countries. In early 2009, when the Chinese government put out bids to build its high-speed rail system, it forced foreign companies to enter into joint partnerships with Chinese companies. The foreign companies could have only a 49 percent equity stake and had to offer their latest designs. At least 70 percent of each system had to be made locally. Today, foreign multinationals still supply some of the most highly sophisticated equipment to China, but for rail transport, they account for only 15 to 20 percent of the market. Chinese companies have already mastered many of the core technologies.

The business relationships that China has created around the world make it easier for Chinese start-up companies to put together efficient supply chains and obtain needed resources, giving the Chinese advantages that competitors in other emerging economies simply don't have. While China still has a pressing need for highly qualified managers, it has been sending thousands of students to the world's best business schools for advanced training, and it is catching up fast.

Within China, the country's amazing growth rate is likely to be prolonged by the rapidly rising level of skill and education of its population and the readiness of recent graduates to work long hours to get ahead. It's possible to hire a college graduate in China for as little as $300 a month, and there are more and more of them. The United States, for example, currently graduates around 40,000 engineers a year. In contrast, China graduates 280,000—more than the rest of the world combined. And all of this is happening in a remarkably short period of time. In 1998, China had around 830,000 students studying in colleges. Today, it has more than 6 million, and the quality of the education being produced by these colleges is very good. It is no secret that China is rapidly moving in the direction of becoming a first-rate power in science and high technology, and some of its leading corporations, such as Huawei, are already there.

In areas like clean energy, China is already taking the lead. President Barack Obama had intended to make solar and wind power a major focus of U.S. investment in technology, but shortly after China began focusing on the market, most of the production had shifted to China.

China's vision of its place in the world is also evolving fast. Chinese companies that conquered China's domestic market a few years ago are now determined to go global and to compete internationally with established Western multinationals. These companies do not really have much choice. Pressure from price wars and intense competition inside China, as well as from the multinationals that gained access to China's internal market when China joined the World Trade Organization in 2001, is forcing China's major companies to expand internationally in order to keep growing.

Western companies that find themselves increasingly challenged by this new situation have the choice of competing head-on or of forming new alliances with Chinese partners. A growing number of these Western companies are being bought outright by Chinese investors. Understanding China's internal frame of reference, what the Chinese are trying to do and why, is increasingly critical to corporate survival.

While a flood of books have described the China phenomenon from a Western point of view, hardly any have been written from the perspective of how China sees the world and how this vision relates to what is actually happening on the ground inside China. This book examines several of China's top companies that are now beginning to create a presence outside China. Each of these companies is a dominant leader in a different segment of China's economy, whether it happens to be energy, electronics, low-cost production, financial services, sophisticated industrial equipment, or household appliances.

It is important for Western businesses to understand how and why these companies function the way they do. China's new entrepreneurs—particularly the ones that have grown up in the private sector following the Open Door Policy initiated by Deng Xiaoping in the late 1970s—are playing by rules that are radically different from the ones that Western corporations and multinationals are used to.

While strategies in the West tend to resemble a chess game, in which powerful pieces attack their target from various directions, the strategy adopted by many of China's new companies more closely resembles the oriental game of Go. In Go, the target is surrounded by pieces that have little strength as individuals but that eventually work together to envelop and lethally submerge the target. In Go, positioning and timing is everything. Mao Zedong used a similar strategy to defeat the Nationalists in China's civil war in the 1940s. He referred to it as "occupy the countryside and surround the cities."

How the West responds to China's emergence as an economic power will have a crucial impact on both international business and the current trend toward globalization. There is a natural tendency in the United States to see Western purchases abroad as investments. Yet when the Chinese try to secure reliable energy reserves or to buy up foreign companies in order to get access to technology, it is often treated as an invasion or a grab for power. But China today is not a monolith, and it is very different from the communist China of the 1950s and 1960s. The Chinese companies that are emerging today as the most competitive are those that have managed to survive in a harsh, free market environment, with little government support to help them get started. Many Chinese admit themselves that they still have a long way to go in terms of development, but they are learning fast.

What makes these companies unique is their extreme readiness to adapt to unforeseen situations, and in many cases to gamble the entire company on a single strategic decision. While major Western corporations have a tendency to diffuse responsibility by turning to committees to set strategies and make crucial decisions, the new Chinese entrepreneurs often act on instinct. The result is that they often close the deal before an unsuspecting multinational competitor can react. Few Western companies would be allowed to take the kind of risks that many of China's best entrepreneurs have engaged in, yet to survive, many Western multinationals may need to learn how to do just that in the future. This book explains why.

No Longer a Shrinking Violet

To be rich is glorious! —Attributed to Deng Xiaoping

XINHUA, CHINA'S GOVERNMENT news agency, used to be known more for what it neglected to say than for breaking news. Not anymore. In New York's Times Square, Xinhua's flashing logo now radiates from a 60-foot-high TV billboard just below a similar spot for Prudential Insurance and right above an ad for Korean TV manufacturer Samsung. The spot—which can be seen by roughly a half-million people every day—had previously been occupied by an ad for the bank HSBC (named for its founding member, the Hongkong and Shanghai Banking Corporation). While HSBC—which briefly moved its headquarters to London after China's takeover of Hong Kong in 1997 and then moved back again—was pondering a new round of layoffs in response to ongoing global financial insecurity, Xinhua was clearly on a roll. Similar display ads in the Times Square spot can cost up to $400,000 a month. Beijing, which previously had a reputation for staying demurely in the background, has discovered the value of building a global brand.

Not all of the new assertiveness from China is as in-your-face as a Time Square billboard. The news that Chinese investors were putting $750 million into a private equity investment fund, J. Rothschild Creat Partners, run by Lord Rothschild, attracted far less public attention, but it is characteristic of a new trend by China's private investors to buy foreign companies in order to operate under an established European name. The Rothschild family invested in China as far back as 1830, and a branch of the family that owns Chateau Lafite Rothschild has been developing vineyards in China. The motivation for the investment in vineyards is not hard to understand. A single bottle of Mouton Rothschild, the ultimate symbol of status for many newly successful Chinese, can easily sell for $2,000.

The Rothschild deal was only a minuscule event in a tsunami of Chinese global purchases. In the first six months of 2011, Chinese investors bought at least 176 publicly traded companies, at least six of them worth more than $1 billion. Many of these purchases were intended to secure access to energy and natural resources, but the Chinese were buying up service industries as well. Purchasing companies not only provides access to new technology—a practice that all companies engage in—but it also enables Chinese companies to sell their own products and services under established brand names that Westerners can recognize. In short, it increases the customer's comfort zone with respect to China's burgeoning global commerce.

Closing the Technology Gap

It should not come as a surprise that the country that invented paper, gunpowder, and civil service examinations should want to resume its natural role as one of the world's economic leaders. China clearly has the intellectual capacity to do so. In November 2010, for example, China announced that it had developed a supercomputer that was 40 percent faster than any other operating at the time. The Chinese model covered a third of an acre and incorporated some 20,000 smaller processing units operating in parallel. What impressed computer experts was the fact that the Chinese had developed some of the components without foreign help. (Six months later, a faster computer was developed by a Japanese computer center, and other supercomputers, many made in the United States, were expected to break the Chinese record as well.) Even more significant than its superfast computer, China launched the Sunway BlueLight MPP supercomputer in October 2011. The BlueLight is capable of making 1,000 trillion calculations, or one "petaflop," per second, placing it among the world's 20 fastest supercomputers. What makes the BlueLight special is the fact that the 8,700 ShenWei SW1600 microprocessors that drive it were designed at a computer institute in China and manufactured in Shanghai.

The bottom line is that China is no longer dependent on Western help to design complex technology. The BlueLight achievement was particularly impressive because only a decade ago, China had no supercomputers capable of competing with the top 500 of the world's fastest computers. Today, it has more than 60 in the top 500, which puts it in second place behind the United States, which has 255.

The design of ultrafast computers is only one area in which China is beginning to excel. At the same time that the United States decided to reduce funding for its space program, the Chinese have been stepping up their program for manned space exploration. Plans are in the pipeline for a Chinese-designed lunar rover and for a manned Chinese space station to be in operation toward the year 2020. True, the Chinese version will weigh only 60 tons, compared to 400 tons for the U.S.-Russian-European international space station that was already in orbit, but China is clearly staking out its claim to be a major competitor in sectors in which the West previously thought that it had a comfortable advantage.

Other Chinese efforts are more down to earth. Less than a decade ago, China's entire rail system was woefully inadequate. Today, China has more miles of high-speed rail lines than Europe, and despite the scandal over a July 2011 rail crash, it will soon have the most extensive network in the world. What is intriguing about that achievement is the fact that the Chinese were able to develop their rail network so quickly. Europe and Japan have been gradually developing their rail networks over the last 20 years. China was able to do it in a fraction of the time. The Chinese were able to obtain some of the core technologies by forcing foreign manufacturers into joint ventures that enabled the Chinese to learn trade secrets. The Japanese conglomerate Kawasaki was particularly annoyed by what it saw as Chinese attempts to profit from its technology. But the Chinese were also able to take the Japanese technology and move it to the next level, so that Chinese trains are much faster than those built by the Japanese. China's are now the world's fastest trains in regular commercial service.

Germany pioneered much of the development of ultra-high-speed magnetic levitation railways that use high-powered magnets to literally lift a train off the ground, virtually eliminating friction. Maglev trains can easily reach speeds up to 270 miles per hour. But today, the Maglev train that most businesspeople know and use is the connection from Shanghai's airport to the center of town—an 18.6-mile, 90-minute trip by taxi, which takes only seven minutes on Shanghai's Maglev. The Germans developed the concept, but hesitated about its economic viability. China took the idea, adapted it to its specific needs, and went ahead and invested the money needed to make it work in a real-life situation. And rail transport is not the only area where the Chinese are making strides through significant investments. Chinese rockets now launch American-made satellites into space for American companies, largely because the United States found that it had to cut back on spending for its own space program.

More and more, new ideas that are invented in the West need to be manufactured in China because the facilities to make them no longer exist in the West. For example, when French farmers tried to restart a high-quality wool industry with Merino sheep, they discovered that the only option for processing the wool was to send it to China. France no longer had any factories capable of processing the quantity that they needed.

Thanks to Western corporations having moved so much of their manufacturing to China, there is almost nothing that is being done in the West that cannot be done cheaper by someone, somewhere in China.

Welcome to Sanlitun Village

The gleaming new glass and steel complex in Beijing's Sanlitun district, which now calls itself "The Village," could easily be a swank shopping complex on New York's Fifth Avenue or in London, Paris, Dubai, or any number of modern global cities. The term village sounds odd in these luxury surroundings, but the irony is not accidental. China is, in a sense, redefining the way the world thinks of it, and Sanlitun Village is not just selling expensive luxury items: It is transmitting a powerful message to the outside world. The period of Western domination, which the Chinese refer to as the "Century of Humiliation," is drawing to a close, and Sanlitun is not a bad place to begin.

The Sanlitun district's center is nearly a mile. A "li," sometimes referred to as a "Chinese mile," is actually 0.5 kilometers. The distance is 1.5 km or 9/10ths of a mile from the Dongzhimen Gate, one of the original entrances to Beijing's ancient city walls. After China's revolution in 1949, Mao Zedong decided to close the old Foreign Legation area and move the foreign embassies that had been located there away from Beijing's center. Sanlitun became Beijing's new foreign enclave.

For the next several decades, while China looked inward and grappled for control of its own destiny, Sanlitun served as an uneasy meeting place between East and West. For a long time, the district had an unsavory reputation for seedy bars, Western-style restaurants, and marginally illicit activities. Then Deng Xiaoping changed everything in China, and in the process, Sanlitun also changed. Today, with Greater Beijing approaching the size of Belgium, Sanlitun no longer seems that far from the city center. Foreigners, treated with suspicion under Mao, are now surprisingly welcome. Beijing's buses and the new metro lines announce stops in both Chinese and English.

The Sanlitun Village shopping mall, which opened in 2008, is an example of China's new openness to the outside world. A gigantic plasma video screen, spanning an elegant stone plaza, broadcasts MTV-style music videos. A few feet away, shoppers scan the offerings of the world's largest Adidas sportswear store. Teenagers equipped with iPods casually stroll into a giant Apple computer showroom. LeSportsac, Fendi, Balenciaga, and Versace compete for the most elegant window displays, and a new multiplex offers the latest films. Smartly dressed toddlers laugh and play next to a futuristic fountain that sporadically spurts multiple jets of water into the air. At a corner of the plaza, a Starbucks coffee shop overflows with café lattés and cappuccinos. The Village, in short, has become a playground for Beijing's new upwardly mobile middle class.

Looking at the Western brand names, it would be easy to conclude that the former colonial powers are once again invading China, this time through consumer materialism. But in fact, the opposite is true. To a large extent, it is China that is conquering the world—at least the consumer world. The brands that have the crowds glued to the showrooms in Sanlitun may have Western names on their labels, but nearly everything offered for sale is made in China. The great multinational names that once dominated the world market are to a large extent converting themselves into repackagers and distributors of China's burgeoning industrial production. Most of these goods are produced in factories and workshops unknown to the public. The latest fashion accessories may have been designed in Paris or Italy, but it is more than likely that they were actually made in China. The Apple iPad is a prime example of the role China now plays in the consumer market. Although much of the world looks on this enormously successful tablet computer as a stroke of genius by a leading Silicon Valley company, the guts of the machine are assembled by Foxconn, an electronics manufacturer in Shenzhen, which until recently most of the world had not heard of.

Instead of signaling a Western invasion, Sanlitun boasts of China's growing dominance in the world economy and the Middle Kingdom's growing importance as the primary source of the world's consumer manufacturing. What Mao failed to accomplish through Marxism, China is managing to achieve today through its own form of "socialized" capitalism.

The average Westerner happening on Sanlitun Village might argue that much of the sophisticated technology there still comes from the West, but that notion is also fast becoming out of date.

China is evolving more quickly than even its most avid proponents expected.

China's feats in high technology are increasingly matched by its development and production of more mundane consumer goods. China's national entrepreneurs are no longer satisfied with simply implementing Western engineering. Given the growing competition from both Chinese manufacturers and the giant multinational corporations that gained access to the Chinese market when China joined the World Trade Organization in 2001, China's biggest corporations are going global. If they want to survive, they have no other choice. Western corporations that had hoped to be able to sell to 1.3 billion Chinese are suddenly discovering that the Chinese are beginning to challenge them on their own turf.

Problems with Speed

The road ahead is not likely to be a smooth one for either China's new entrepreneurs or the multinationals that will need to learn how to compete with them. The accelerated pace of development can create problems of its own. Success comes rapidly, but there is less time to identify and respond to the pitfalls. In a sense, the "village" is a metaphor. Traditional villages in both China and Europe developed by trial and error over centuries. As a result, the most serious mistakes were smoothed out and eliminated along the way. When development takes place at exponential speed, however, there is less time to assess what is likely to go wrong.

The surge in worker suicides at Foxconn in 2010, which made international headlines, is a case in point. Low pay and long working hours were clearly a cause of dissatisfaction, and the company moved quickly to improve salaries, but it is also clear that the company faced serious internal management problems that went beyond salary issues and created a working environment that employees ultimately found psychologically intolerable. The fallout not only threatened Foxconn's future but also had potentially serious repercussions for the brand image of its U.S. clients.

Western corporations have evolved management structures and employer-employee relations over the last century, often with painful periods of friction and miscalculations on both sides. The lessons learned from these experiences are now taught in MBA courses at leading business schools. The new Chinese private sector entrepreneurs have not been given time to absorb that accumulated knowledge. They have largely been forced to develop their operations relying mostly on intuition and with very little outside guidance.

Illusions About the China Market

International companies competing in China tend to blame their lack of increased market share on government rules that favor Chinese companies, particularly when it comes to government purchasing. But this is hardly different from the situation in the United States or Europe. Most governments give preference to their own companies. A more serious charge is that in order to get access to foreign technology, China enticed international companies with dreams of selling to 1.3 billion potential customers. Once it had the technology, it simply rebranded it and froze the foreign companies out.

Many Chinese CEOs admit openly that their strategy from the beginning was to learn from the West, master the technology, and then develop their own products that took the technology further. What makes these companies such formidable competitors is the fact that they grew up as independent entrepreneurs in a hostile environment that neither understood private enterprise in its early days nor supported it. To survive, these entrepreneurs had to understand their own markets and teach themselves how to grow a company without access to the financial cushioning and venture capital facilities that business can rely on in the West.

Finding Profit in Markets That the West Overlooked

Where China's new entrepreneurs excel is their readiness to plunge into markets and new technologies with a speed and flexibility that the giant multinationals find difficult to match. In many cases, Chinese companies have moved into markets that the major multinationals did not think worth the effort, and they have proved that these sectors can, in fact, be very profitable. Haier, a Chinese manufacturer of air conditioners and refrigerators, slipped into the U.S. market by selling compact refrigerators for dorm rooms, wine cellars, and other specialty uses—mostly through low-price chains like Costco, Best Buy, and Walmart. The big players in the field hadn't thought the sector worth bothering with. By the time they finally realized that Haier was beginning to cut into their market share, it was too late—Haier was already a player. When it looked as though Haier was about to buy cash-strapped Maytag in order to get control of a brand name that Americans were more likely to recognize, Whirlpool—the market leader—was forced to step in and pay more than analysts felt that Maytag was worth. Whirlpool's move was aimed far more at keeping Haier at bay than it was at gaining Maytag's assets. (This is discussed in further detail in Chapter 10.)

U.S. corporations are just beginning to discover that Chinese-manufactured products are not only less expensive than products made in the United States but of very good quality. The products of Chinese technology giant Huawei started off as low-cost alternatives to more costly Western telecommunications systems, but after the company spent heavily on R&D, it became a leader in advanced technology. In fact, AT&T and Sprint tried to award Huawei the contract to design a major part of the next-generation 4G telecommunications system in the United States. The only thing that stopped the deal from going through, in late 2011, was concern from the Pentagon that U.S. strategic interests might be damaged if the contract went to a company with strong ties to China's military. (This is discussed in Chapter 3.)

Intelligence and Flexibility at a Bargain Price

A highly educated workforce willing to work long hours at relatively low wages is an obvious advantage, but the most successful Chinese companies offer more than that. Chinese corporations frequently win major contracts not only because their products are cheaper but also because they can be delivered in a fraction of the time required by many of the large multinationals. Many European and American companies have lapsed into a "take it or leave it" approach, which leaves customers with requirements that may be only partially satisfied. In contrast, the best Chinese companies make a point of quickly adapting themselves to specific customer demands, often making alterations while equipment and systems are actually being used on a site, essentially doing their research and development on the fly. Often, this is because the company didn't have the funding to finance major R&D in advance, but the effect is to make these companies pay close attention to the specific needs of individual clients. The end result is that Chinese corporations are increasingly a force to be reckoned with in many of the high-value sectors that Western corporations cherish the most.

When President Barack Obama took office, he listed clean energy as a major potential source for new U.S. jobs, but Obama soon ran into resistance from conservative members of Congress. The delay opened the way for China to get a head start on what it saw as an important component in its future supply of energy. In 2010, the United States offered roughly $4 billion in grants to American companies developing clean energy, and it made available $16 billion in loan guarantees. In contrast, the China Development Corporation lent $35.4 billion to Chinese wind and solar companies and sank another $54 billion into Chinese equity and project debt for clean energy.

Only five years earlier, China had practically no significant experience in solar or wind energy, but by 2010, it was responsible for 58 percent of the world's production of solar cells and almost half of its wind turbines. A new wind turbine was going on line somewhere in the world every 30 minutes, and one out of three of them were manufactured in China. By 2010, China had doubled its wind capacity to 25.1 gigawatts (a gigawatt is equal to 1 billion watts). In contrast, U.S. wind power in 2010 added up to only 35 gigawatts. The difference is that while U.S. energy companies and conservatives in Congress pondered whether climate change should really be considered a threat, the Chinese were quietly planning to increase their wind power capability by up to ten times by 2020. The worldwide wind power industry currently employs around 600,000 people. That figure can be expected to increase dramatically in the future, and much of it will likely be in China.

Solar power is another technology that the West appears to be ceding to China. In March 2010, BP Solar—a pioneer with 37 years of experience in the solar field—announced that it was closing its solar panel manufacturing plant in Frederick, Maryland, and moving to China. Only three and a half years earlier, BP Solar had announced a $70 million plan to double the Maryland plant's capacity. Despite this, it said in 2010 that it would lay off 320 workers, leaving only a reduced staff of 100 employees to stay behind to work in research, sales, and project planning. BP Solar estimated that by moving to China, it could cut unit costs by up to 45 percent. The cost of manufacturing in China was so low in comparison to anywhere else that it seemed impractical to try to develop one's own technology. The former chairman of BP, Sir John Brown, once commented in an interview that if anyone could get a jump on controlling the energy of the future, it would be worth trillions of dollars. It looks very much as though those trillions are now likely to be Chinese.

The Downside of Exporting Manufacturing

The rush by Western multinationals to take advantage of the lower cost of human capital at all levels in China resulted in a tectonic shift in the global economy. Not too long ago, China manufactured 6 percent of the goods sold in the United States. Today, the figure is closer to 40 percent. While inexpensive Chinese labor has made Western distributors like Walmart and Costco extraordinarily wealthy, the broader impact is just beginning to become evident. Innovation tends to follow manufacturing. You have to be part of the process in order to know how to make the process better.

Once it became apparent that even the most advanced industrial economies could meet severe difficulties in an unrestrained global free market economy, the ardor for globalization began to cool. Former free marketers who suddenly realized that they might be losing in the exchange began to have second thoughts, and not surprisingly, their skepticism focused on China.

Learning Through Copying

Although Chinese companies unabashedly copied Western products when they were just getting started, China's entrepreneurs are fast moving past that stage into the next phase of their development. Their goal is to turn out products that are less expensive than the competition's—and also better.

Two powerful forces are driving the Chinese to try harder. The first is competition from inside China, which is increasingly moving up the value chain to find new customers in saturated market sectors. The second is competition from the foreign multinationals that gained access to the Chinese market under the terms of the World Trade Organization. Not long ago, foreign companies were interested in selling mainly to other foreigners operating in China, but these companies are now beginning to compete head-on with domestic Chinese companies in a fight for market share as China's domestic population begins to have more spendable income. According to *Forbes* magazine, China is already just behind the United States when it comes to number of billionaires, and the rate at which new billionaires join the list has been nearly doubling yearly with the exception of 2009, when 19 Chinese billionaires dropped off the list, and the list itself contracted by 30% due to the global financial crisis. The key advantage, though, is that the Chinese are simply endowed with a greater hunger for success than many Westerners, and they are ready to do whatever it takes to achieve it. The Chinese term that well describes this trait is *chi ku*, or to "eat the bitterness that life offers." The risk, of course, is that some companies will go too far and cut too many corners in order to get a competitive edge. Scandals over tainted milk and lead paint on exported children's toys, and the labor problems at Foxconn, all threaten to damage the image of Chinese products in international markets. As that danger is realized, controls are likely to be tightened. The bottom line, however, is that the Chinese are willing to make the extra effort and go the extra distance that is necessary to close a deal. That in itself makes them formidable competitors.

The Wenzhou Model

Nowhere is the competitive spirit more in evidence than Wenzhou, a manufacturing center roughly 300 miles south of Shanghai. Wenzhou is generally acknowledged as the birthplace of China's private sector economy. Today, it produces some 70 percent of the world's cigarette lighters and about half the world's cheap shoes, as well as much of its bra parts, plastic leather, and zippers. The population of the greater Wenzhou metropolitan area is estimated at 7.7 million, roughly equivalent to the population of New York City.

Wenzhou's claim to launching capitalism in China stems in part from the fact that the first official license to engage in private commerce was issued to a Wenzhou resident, Zhang Huamei, in November 1979. Zhang admits that she was already doing business, selling toys in front of her house, before it became legal. Today, more than 95 percent of Wenzhou's economy is in the private sector.

The city's reputation for spirited private enterprise is famous throughout China. Since the region was poor, many of its citizens left to try their luck in other parts of the country. They ultimately linked up with each other to establish a formidable business network and powerful commercial connections, based on social relationships already established back in Wenzhou. Estimates are that about 2 million former residents of Wenzhou are now strategically positioned across China, and another 500,000 are doing business in 70 countries around the world. Roughly 100,000 of them are in the United States.

Economic success has led to shopping malls in Wenzhou being stuffed with luxury goods. A Wenzhou company tried to take over Pierre Cardin, and another attempted to buy Michael Jackson's Neverland Ranch so that it could be dismantled and transported to Wenzhou. A new airport and opera house in Wenzhou were designed by Uruguayan architect Carlos Ott. Not surprisingly, sales of BMWs, Audis, Maseratis, and Porsches in Wenzhou increased substantially during the economic boom.

The flip side was that as the global economy began to slow substantially, many of the Wenzhou entrepreneurs found themselves strapped for cash. Many had borrowed from what is known as the "curb market"—a system of informal lending in which loan shark rates can range from 20 to 40 percent, depending on the number of intermediaries involved. For more than two decades, the importance of family honor, combined with the fear of social ostracism if a debt failed to be paid off, was enough to keep Wenzhou's curb market relatively dependable. But the interest rates were hard for businesses to sustain over a long period of time. Between April and November 2011, at least 90 small and medium enterprises (SMEs) in Wenzhou collapsed and went into bankruptcy. Alarmist news accounts, combined with the fact that Chinese banks were also tightening credit, increased the pressure on SMEs to find new credit. It wasn't the first time that Wenzhou had faced this kind of pressure, and it was a situation that China's financial institutions could easily reverse if they decided to do so.

Size Counts

While China's newly released entrepreneurial spirit is unquestionably an important factor in the country's success, China's immense size also helps. The United States became an industrial powerhouse largely because it had a huge, relatively homogenous population that provided both an enormous pool of talent and a unified market to finance the development of products that could eventually be peddled to the rest of the world. China is poised to match the U.S. model on steroids. It has nearly four times as many people from which to choose its best and brightest.

The global free market cuts both ways, of course. Coca-Cola currently dominates carbonated drink sales across the China market. Nokia, Cisco Systems, IBM, and others have also been extremely successful in the Chinese marketplace—not to mention McDonalds, Kentucky Fried Chicken, and Burger King. The bottom line is that China still promises significant profits to those companies that meet the specific demands of China's market.

How the rest of the world adapts to these challenges will to a large extent determine the future of the global free market economy. As China begins to connect with the outside world, it is emerging as a force that will eventually also need to be reckoned with in international affairs. It is time for a clear-minded reassessment of where

China is heading and a deeper look at the factors that have not only shaped China's thinking up to now but have also shaped Western perceptions of China.

Different Attitudes About China

Western attitudes toward China often seem schizophrenic. On the one hand, the United States and Europe often seem dazzled by China's immense potential as a market for Western goods and services. In a global market where competition is fierce, who can ignore 1.3 billion potential customers? The expectations are not far-fetched. For example, despite the high cost of Swiss watches—around $550 each—more than 40 percent of the roughly 26 million Swiss watches exported annually are bought in Asia.

On the other hand, China's sheer size and energy can appear threatening, not just to Westerners but to the Chinese as well. But the Chinese are looking at the situation from a very different perspective than that held by most people in the West. Thirty years of isolation, extreme poverty, and deprivation have created an enormous pent-up demand for a broad range of consumer products. While many Westerners focus on their leisure and quality time, most Chinese are now obsessed with catching up and getting ahead no matter what the cost. At the same time, most are intensely patriotic and proud of their recent achievements.

POLITICAL VIEWS WITHIN CHINA

While the West frets about political issues such as censorship on the Internet and freedom of expression, many Chinese see their current relative political stability and increased opportunity for advancement as welcome changes from the chaos of the past, which for many people is still a vivid memory. It is not that the Chinese do not care about politics or democracy—it is that for the time being, they care more about getting ahead, which translates as making money. If you ask most Chinese people about the turbulent recent past, they will respond by asking what profit they are likely to get from dwelling on the past. For most Chinese, reality is now, and the future looks promising. That is not to say that the Chinese do not care about human rights or government corruption. Public outrage was certainly sparked by scandals over infant deaths resulting from tainted milk and over buildings that collapsed because of faulty construction during the 2008 Sichuan earthquake. Internet bloggers have increasingly pressured for government reform, even at the price of facing jail terms. (The government is trying to control expression on the Internet and in the media, but it is questionable how successful it will be at shutting down dissent.)

Foreigners visiting Beijing today are often surprised at how outspoken the Chinese are on an individual basis. However, while it may be acceptable to make comments in a coffee shop, when the criticism goes out to the blogosphere over the Internet, those in power become visibly nervous. Instead of openly inciting authorities and upsetting the current period of relative freedom, many Chinese now seem to prefer evolution to revolution. They are going for incremental change within recognized limits that they expect to expand gradually. Above all, they want the changes to come from within China itself, not to be dictated by foreigners.

The Internet is emerging as a powerful tool both for communications and public expression, despite the government's efforts to control it. At least 400 million Chinese are currently connected to the Net. In place of shutting it down, various government organizations have tried to flood social networking sites on the Net with their own points of view. A recent military-sponsored blog, for instance, criticized the social networking site Twitter for helping to incite violent street demonstrations that followed Iran's 2009 presidential elections. As the blogger saw it, inflammatory comments on the Net simply made the task of running a stable administration all the more difficult, which seemed to the blogger to be an argument in favor of maintaining better control over public communications.

It is obvious that China's current views on politics are often at variance with the West's democratic ideals. But having experienced a century of colonization by the West, the Chinese also tend to view some of what they hear coming from the West with a certain degree of skepticism. One person's defender of democracy, in short, is likely to be another's political agitator and source of civil disorder.

Most young Chinese show more passion about getting on with life than engaging in politics. As long as the system offers jobs and a possibility of a promising future, they are content to deal with it. China, in short, is changing. There is considerable internal debate over its future, but most of the debate these days is about how to make the country more successful. For any Westerner hoping to understand the changes taking place, it is counterproductive to look at China's government as a static monolith rooted in the missteps and false directions of the past.

The West expects China to move in a straight direction, but the complexity of China's politics and culture often make survival for government leaders dependent on a path that is filled with twists and turns. What is clear is that a new generation is gradually moving into power with new ideas and new approaches. It makes sense for Westerners to judge China on its own merits rather than on its past.

THE EFFECT OF HISTORY

China's history with the United States over the last two centuries has been a roller coaster of changing attitudes. The first influx of Chinese immigrants into the United States occurred during the Gold Rush in the western United States in the late 1840s. Chinese adventurers who arrived to work in the mines referred to San Francisco as the "hills of gold." As competition in the gold fields increased, the Chinese gradually moved into small businesses, especially restaurants and laundries. Then came the first Transcontinental Railroad connecting the eastern United States to California. Leland Stanford, the railroad magnate, saw the Chinese as diligent workers and imported thousands of Chinese to work on the project. The sudden influx of Chinese coincided with massive immigration to the United States from Ireland, which had been stricken by the potato famine. Denis Kearney, a labor leader and populist originally from Ireland, saw the Chinese as eventual competitors for entry level jobs and decided to use the issue to build political support for his own Workingmen's Party. Kearney's argument, expressed in a vitriolic, racist campaign, was that the Chinese were prepared to work for wages low enough to make it impossible for anyone else to compete. Kearney's efforts and those of others like him eventually led to the Chinese Exclusion Act of 1882, which restricted Asian immigration into the United States until the 1965 Immigration Act.

For the most part, the West has tended to look at China as an ancient empire that never quite managed to adapt to the modern world. The fact is, however, that China, in its unique way, had been the equal and often considerably in advance of the West for centuries. As previously stated, the Chinese not only invented gunpowder and paper but also developed the first effective civil service system based on examinations. Their philosophers were the equals of any in the West, and when it comes to business, the Chinese were there at the start. For example, the round Chinese coins known as "cash," which have a hole in the center to enable them to be strung together, began to be used as early as 1200 BC. The English term "cash" is an evolution of the French word "caisse," or "money box," which dates back to 1590. (The word eventually referred to the money, or symbolic value of the tokens inside the box, rather than the box itself—a sophisticated concept that came into widespread use in the West a few centuries ago.) The word cash is virtually the same in Chinese and English, except that the Chinese were there at the beginning and have understood its meaning continuously ever since.

Where the Chinese unquestionably missed out in history was the industrial revolution that ushered in the modern age. Historian Mark Elvin, who has developed a theory called the High Level Equilibrium Trap, contends that China never experienced its own organic industrial revolution precisely because the agricultural and social systems that were already in place in China were so successful, and the workforce so plentiful, that there was no commercial incentive to turn to machinery to do the job.

China's lack of technology put the country at a disadvantage when it was eventually driven into armed confrontation with the West. Colonialist attempts to dismember China reached a high point in the 1850s, when the British forced the Chinese to open their doors to foreign merchants, including those selling opium, in order to offset the balance of payments deficit that had resulted from the English obsession with Chinese tea. The British were concerned that they were losing too much silver in payments for tea, and by inflaming a Chinese addiction to opium (which was easily obtained from their concessions in India) they could stop the outflow of hard currency to China.

The British-inspired Opium Wars of the mid-1800s forced China to cede Hong Kong as a Western trading port for the next century and a half. The military victories by the British and other Europeans over China, combined with the court intrigues of the Dowager Empress and the last Emperor, Pu Yi—who eventually became a pawn of the Japanese—reinforced the impression that China was weak and somewhat backward. Seen against the last 3,000 years of Chinese history, however, the late 19th and early 20th centuries looks like a brief, albeit troubled, intermission in a highly sophisticated civilization's relentless drive forward.

Globalization Flickers, Then Flames Out

In 1925, Chiang Kai-shek, a relatively young army general, replaced Sun Yat-Sen, the first leader of the post-imperial Republic of China. Chiang quickly drove out the Soviets who had tried to gain influence with Sun by providing funding and advice. The Soviets were mainly interested in their struggle with the Japanese over the territory to the north of China, which the Japanese insisted on calling Manchukuo, and which the Soviets wanted to annex to their own Siberia.

Until Japan occupied eastern China in 1937, China was relatively open to Western business as long as bribes were paid to the relevant officials. Many of the world's major corporations piled into China. They included Standard Oil, Bethlehem Steel, British American Tobacco, Siemens, and IBM. AIG, which was to become one of the world's leading insurance companies, was founded in Shanghai in 1919, and Coca-Cola entered the Chinese market for the first time in 1927.

Modern Chinese corporations also began to emerge during the 1930s. The top management was usually European or American. Meanwhile, new technical schools undertook the task of training a new class of Chinese industrialists. While some of these companies were successful, political power fragmented, and large parts of the country were left to the mercy of competing warlords, whose corruption resulted in unspeakable poverty and periodic starvation for much of the country's neglected rural population. The inability of the nationalists to deal with these problems fueled the rise of the communist party led by Mao Zedong. Mao dispatched troops to fight the Japanese occupation in World War II, but Chiang Kai-shek refused to commit his resources. He knew that the real struggle for power would follow the end of the war with the collapse of Western colonialism.

By 1949, Mao's forces had driven Chiang's Kuomintang Party from the mainland. China entered a period of isolation from the West, which lasted from the 1950s through the 1970s. While China grappled with trying to establish a viable political system, it was largely cut off from much of the technological revolution that was having an enormous impact on the rest of the world. As earlier emperors had found, isolation can exact a heavy price in terms of national survival. Napoleon Bonaparte had famously commented that China was a giant, but that it was a sleeping giant. By the start of the 21st century, it was clear that the giant had already started to awaken.

The New Silk Road

The breakthrough, liberating China's innate entrepreneurial spirit and opening the doors to the outside world, came in 1978, when a new generation of Chinese leaders under Deng Xiaoping began gradually nudging China from collectivism toward a market-oriented economy. To make certain that everyone was sure of the change of direction, Deng reportedly declared, "Poverty is not socialism. To be rich is glorious."

Deng's reforms had the effect of green-lighting a new generation of Chinese entrepreneurs and at the same time opening the doors to Western multinational corporations that wanted to do business in China. China increasingly provided battalions of inexpensive labor, effectively turning itself into a factory for the world, and it has had a seismic impact on much of the world's economy. The impact on China itself has been equally dramatic. At least 300 million in China—roughly equivalent to the population of the United States—have been boosted from poverty to middle class status. China's low-cost production has made thousands of types of goods available to markets that never could have afforded them before. Services have also been made more widely available. For example, the collaboration of Huawei, one of China's leading telecom network systems manufacturers, with France's Neuf SFR, a leading European competitor, have driven down prices for basic services in much of the West, making them affordable to the average consumer and not just a privileged class.

China's purchase of U.S. treasury bills has inextricably intertwined China's fate with that of the United States, linking their futures together and thus making both major powers more cautious and consequently more responsible in their approach to international politics.

Within China, the new openness to the rest of the world has brought a dramatic influx of new technologies and ideas about modern management. For some of the largest multinational corporations—General Electric, Microsoft, LVMH, and Cisco Systems—China looks as though it is delivering on its promise as the world's most exciting emerging market.

The experience of the last 30 years has shown, however, that both multinationals and China's homegrown entrepreneurs enter this new relationship with respective advantages. Established multinational corporations have thrived in China primarily in industries that depend heavily on developing new products and technologies and on brand management. Chinese-owned companies tend to be leaders in industries that depend heavily on low-cost labor and materials and that demand large production facilities and close connections with local political power structures.

Most analysts assume that Chinese companies will use their newly earned wealth to move up their respective industry's value chains in China where they have a "home-field" advantage. But we believe that the situation is likely to evolve with a much broader scope than the Chinese domestic market. Our research shows that Chinese-owned corporations are currently rewriting the rules for how an emerging market corporation adapts and operates in the 21st century. The experience of the first wave of emerging Chinese multinational corporations indicates that tomorrow's corporate giants will challenge the world's established multinationals in knowledge-intensive and technology-intensive businesses, and that they will strike in the West's home markets with extensive R&D and quick-learning and quick-strike capabilities.

Globalization Without Trust

The sheer scale of China's economic and political ascent in the 21st century makes it a formidable force. In the long run, Asia is likely to be the center of gravity for the world's economic expansion simply because it is already the center of gravity for the segment of the world's population whose needs are expanding the fastest. When Asia's share of global income reaches 54 percent in 2050, after it is expected to hit 49 percent in 2025, it will merely be returning to its historical past. In 1820, China and India represented roughly 56 percent of the global economy.[1]

The influence of China's 1.3 billion population is likely to be felt in global politics, much as the rise of the United States was in the 19th century and the rise of Germany and Japan were felt in the early 20th century. Even if China were to adopt a policy of isolationism as the United States did at various points in its history, the world would still feel the impact of China's rising standard of living. A billion people driving cars, for example, are likely to have an impact on the climate that the planet simply can't ignore. The competition for resources to meet the standard of living enjoyed in the West is also impossible to ignore. Although China has invested heavily in developing alternative energy, such as wind and solar power, it has no illusions about needing conventional fossil fuels and nuclear power to fulfill its needs. Estimates are that alternative energy will probably supply only 15 percent of the country's needs.

As a result, China is actively looking to international markets and foreign alliances to secure vital primary resources for the future.

This is where the CEOs of China's emerging multinationals come in. In 1979, at the beginning of the Open Door and Reform Policies, China's annual outflow of foreign direct investment (FDI) was virtually zero. The Chinese government continued to keep its outflow of FDI low throughout the 1990s largely because it feared an illegal flight of capital out of the country. Since China became a member of the World Trade Organization in 2001, the situation has changed dramatically. The government is now clearly willing to help Chinese companies become globally competitive.

Attracting FDI into China is the first stage of globalization for Chinese companies. Actually going global is step two, and this is now in full swing. The government has decentralized approvals for applications for overseas investments, and as a result, decisions are being made much faster at the local level. In addition, the Ministry of Commerce of the People's Republic of China (MOFCOM) has created a database on market opportunities as well as investment and tax law in foreign countries. The government is also providing subsidies, including easy access to low-interest loans and credit lines.

This important change in the direction of China's policy has already had a noticeable impact. From 2005 through 2006, China's outward FDI grew at a rate of 60 percent or more annually. In the first eight months of 2007, according to the latest figures from MOFCOM, the turnover of contracts for Chinese projects overseas amounted to $22.66 billion, an increase of 32.5 percent over the previous year. New contracts were worth $41.6 billion, an increase of 27.1 percent. To put matters into perspective, the China Develop - ment Bank Corporation alone had twice the assets of the World Bank. By the end of August 2007, at least 239,000 Chinese personnel were working overseas, an increase of 6,000 over the same period in 2006.

Brand building, often seen as a weakness of Chinese corporations, has begun to thrive. In the first eight months of 2007, the turnover of China's design and consultant services overseas amounted to $179 million, an increase of 2.8 percent. At least $404 million in new contracts were signed, an increase of 48 percent over 2006. By the end of 2007, the accumulated turnover in overseas design and consultant services amounted to $1.91 billion. Newly signed contracts reached $3.15 billion.

Chinese investors and public-private entities have clearly been spending money at a dizzying clip in a frantic effort to acquire the design know-how and technology needed to compete in a global marketplace.

The reactions to this burst of energy tend to run the full spectrum. Some observers in the United States hail China as a true champion of globalization. William Overholt, the Asia policy chair of the RAND Corporation, told the U.S.-China Economic and Security Review Commission in 2005 that China had managed to transform itself from an opponent of globalization to one of the United States's best partners in promoting liberal economic and democratic values and policies in Asia, Africa, and Latin America—in short, where China does business.

Others see these developments more darkly. A number of recently published books aggressively challenge China's motives. The titles range from *The Coming China Wars: Where They Will Be Fought and How They Can Be Won* to *Showdown: Why China Wants War with the United States* and *America's Coming War with China: A Collision over Taiwan.*

Regardless of how one interprets China's long-term objectives, it is clear that from a purely business point of view, the single greatest challenge for Chinese corporations seeking to expand overseas will be winning the trust of a public that is already experiencing misgivings about globalization and especially about China's role on the world stage. As the Chinese are learning quickly, corporate growth in the next few decades is likely to be as much about managing geopolitical risk and foreign policy considerations as it is about best practices in business.

Working Toward a New Model of International Relations

While we live in an increasingly interconnected global economy, it is one in which global societies remain sharply divided. The fierce global competition that has brought us to this point also threatens to tear us apart, and it is limited as a tool for problem solving. It is clear that we need a new model for international relations.

What appears to be a paradox can also be an opportunity. The rise of China, the threat posed by climate change, the ballooning world population, and the poverty that has trapped a billion people are powerful incentives to rethink global cooperation and existing power relationships. Cooperation between U.S., European, Japanese, Brazilian, Indian, African, and Chinese institutions will need to become the norm if we are to survive the seismic events that will characterize the 21st century.

The readiness of the United States to come to terms with China's increasing influence is critical to the shape that international affairs will take over the next decades. History so far has shown that bloodshed has often accompanied major shifts in the fortunes of the great powers. It remains to be seen whether the next few decades will see genuine progress toward greater international harmony and cooperation or a regression toward a potentially cataclysmic conflict.

Learning how to thrive despite these geopolitical challenges and being nimble enough to quickly understand and adapt oneself to differences in cultural perceptions are the qualities that distinguish a global multinational from a company that confines itself to a domestic market. Learning to adapt to this much more complex and potentially dangerous environment is the principal hurdle that China's successful privately owned national companies need to master as they contemplate the transition to multinational status. In the next chapters, we will look at how Chinese corporations, having achieved success in their own domestic markets, began making their first tentative steps toward asserting their place alongside the world's other leading multinationals in the profitable but dangerous waters of the global free market—and in the process, set about constructing what amounts to a new virtual Silk Road.

As we will show in the next chapters, the entry of China's new private-sector entrepreneurs on the world stage promises to be the most significant development in global business in the next few decades. At the same time, both these companies and their competitors have a steep learning curve and very little time to master it.

The multinationals that have dominated the world market for the last 50 years have largely defined the rules for global competition until now. Although they have competed with each other, they have generally played by the same rules in which size counts. The Chinese companies that are emerging as newcomers on the global scene are changing the rules of the game. They operate with a lean cost structure. They approach innovation differently. They do not have legacy systems to hold them back. They are very aware that they are going to have to operate differently if they want to catch up. They cannot compete on size, so they compete on speed, flexibility, and faster reactions than the competition. If size is the determining factor in Western countries, in China, speed is the new rule of the game.

NOTE

1. Angus Madison, *The World Economy: A Millennium Perspective* (Paris, France: Development Center of the Organization for Economic Cooperation and Development, 2001).

TWO

Coca-Cola, Huiyuan Juice, and CNOOC
Protectionism on Both Sides of the Pacific

He will win who knows when to fight and when not to fight.
—Sun Tzu, *The Art of War*

AS THE WORLD'S LEADING ECONOMIC giants, both the United States and China have a great deal to gain from a free market economy that allows their products to be sold in other countries. The passion for a free market diminishes considerably when it begins to look as though the free market is going to give a competing country a substantial foothold on your own territory. China saw Coca-Cola's attempts to buy one of its leading beverage providers as just such a threat. The U.S. was equally upset when China's National Offshore Oil Company, CNOOC, attempted to buy UNOCAL, a U.S. energy company that had fallen on hard times but still had access to substantial oil resources, even though most of these were in Asia.

Coca-Cola and Huiyuan Juice

Coca-Cola was one of the first multinational giants to enter the Chinese market, and it did so long before most other countries saw China as a promising opportunity. The soft drink that came to be known as Coke had started its career as a medicinal tonic invented in 1886 by a pharmacist, John Stith Pemberton. It was originally marketed as Pemberton's French Wine Cola and sold in drugstores for 5 cents a glass. Pemberton, who eventually became a morphine addict, sold the formula to several different people, including his own alcoholic son, Charlie. In 1892, Asa Candler, one of the purchasers of the original formula, beat off his competitors and founded the Coca-Cola Company. Two years later, the drink began to be sold in bottles. Sales accelerated when Fulton County and Atlanta, Georgia, where Coca-Cola was based, instituted their own prohibition laws against alcoholic beverages. Coke became the optimal replacement, and over the next century, the company grew into one of the world's largest producers of soft drinks and juices. The company eventually emerged as one of the world's most formidable multinational giants. Now, Coca-Cola's worldwide earnings exceed the wealth of many of the countries where it markets its products. Today, the company sells 500 different brands in 200 countries.

A LONG HISTORY OF COCA-COLA IN CHINA

Shortly after the end of World War I, Coca-Cola was selling soft drinks in China's major cities, and in 1927, it opened its first bottling plants in Tianjin and Shanghai. In 1948, Shanghai became the first location outside the United States to sell more than a million cases of Coke per year (ref: Enterprise China, http://enterprisechina.net/content/serving-coca-cola-shanghai). A year later, though, civil war forced Coca-Cola and other foreign companies to suspend operations in China.

As soon as Deng Xiaoping opened the door to foreign investment again in 1979, Coke was back, opening a bottling plant in Beijing in 1981. It now has 35 joint venture bottling plants across the country and controls slightly more than half of China's market for carbonated drinks. China is currently Coke's third most important market after the United States and Mexico, and it is very likely to become the company's leading market in the future. According to Coca-Cola's figures, consumption of Coca-Cola's many offerings in China soared from three 8-ounce cans or bottles per capita in 1998 to 28 in 2008. When you talk about a population of 1.3 billion people, that kind of growth in per capita sales attracts attention.

THE CHINESE JUICE MARKET

Impressive as Coca-Cola's results sounded, it wanted more. While overall soft drink sales in China have grown by 42 percent since 2004, the increase in sales of fruit juices have increased by 89 percent. It didn't take much to convince Coca-Cola that the juice business was the way to go. The dominant player in China's juice market is the Huiyuan Juice Group, and in September 2008, Coca-Cola offered $2.4 billion for the company. It promised to be the most expensive acquisition that Coca-Cola had ever made. At the time that Coca-Cola made its offer, Huiyuan controlled around 40 percent of China's market for non-concentrated juices. The company was launched in 1992 by Zhu Xinli, and its history is remarkable.

Zhu was the second son in a large farming family in a small village in Huiyuan county, in the northeastern coastal province of Shandong. His father was a follower of Confucius and named each of his sons after a Confucian ideal. Zhu's given names signify "new" and "appropriateness."

At the age of 36, Zhu studied economics at a local college and soon was put in charge of economic development for Huiyuan county. In 1992, he decided that he had had enough of working in administration and asked local authorities to let him take over one of the most troubled companies in the area. He got his wish and assumed control of a nearly bankrupt canning factory with 110 employees. Instead of despairing at the factory's plight, Zhu used his position to travel to Switzerland and Germany to see how food packaging was being handled in the world's most sophisticated markets. It didn't take him long to realize that he needed the latest technology to compete. Zhu made a list of the necessary equipment and estimated that it would cost around $10 million. Zhu's factory was already on the edge of bankruptcy and he didn't have the capital, so he talked a German company distributing fruit juice into providing it on the basis of a production-sharing agreement. The Germans would set up the operation and be paid in canned juice produced by the factory. The most important part of the deal was that the Germans agreed to set up the equipment in China. More than 200 German technicians flooded into the sleepy county for nearly six months to get the work done.

Zhu's second stroke of genius was to ask the Germans to keep a technician behind to guarantee quality control. The engineer's monthly salary added up to more than the combined annual salary of the factory's entire Chinese staff. Zhu was convinced, however, that the expense was worth it, and he was proved right. By 1994, orders for Huiyuan Juice began flooding in from Switzerland and Germany.

Zhu's next step was to create a Chinese market for fruit juice. China was accustomed to a culture of tea, and most people had no idea that juice was popular in Europe and the United States, but Zhu was convinced that if juice sold so well in other countries, the Chinese would adapt to it quickly. To launch a national strategy, Zhu moved his headquarters to Beijing. The company adopted the slogan, "100% of China drinking 100% pure juice."

In November 1996, Zhu decided it was time to make his brand recognized across all of China. He gambled the company's future by purchasing several five-second TV commercials programmed to run on Chinese New Years 1997 in prime time immediately after the evening news and between the top-rated national network shows. The commercials cost more than $8 million, more than the company's revenues for the entire year, but the gamble paid off, and Huiyuan emerged as a national brand and a leader in its field. Zhu eventually managed to make Huiyuan the first Chinese beverage company to be publicly listed on the Hong Kong Stock Exchange.

COCA-COLA'S INTEREST IN HUIYUAN

Coca-Cola saw Huiyuan as the obvious target for an acquisition. Most analysts assumed that Muhtar Kent, who had taken over as CEO of Coca-Cola in July 2008, saw it as the key to cementing his leadership over the corporation. Kent—a Turkish-American who was born in New York, where his father was Turkey's consul general—had started his career at Coca-Cola in Turkey. There, he initially drove delivery trucks around the country, an opportunity that had allowed him to learn Coca-Cola's distribution system from the ground up. By the time Kent took over the company, only 22 percent of Coca-Cola's revenues were coming from North America, where it had been losing market share, especially after its fiasco with New Coke in 1985.

What Kent had not bargained for in his effort to take control of Huiyuan, however, was the reaction of a newly confident Chinese public that saw Huiyuan as a homegrown national achievement. Coca-Cola, whose strategy for emerging markets is "think local, act local," suddenly found itself under attack by Chinese Internet bloggers charging it with "Coca-colonization."

Zhu was initially hesitant about selling the company, but he eventually decided that Huiyuan was reaching a sales bottleneck and that Coca-Cola had the resources to help it to move forward. Before Zhu could agree to the deal, however, China's Ministry of Commerce vetoed it on the grounds that the arrangement would enable Coca-Cola to get an unfair monopoly over China's beverage market and stamp out competition.

China was not the only country to come to the conclusion that Coca-Cola might be a dangerous competitor. An earlier attempt by Coca-Cola to get a controlling interest in Cadbury Schweppes PLC had been blocked by European regulators for the same reason. Huiyuan's shareholders, on the other hand, were less certain that turning down Coca-Cola was such a good idea. Lehman Brothers collapsed in September 2008, shortly after the offer was made, signaling the start of a worldwide economic downturn, and Huiyuan was coming under intense competition from other competitors besides Coca-Cola. Pepsi, for example, had invested $1 billion in the Chinese market, and other multinationals as well as Taiwanese food and drink companies were closing in. It was far from certain whether Huiyuan would be able to expand its market share further or even maintain it at its current level. More than that, the government veto was interpreted by some multinationals as a signal of an overall policy change aimed at freezing foreign companies out of China's domestic market. The multinationals, Coca-Cola included, did their best not to see it that way.

FURTHER EFFORTS BY COCA-COLA IN CHINA

Kent expressed disappointment that the sale hadn't gone through, but he appeared determined to follow through on an earlier commitment to invest $2 billion in China over the next three years.

At a regional meeting of the World Economic Forum in Tianjin, China, in September 2010, Glenn Jordan, president of Coca-Cola's Pacific Group, said that the lesson that Coca-Cola had taken from the affair was that it had to play by the rules of the game, and in

China those rules meant that Coca-Cola would have to invest in its own plants and grow organically. Jordan maintained that the rejected takeover bid would not slow Coca-Cola's efforts to expand in China. "It did not in any way break our determination to proceed in China one way or the other," he said.

Coca-Cola had already opened a $90 million innovation lab in Shanghai in 2009. In late October 2010, Kent, on a trip to Inner Mongolia, announced that Coca-Cola would spend $240 million to build three new bottling plants as part of the previously announced $2 billion expansion plan, which would effectively double Coca-Cola's investment in China to $4 billion. Coke is about people, Kent told reporters on the trip, and China had more people than anywhere else. Kent suggested that sales of Coca-Cola in China could eventually even surpass those in the United States.

CNOOC and Unocal

While the failed Huiyuan deal highlighted the readiness of China's government to step in and prevent what it considered to be a foreign takeover of an important domestic asset, the case of China's National Offshore Oil Corporation (CNOOC)'s failed attempt to buy a troubled U.S. oil company, Unocal, showed that where energy is concerned, the United States could be just as protectionist.

AMERICANS FEEL PROTECTIONIST ABOUT OIL, EVEN WHEN MUCH OF IT IS IN ASIA

In late 2004, Fu Chengyu, president of CNOOC, made an $18.5 billion bid to buy Unocal, a faltering U.S. petroleum company, whose owners were only too happy to sell. Before the deal could be completed, it sparked an unprecedented political firestorm that resulted in a Republican congressman, Joe Barton of Texas—the head of the House Energy Committee—writing a letter to then President George W. Bush, warning that the U.S. economy was being threatened by "China's aggressive tactics to lock up energy supplies around the world that are largely dedicated for their own use." A newspaper headline put it more bluntly: "The Chinese are coming for an American oil company!"

A U.S. COMPANY IN TROUBLE

The subject of these outcries was Unocal, a relative midget in terms of the U.S. energy market. At the time, Unocal's North American fields were responsible for just 0.2 percent of daily U.S. use of oil and 0.7 percent of natural gas. An independent oil and gas company based in California, it had U.S. reserves of only 447 million equivalent barrels of oil, known in the business as "boe" (a boe can be either a barrel of crude oil or 6,000 cubic feet of natural gas), and it produced an average of 136 million boe per day from the Gulf of Mexico and Alaska's Cook Inlet. Unocal's major reserves of 980 million boe were located in Asia, where it had been active for more than 40 years with various interests in Thailand, Indonesia, Azerbaijan. and Vietnam. Unocal's Asian production averaged 222 thousand boe per day compared to only 132 thousand boe a day in the United States.

In addition to being a relatively minor player in the U.S. market, Unocal found itself tied up with legal tangles concerning its obligations under recent legislation to clean up hazardous waste. If that was not daunting enough, the company's corporate image was under attack because of allegations that it might have been complicit in human rights abuses in Burma, where some of its reserves were located. Added to a long list of problems, Unocal's executives were convinced that the company had reached the limit of its ability to develop larger fields on its own. By 2004, Unocal had clearly become an obvious candidate for a merger.

Inside Unocal, the argument for concluding a sale quickly was based partly on the fact that the price for a barrel of oil had soared from $10 in 1998 to nearly $60 in 2005, an increase of 500 percent. Since China, India, and other fast growing emerging economies were going to need more oil to support their growth, many analysts, speculators, and investors were predicting that oil would soon reach $100 a barrel. To the shareholders of Unocal, it looked like a narrow window of opportunity to dump their holdings in a tarnished company for a maximum profit.

CHINA'S POINT OF VIEW

From China's point of view, the deal was part of a growing realization that if the country was going to handle a significant amount of the world's manufacturing, it had better nail down future energy supplies now. In that respect, Joe Barton's analysis that China wanted to secure oil for itself was accurate. What Barton had failed to note, however, was that it was the mad scramble by major U.S. corporations to take advantage of inexpensive Chinese labor that had led China to seek dependable energy reserves outside China. Chinese companies were reaching out beyond China's borders precisely because the production demands that were already being placed on them could be met only by gaining access to resources on a global scale. Barton, of course, failed to mention that American oil companies had signed deals around the world during the 20th century for precisely the same reason: American manufacturing needed guaranteed access to energy in order to function. Barton had also neglected to mention that most of Unocal's oil was in Asia, not in the United States.

As demands on China's manufacturing rose, oil was becoming increasingly essential to China, not just as fuel for transportation but also to run electric power plants during coal shortages and blackouts. In 2007, China had proven oil reserves of 16 billion barrels spread over six large regions. This was pitifully small in comparison to countries like Saudi Arabia, Canada, Iran, Iraq, and

Kuwait that each had proven reserves of well over 100 billion barrels. China was producing under 4 million barrels per day, but consuming more than 7 million.[1]

China had the world's fastest growing major economy, averaging above 10 percent growth per year. The country was rapidly transforming from rural agriculture to industrialization. In the process, China had transitioned from a net oil exporter to a net importer. At the time of the Unocal deal, the predictions were that the gap between oil supply and demand would increase to around 100 million tons by 2010, and the imported share of oil consumption would double to around 40 percent.

If you divided the world's oil reserves by the amount produced annually, it seemed reasonable to predict in 2008 that the world would run out of oil in roughly 54 years, if not sooner. Clearly, if China were to depend on importing oil from foreign companies to fuel its economic growth, it would be taking a significant risk. Long-term procurement contracts with foreign-owned oil companies could never be considered bulletproof. To attain self-sufficiency, China needed direct ownership of its overseas energy reserves, which is precisely what the United States had sought through companies like Unocal, when it secured long-term access to oilfields in Asia and the Middle East. Those fields were now considered U.S. property, even though they were nowhere near the United States.

CNOOC IS BORN AND GROWS

China's first step in securing expanded access to energy had been to find partners to exploit the oil adjacent to China's coastline. CNOOC had been created in 1982 with a mandate to negotiate and administer offshore petroleum operations with foreign oil and gas companies, and it eventually became a majority shareholder in three companies that were publicly listed and open to foreign investment. These were China Oilfield Services, CNOOC

Engineering, and CNOOC Ltd. The latter was incorporated in Hong Kong in 1999 and listed on both the New York and Hong Kong Stock Exchanges in 2001.

CNOOC operated primarily offshore in China and Indonesia and maintained a number of production sharing contracts with foreign partners. These contracts usually consist of concession agreements between international companies and host governments, in which the host government owns the mineral rights, while the foreign company retains part of the production while sharing the rest with the respective host government. CNOOC Ltd. had negotiated sole "back in" rights for the Chinese government. Essentially, the "back in" rights permitted CNOOC to acquire up to 51 percent of any successful discoveries that foreign partners made off China's coast at no additional cost.

CNOOC Ltd.'s total worldwide reserves were equivalent to 2.23 billion boe with nearly all of its holdings—2 billion boe—near China's shoreline. The company's reserve replacement rate was nearly 150 percent. The company's overseas reserves were limited to 156 million boe, mainly in Indonesia, with a daily production of 44 thousand boe. While production along China's coastline cost roughly $5.31 per barrel, international production cost $10.72 per barrel. According to a Nomura Group report in 2005, CNOOC Ltd. had already locked up 89 percent of China's offshore exploitable territory likely to contain oil.[2] To maintain its reserve replacement rate and reduce its international production costs, the company was literally being forced to become an international player.

As a pure exploration and development company, CNOOC had no refineries, which meant the company's growth depended largely on a high reserve-replacement rate at a competitive cost. "CNOOC is pure upstream," Mark Qiu, CNOOC's chief financial officer, explained. "That forces me to look anywhere that I can find oil or natural gas." Although CNOOC was smaller than its main Chinese competitors, Sinopec and PetroChina, it had been looking globally for oil and gas from its inception.

In 2002, CNOOC acquired the main assets in Indonesia of Repsol YPF for $600 million. The deal made it Indonesia's largest offshore operator. In the same year, the company signed a term agreement to acquire a 5.3 percent interest in Australia's North West Shelf Gas Project. A year later, it acquired a 12.5 percent interest in Indonesia's Tangguh Liquefied Natural Gas (LNG) Project. Also in 2003, CNOOC entered an agreement with Unocal, Sinopec, and Shell to explore and develop the Xihu Trough in the East China Sea, about 250 miles from Shanghai.

In 2004, CNOOC's wholly owned subsidiary, CNOOC Muturi, completed acquisition of an additional 20.8 percent interest in the Muturi Production Sharing Contract (PSC) from BG Group for a total consideration of $105.1 million. This purchase increased CNOOC's interest in the Muturi PSC from 44 percent to 64.8 percent, and its interest in the Tangguh LNG Project increased from 12.5 percent to 16.9 percent. In 2004, CNOOC also signed the second deepwater contract with Husky Oil China.[3] In short, CNOOC had gone on a worldwide purchasing binge.

Despite its phenomenal growth, however, CNOOC faced tough competition in its domestic market. In 2005, it lost its monopoly over offshore explorations. Its largest domestic rivals, CNPC and Sinopec, were granted permission to begin their own explorations in what had previously been CNOOC's territory. Smaller domestic players also began pushing against the monopoly held by PetroChina's parent, Sinopec, and CNOOC.

While all this was going on, China's entry into the World Trade Organization radically changed the rules of the game. China was suddenly obliged to let international oil companies compete in its own domestic retail and wholesale markets. Thus, CNOOC found itself competing on its own turf not only with its larger domestic rivals, PetroChina and Sinopec, but also with the much larger international companies such as ExxonMobil and BP. The message to CNOOC's executives was clear: Either the youthful company needed to make a substantial effort to grow bigger and stronger or it faced being overwhelmed by competitors at home and abroad.

CNOOC GETS THE MANDATE TO BECOME A GLOBAL COMPANY

The key architect of CNOOC's push to expand internationally was Fu Chengyu. Born in 1951, Fu had received a master's degree in petroleum engineering from the University of Southern California. He spoke English fluently and besides his U.S. training, he had acquired more than 30 years of experience in China's oil industry.

Fu joined CNOOC in 1982 and worked on joint ventures with foreign companies almost from the start. The foreign companies that he was familiar with included Amoco, Chevron, Texaco, Philips, and Shell. Chevron was later to bid successfully against Fu in the struggle to take over Unocal.

Before assuming the leadership of CNOOC, Fu had successfully restructured CNOOC's two major subsidiaries, CNOOC Ltd. and China Oilfield Services. He was promoted to the post of chairman of China Oilfield Services in August 2002. When CNOOC's CEO at the time, Wei Liucheng, left CNOOC to become the governor of Hainan Province, Fu was chosen to be both chairman and CEO of CNOOC Ltd. Wei had been campaigning for some time to turn CNOOC into an international company. "The only way to meet the demands of a rapidly changing market and the company's evolving goals is to continuously adapt ourselves," he explained. Fu, with his fluent English and international background, looked like the perfect candidate to expand CNOOC beyond China's national boundaries. When he took over leadership of the company, his mandate was to build CNOOC into one of the world's leading oil companies.

Fu immediately began modernizing CNOOC's operations, placing a heavy emphasis on transparent management, governance, and maximizing shareholder values. Together with his team, he initiated several overseas acquisitions leading to the bold attempt to buy Unocal. While Unocal looked only mildly interesting to the major multinational oil companies, it promised to be the biggest foreign takeover that any Chinese company had attempted until then.

THE BIDDING WAR BEGINS

Beginning in December 2004, CNOOC engaged in a flurry of activity aimed at eventually taking over Unocal. Before either side had a chance to engage in detailed discussions, news leaked to the press that something unusual was about to happen. On January 6, 2005, the *Financial Times* reported that CNOOC was planning to bid more than $13 billion for Unocal, making it the largest and most significant overseas acquisition by a Chinese company.[4] The trouble was that CNOOC was still not exactly sure what kind of offer it wanted to make. Even more troubling, its board remained divided about the wisdom of making any offer at all. In addition, Fu seemed to have miscalculated the political sensitivity in the United States to a Chinese company taking over an American oil company, even a relatively minor one. Fu had failed to grasp the complexities of the deal before revealing his intentions. He had essentially alerted his competition that Unocal was up for sale, before being sure how he or his board wanted to proceed.

Sensing that Unocal was now on the market and that a political firestorm was about to erupt, Chevron's chief executive, David O'Reilly, called the head of Unocal, Charles Williamson, to ask whether he might consider a friendly takeover offer.[5] The immediate effect was to up the ante required from CNOOC, if it wanted to stay in the game.

In April 2005, Chevron offered to purchase Unocal for $16.8 billion. With sales of $155.3 billion in 2004, Chevron was the second-largest integrated oil company in the United States, surpassed only by Exxon. Chevron had reserves of 11.25 billion boe and produced 2.37 million boe per day. It was five times the size of CNOOC in terms of worldwide reserves. Chevron's exploration and development costs were about $14 per barrel, $6 higher than that of CNOOC. Although Chevron posted increased income most years, much of that was as a result of the steady increase in the price of oil. The company's production had actually fallen by 14 percent since 2000, and its replacement rate was just 18 percent—one of the worst showings by a large oil company in recent years. Chevron had clearly been left behind. The company needed new oil reserves to support its growth, or it risked pumping itself out of existence. From Chevron's point of view, Unocal suddenly began to look like an attractive target for acquisition. Chevron couldn't depend on rising oil prices to shore up profits indefinitely, and Unocal's untapped reserves offered a partial solution. CNOOC, by failing to be discreet about its intentions, had made the mistake of alerting Chevron that Unocal was up for grabs.

David O'Reilly of Chevron calculated that the Unocal takeover would increase Chevron's reserves by 15 percent and its oil and gas production to 3 million boe per day. "Chevron wants it badly because they don't have near-term production growth," observed Jay Saunders, an oil analyst at Deutsche Bank. "The fact they had to do this offer is a reflection of Chevron's challenges that its rivals don't have."[6]

On April 4, 2005, Chevron announced its offer to acquire Unocal for $16.5 billion. The deal was structured to be 75 percent stock and 25 percent cash, valuing the company at $62 per share. The transaction was subject to Federal Trade Commission antitrust review and Unocal shareholder approval.

CNOOC'S REASONS FOR TARGETING UNOCAL

CNOOC had done its original homework brilliantly in identifying Unocal as a potential target. CNOOC's internal research projected that with the price of oil and natural gas reaching new highs, purchasing energy assets was likely to become increasingly difficult and costly. CNOOC decided to focus on acquiring an undervalued energy company with proven and potential reserves, and it short-listed dozens of independent oil companies. It made its selection according to four criteria:

1. Valued below $20 billion

2. Reserves and production potential

3. Liquid natural gas business related to China

4. Affordability and accessibility

Following these criteria, Unocal was clearly the best potential acquisition. The deal promised both to double CNOOC's production and to increase its reserves by 80 percent. Unocal had significant assets in Asia, and some of its projects were particularly attractive to China. The assets of the two companies complemented each other: 60 percent of Unocal's reserves were natural gas, and 35 percent of CNOOC's reserves were gas. The combined company would have a more balanced portfolio with 53 percent oil and 47 percent natural gas. The improved balance of the asset portfolio promised to significantly reduce the cyclical variations of commodity prices. Another positive aspect was the potential for synergies generated by the combined exploration and capital investment programs. Unocal's excellent operational management team and deep water drilling and production expertise were added bonuses.[7]

PROBLEMS CLOSING THE DEAL

Although CNOOC had made the right choice, it lacked the experience needed to close the deal. In December 2004, Fu approached Unocal's Charles Williamson and initiated several weeks of general discussions with Unocal's senior management. Almost immediately, a story leaked to the *Financial Times* identifying CNOOC as the buyer and Unocal as the target of the acquisition. The *Financial Times* also revealed the proposed price, which led Unocal shares to shoot up 7.7 percent to $44.34, the biggest one-day gain for Unocal shares in six years. The *Financial Times* article also launched a bidding war with Chevron's O'Reilly. The Italian company Eni also began expressing an interest in Unocal.

CNOOC needed to make an immediate formal proposal to Unocal or dramatically revise its original plan. The company failed to do either. In addition, the idea of teaming up with an American company to avoid a bidding war and to soften the political implications of a Chinese takeover doesn't seem to have occurred to anyone at the time. To make matters worse, CNOOC failed to make a serious offer within the set time limits. Ultimately, CNOOC's indecision effectively handed the deal to Chevron.[8]

On February 25, 2005, CNOOC told Unocal that it had "strong interest" in more detailed talks and signed a confidentiality pact. It followed this up on March 7, with a proposed bid of $59 to $62 per share in cash. A team from Unocal, headed by Williamson, arrived in Beijing to continue the negotiations. The deadline for final offers was set for March 30, but CNOOC then told Williamson that it could not make the deadline and that it would take at least several more weeks to confirm the offer.

On March 30, the Unocal board gave CNOOC a new deadline of April 2, but CNOOC still hadn't been able to make a final decision. Instead, it announced that it would consider "future discussions." On March 31, Unocal's board received Chevron's offer.

The major obstacle on CNOOC's end was its own board of directors. According to *Time* magazine's account at the time, the plan to buy Unocal ran into resistance from nearly all of CNOOC's board members who complained that CNOOC was offering too much money for a company lacking a bright future. During a board meeting on March 30, four of CNOOC's independent board members refused to vote on the bid at all, complaining that they didn't have enough time to understand the issues fully and were concerned about the price being offered. What was especially embarrassing for CNOOC was that after each board meeting, precise details of the discussions were immediately leaked to the media. Reporters might as well have been allowed to be present in the room. CNOOC somehow never managed to control the leaks.

During the April bidding, despite the abstentions by the independent directors, CNOOC kept insisting that it was still interested in Unocal, although it was still a long way from a final decision. The company issued a statement saying that it was "continuing to examine its operations with respect to Unocal" and that "these options included a possible offer by the company for Unocal." The bidding war was looming.

THE BIDDING WAR TAKES ON A POLITICAL DIMENSION

On June 22, 2005, CNOOC offered $67 per Unocal share in an all-cash transaction valued at $18.5 billion, excluding debt. Although CNOOC's all-cash offer looked more profitable than Chevron's on the surface, it was far from certain that it could ever be completed.

Meanwhile, Chevron had obtained approval for its deal for Unocal from the Federal Trade Commission and the Securities and Exchange Commission in record time, while CNOOC's proposal still needed to be reviewed by the U.S. Treasury Department's Committee on Foreign Investments. The committee was charged with assessing the deal's impact on U.S. national security.

For CNOOC, the takeover attempt had come at a bad time. It coincided with mounting friction between Washington and Beijing over trade imbalances and China's refusal to revalue the RMB (renminbi), all of which CNOOC seems to have been oblivious to. Although Fu had anticipated some opposition, he failed to understand the deal's political dimension or the growing uneasiness among American workers over losing jobs to China and concerns about the waning influence of the United States in the world. In retrospect, it was not the best moment for a Chinese government–owned company to launch the biggest foreign takeover attempt in history of a U.S. energy company, but Fu seemed oblivious to U.S. concerns.

The deal quickly became a political issue, with a bipartisan group of 41 members of Congress demanding a rigorous review of CNOOC's bid. They argued that the offer was not a free market transaction and that it was part of an attempt to control energy resources and influence in Asia.

The foreign ownership of oil assets, the critics argued, would constitute a regional and economic security risk. The U.S. Department of Defense warned that it might open the door to sensitive deep-sea exploration with drilling technology that could have dual-use applications for military purposes. From that perspective, the Pentagon argued, communist ownership of a U.S. oil company could present a national security risk. There was a call in Congress for more research, which threatened to lengthen the review process and, in the eyes of Unocal shareholders, make the CNOOC bid an even riskier proposition.

In July 2005, Senator Byron Dorgan (Democrat of North Dakota) submitted a bill to the Senate that would have kept CNOOC from buying Unocal. "This really isn't very complicated," Dorgan explained. "Unocal is located in the United States and has approximately 1.75 billion barrels of oil. It would be foolish, to say the least, to allow a foreign government . . . to own that much of such a strategic resource so vital to the U.S. economy and the national defense." The fact that more than half the oil was actually in Asia didn't seem to have made much of an impression on Dorgan.

To ram its point home, Chevron argued in the media that CNOOC's bid had been financed by cheap loans and subsidies from the Chinese government and was consequently against the principles of free trade. "CNOOC clearly isn't a commercial company," pleaded Peter Robertson, ChevronTexaco's vice chairman. "We're up against the Chinese government." There were also attempts to associate CNOOC with the debate over China's human rights record. After a successful lobbying campaign by Chevron, opinion polls conducted by the *Wall Street Journal* showed that 74 percent of the public opposed the deal with CNOOC. Another element adding to anxieties about the deal was the suggestion that it would dramatically increase China's leverage over Southeast Asia and subsequently its leverage over U.S. interests in the region.

While Chevron made no secret about its intention to reduce Unocal's workforce, it was careful to promise senior managers that they would not only hold on to their positions and benefits but would get increases once the deal went through. Also, although it was offering up to a billion dollars less than CNOOC, Chevron argued that its offer had a much better chance of actually getting through the U.S. regulatory process.

Chevron had mounted a sizeable internal team along with outside lobbyists and policy advisers to make its case in Washington. The main theme that it kept hammering at was national security. The lobbying effort successfully shifted the focus from the relative merits of both offers to one of national defense. Frank Gaffney, the ultra-conservative head of the Center for Security Policy, argued that CNOOC's offer was part of a larger Chinese long-term strategic plan aimed at eventually securing control of the world's energy and resources. Besides oil, Gaffney also raised the specter of what he saw as a Chinese attempt to corner the market for rare earth, a classification of certain metals that are essential in the manufacture of strong magnets and various electronic components. The main company mining rare earth in the United States, Molybdenum Corporation of America, had been sold to a Chinese company. Although it was closed, one of the world's two major mines for rare earth belonged to Unocal.

"Unfortunately, Communist China's play for Unocal's energy and rare earth mineral assets is no more an isolated incident than it is, as the Chinese insist, a "purely commercial transaction." Rather, it falls into a pattern of PRC activity around the globe that is clearly deliberate, well-thought-out, and ominous in its implications," Gaffney told a Congressional hearing on July 13, 2005.

"This activity is guided by a long-term strategy," Gaffney continued. "It involves the dominance of strategic energy resources, materials and minerals, technologies—all aimed at providing a civilian economy that will, consistent with Deng Xio Peng's famous "16 Character" dictum, serve China's military needs." For good measure, Gaffney paraphrased an old quote from Lenin: "It is an irony not lost on the Communist Chinese that they have done Lenin's putative dictum one better: We are paying for the rope they will use to hang us. In addition to our money coming back in the form of weapons designed to kill Americans."

Gaffney's outrage at Chinese government support to China's oil companies ignored the fact that the U.S. government provides considerable support and takes a major interest in American oil companies in much the same manner, or that in both Bush administrations, a number of former oil company executives held critical government positions.

The crucial point, and the one that Fu had failed to grasp fully when CNOOC approached the deal in the first place, was that in the climate that existed just four years after the 9/11 attack on the World Trade Center, the mere suggestion of a threat to U.S. national security would be sufficient to slow the bureaucratic process long enough to give Chevron the advantage it needed. Chevron was playing hardball, and CNOOC was only beginning to understand how the game was played.

CNOOC WITHDRAWS, CHEVRON WINS

Although Unocal's board was beginning to lean toward Chevron's offer, Chevron made no effort to put a halt to Unocal's negotiations with CNOOC, which continued to try to win over Unocal's board. On July 19, 2005, Chevron increased its offer to $63.01 per Unocal share. That raised Chevron's overall offer to $17.8 billion. Chevron's proposal was restructured with 60 percent stock and 40 percent cash. Unocal's board endorsed the new offer and recommended that its shareholders approve it.

CNOOC debated whether to raise its offer again, but with increasingly vocal opposition from members of Congress, it decided that the struggle was no longer worth the effort. The company announced that it was no longer bidding. On August 2, 2005, CNOOC withdrew its $18.5 billion bid, saying that it could not overcome the political resistance. Unocal shareholders approved Chevron's increased offer on August 10. "It serves as a stark reminder that it isn't always just about price," said Stefan Selig, vice chairman of Bank of America Securities. "Timing and tactics matter."

The high prices for oil and gas had also worked against Fu. Mario Traviati, an oil and gas analyst at Merrill Lynch, Singapore, had warned CNOOC that the high-cost energy environment had created a situation in which buyers outnumbered sellers and that it was not the best moment to launch into a program of acquisitions. "It's a very dangerous strategy to pursue in enhancing shareholder value," Traviati said. "The best way to grow in the oil and gas business is through exploratory and development success, rather than acquisitions."[9]

To add to the multipronged campaign it had launched against CNOOC in the United States, Chevron deftly mounted a counterattack against CNOOC in China. Chevron approached CNOOC's domestic competitors, PetroChina and Sinopec, and encouraged them to engage in offshore explorations in the territory that had previously belonged solely to CNOOC. The tactic safeguarded Chevron's key interests in China and forced CNOOC to defend itself in its home market.

In *The Art of War*, Sun Tzu, China's most famous military strategist, lists five factors that are essential to victory. The first is knowing when to fight and when to withdraw. Picking the right place also counts. During the bidding war, Chevron fought against CNOOC on Chevron's home turf, which turned out to be the right place, and the political frictions with China, along with doubts about China's record on human rights, combined to make it the right time. Working its home advantage where it knew the terrain and could muster the most support, Chevron was able to exert maximum influence on the public, legislators, Unocal shareholders, and Unocal senior managers—the critical stakeholders in the deal. Once it had locked up the home front, Chevron went further by allying itself with CNOOC's domestic rivals. It is hardly surprising that Chevron won that round.

From a purely business point of view, CNOOC's campaign had appeared to make sense, but CNOOC had underestimated the emotional, cultural, and political factors that can tip the scales in an extended bidding war. CNOOC emphasized reasonably enough that 70 percent of Unocal's oil and gas reserves were in Asia, and Unocal's U.S. oil and gas production accounted for less than 1 percent of U.S. consumption. The argument was reasonable, but as it turned out, it was only a small part of the picture.

When Chevron shifted the debate to political and military anxieties as well as CNOOC's motives, CNOOC's initial arguments suddenly seemed irrelevant. CNOOC could have invited an American company to join its bid, which would have defused the political opposition and allayed some of the anxieties about China's overall intentions, but the company failed to correctly identify and analyze Chevron's strategy, and it was too slow when it came to changing course and adapting its own strategy to the new challenges.

A number of CNOOC's other arguments appeared not to have been fully thought through. CNOOC had pledged to sell the oil and gas produced from Unocal's U.S. properties in U.S. markets, but that promise was virtually meaningless since Unocal's U.S. oil and gas accounted for only a tiny portion of local consumption. CNOOC said that it would try to retain nearly all Unocal's employees, including those in the United States, but that offer undercut CNOOC's claim that the primary motive for the acquisition was commercial. CNOOC also offered to make Unocal's senior executives part of the management team of the combined company, but in contrast to Chevron, CNOOC neglected to offer promotions or substantially increased benefits.

LESSONS LEARNED

As CNOOC found out, when the stakes are high enough, America's commitment to a genuinely free market can be variable at best. As T. Boone Pickens told *Oil & Gas Investor* following the affair:

> To me it was very simple—if Chevron wanted it they would have to bid more than the Chinese. It is not up to

the government to step in front of the deal. Chevron did what most companies do—which is, when they get in trouble, they run to Washington. We don't have any problem with the Chinese buying federal bonds. Nobody says anything about that. Unocal is so small in the world oil picture; it's a brouhaha over nothing.

The need to act quickly and to adapt to new situations faster than the competition is an important lesson that CNOOC should have, and ultimately did, learn from the experience. The company had identified Unocal as a potential acquisition as early as December 2004, but it took CNOOC much longer than any of its competitors to make an actual offer. CNOOC's fatal flaw was that it lacked a mechanism to manage the acquisition process discreetly and rapidly.

Another important lesson is that in foreign acquisitions, political factors need to be taken into consideration from the beginning. Both the company and the acquisition can require an intensive public relations campaign and lobbying effort right from the beginning of the process, and that can require help from experts on the spot. Chevron is an American company, but it still went to outside consultants and professional lobbyists to get its message across.

Despite its failure to acquire Unocal, both Fu and CNOOC profited from the public attention that had been stirred up. As it turned out, the exercise of attempting to buy Unocal had effectively been a win-win proposition from the start: a great win if the company could acquire Unocal, and a small win if the negotiations put the company on the map in a positive way. In the end, the bid for Unocal proved both CNOOC's financial stability and its determination to grow rapidly. More important, it demonstrated Fu's boldness in taking on the world's leading oil giants on their own turf. After the deal fell through, CNOOC's market capitalization continued to increase by $7 billion.

Fu found that at least in China he was seen as a hero for having pushed CNOOC to take the gamble. CNOOC's new assertive profile made it instantly recognizable as an emerging multinational player, and the positive change in CNOOC's image abroad cost the company practically nothing in financial terms. Fu immediately found it easier to expand aggressively on other projects. His experience would ultimately prove to be valuable lesson for other Chinese companies going global. It proved that boldness and initiative would ultimately pay off.

In 2006, with cash reserves of $2.3 billion, CNOOC launched a series of acquisitions outside the United States. First, it acquired a 45 percent working interest in an offshore oil-mining license in Nigeria. In the same year, CNOOC Africa signed production-sharing contracts for six blocks of territory for exploitation in Kenya. In 2008, CNOOC tried to acquire Russia's STU, a unit of the Russian oil company TNK-BP. The Russian government blocked the deal.

In July 2008, China Oilfield Services, the oil-services arm of CNOOC, spent $2.5 billion to acquire the Norwegian offshore oil company Awilco, which owns the world's eighth-largest fleet of oil rigs. It marked the company's first successful acquisition of a Western oil enterprise following the Unocal fiasco. That year, CNOOC reported a profit of nearly $10 billion, with revenue rising 22 percent.

Fu also found that with the right timing, he could work profitably on U.S. territory. CNOOC signed production-sharing agreements with both Chevron and BP for exploration in the South China Sea as well as a $2.2 billion deal to buy a third of the oil and gas assets of Chesapeake Energy, the second-largest producer of natural gas in the United States, based in Texas.

The Chesapeake energy purchase raised many of the same objections that conservatives had used to block the Unocal takeover.

The deal promised to give CNOOC access to advanced technology as well as deep sea drilling, but in contrast to the failure five years earlier, most analysts had expected the CNOOC bid to go through when it was announced. For once, the timing was right. CNOOC was not in competition with other buyers, and there were no media leaks.

As it turned out, CNOOC had learned quite a bit from its failed attempt to buy Unocal. Probably the most important lesson was that energy is such an important factor in the economy of every country that government involvement and national security considerations are inevitable. To succeed, any takeover strategy needs to weigh these sensitivities in order to succeed. When it comes to oil, political pressure is a fact of life. When your own country buys oil rights on foreign territory, it is usually seen as an investment. When the reverse is true, it can be seen as an invasion. Oil is not the only sector where this occurs. In Chapter 3, we will show the impact that politics and national security concerns can have on the market for high technology.

NOTES

1. Energy Information Administration, tonto.eia.doe.gov.

2. Nomura, "CNOOC Limited: Offshore Overseer," December 5, 2005.

3. Datamonitor.

4. Francesco Guerrera and Joseph Leahy, "CNOOC Considers $13bn Bid for Unocal," *Financial Times*, January 6, 2005.

5. Mouawad, Jad, and David Barboza. "Chevron Risks China Ties in Fight for Unocal," July 6, 2005, www.iht.com.

6. Mouawad and Barboza.

7. "The Acquisition of Unocal Corporation," Insead Case, 106-021-1.

8. SEC Form DEFM14A, Unocal Corporation, filed on July 1, 2005.

9. Abe De Ramos, "The Explorer," November 2003, www.cfoasia.com.

Huawei
Technology Dictates, but Politics Still Counts

Use the countryside to surround the cities.

—Strategy attributed to Mao Zedong

IN EARLY NOVEMBER 2010, executives at China's Huawei Technologies anxiously awaited the fate of their bid to upgrade the wireless network for Sprint Nextel, one of the largest telephone companies in the United States. With worldwide sales of roughly $30 billion a year, Huawei already provided some of the world's most advanced telephone switching gear to 45 of the world's top 50 telecom companies, including BT (British Telecom), Orange (part of France Telecom), Vodafone Spain, Telefonica, and KPN, as well as carriers in a number of emerging markets in Eastern Europe and the Pacific Rim. The company had 60,000 employees, nearly half involved in R&D, and had taken on an increasingly international personality. "We used to recruit mainly in Beijing and Shanghai," said Edward Deng, the company's chief of European operations. "But now, we also recruit in New York, London, Paris, Canada, and Australia."

Entering the Market Through the Back Door

But for all of Huawei's growing reputation abroad, it had been forced to enter the U.S. market through the back door. Although Huawei was quietly generating sales in the United States worth around $400 million a year, its business was limited to small and medium-size enterprises. The major players—Sprint Nextel, AT&T, and Verizon—and the high-end contracts were effectively off-limits. No formal declaration excluded Huawei from the market, but every time the company tried to close a major deal, a discreet phone call from a U.S. government agency would warn the potential client that if it went to a Chinese company to manufacture its equipment, it risked losing its most valuable contracts with the U.S. government.

What was particularly galling to Huawei was the fact that the largest competitor in the field—Cisco Systems, with sales of $36.1 billion in 2009—had been manufacturing much of its equipment in China for years. Cisco was the main company involved in creating the first generation of equipment giving China access to the Internet, which came to be known as the Great Chinese Firewall. It was difficult, Huawei's supporters argued, to see much difference between the two companies unless it came to who owned the stock. Opponents of the 2010 deal between Huawei and Sprint Nextel implied darkly that Huawei's close connections to the Chinese military and government agencies might make Huawei vulnerable to pressure to insert spyware or even a "software bomb" into the vital communications networks of the United States.

By the time the Sprint Nextel bid emerged, Huawei was already experienced at dealing with America's political sensitivities toward China, especially on the part of the Republican Party and Washington's right-wing policy organizations, which were to a large extent still mentally rooted in the Cold War.

Ren Zhengfei, Huawei's founder and chairman, had already made headlines in 2000, when the CIA flew into a rage over Huawei's readiness to bypass international sanctions and sell a communications system to Baghdad. For its part, Huawei had seen little reason at the time why a Chinese company's client list should be limited by what it saw as U.S. foreign policy interests. This was especially true to Huawei since Halliburton, the oilfield services company that was then headed by Dick Cheney (the future vice president of the United States), had purchased a subsidiary, Dresser Industries, which had sold $73 million worth of oilfield equipment and parts to Saddam Hussein's Iraq regime through another subsidiary that it jointly owned with another major American equipment company, Ingersoll-Rand. (Cheney denied direct knowledge of the Iraq sale at the time, but Colum Lynch, reporting in the *Washington Post*, quoted two senior executives who had served under Cheney as saying that the company had no policy that they knew of that would have prevented them from doing business with Saddam's Iraq.)

The flap over Iraq underscored a fact that was just beginning to dawn on American politicians, that although the United States might still be the world's only superpower, it could no longer claim a monopoly in shaping international politics. The emerging markets—particularly China and India—still lacked the power to set policy themselves, but they were increasingly in a position to veto someone else's policy plans. The new state of affairs was beginning to endow China with the political weight that it had long sought. For private businesspeople like Ren, it meant that the world had suddenly become a lot more complicated.

Hitch Your Star to a Global Brand: Huawei, 3Com, and Cisco

In 2002, Huawei had begun putting together a joint venture with 3Com, an American pioneer in developing wireless Internet routers, the switch boxes that enable computers to network together. Although 3Com was critical in launching the technology, it had had trouble keeping up with the fast-changing market.

The joint venture was intended to build network routers in Hangzhou and sell them in the United States. 3Com, founded in 1979, had entered the Chinese market in 1994 and built a business selling its innovative networking solutions to small and medium-size businesses worldwide. By 1995, it had a broad distribution network throughout China, but as competition from Chinese companies picked up, 3Com's market share began to decrease. By the time that Ren approached 3Com's CEO, Bruce Claflin, about forming an alliance, the company had slashed its staff from a peak of 10,000 employees to just 3,400. Although industry observers were convinced that Huawei wanted to gain access to 3Com's technology, 3Com had lost so much staff and was under so much financial pressure that it stood to gain much more than it had to offer from access to Huawei's technology and formidable capacity in R&D.

For his part, Ren wanted a recognizable global brand to make Huawei's products more attractive to American and European clients. Most important of all, however, Ren and Claflin were mutually impressed with and liked each other.

OPPOSITION FROM CISCO

The joint venture soon ran into trouble when Cisco Systems, the market leader, filed a suit against Huawei on January 23, 2003.

Cisco accused Huawei of violating its intellectual property rights by copying its software and some of the terminology in its user manuals. Huawei immediately removed the suspect products from the market, but Cisco then accused Huawei of trying to remove evidence. Ren suspected that Cisco was not as concerned about a few lines of software code as it was about the prospect of entering into long-term competition with a Chinese company that employed thousands of brilliant engineers who were hungry for success and willing to work for a fraction of the salaries paid in the United States.

At the time, Cisco, which had begun producing network routers in 1986, was the leader in the field. It had 68 percent of the market for Internet routers in China, compared to only 13 percent for Huawei. But Cisco was already beginning to feel pressure from the same competition in China that was driving Huawei toward the international market. China represented 5 percent of Cisco's worldwide sales in 2002, but it was not clear how long that would continue.

Cisco's suit was based on several lines of its code that had appeared in some of Huawei's software. Huawei countered that it employed more than 10,000 engineers and didn't need to copy anyone else's software. Since Cisco was employing Chinese engineers itself, it was difficult to tell whether the code had accidentally slipped into Huawei's software or had been intentionally copied. Eventually, Huawei admitted that some 2 percent of its routing operating software had come from Cisco, but Huawei insisted that the code had been accidentally introduced by an employee without the knowledge of Huawei's top management. The suit was settled out of court. For Huawei, though, the fact that the suit had coincided with its developing relationship with 3Com was a signal that Cisco was determined to keep Huawei from competing directly in the American market.

3COM DROPS OUT OF THE PICTURE

Huawei eventually went ahead with its joint partnership with 3Com, which was called H3C (Huawei-3Com). Before long, 3Com was well on its way to changing from an industry innovator to a mere distributor of Chinese products to be sold in the United States. Huawei contributed 1,000 employees to the venture, while 3Com contributed only 50. After two years, 3Com exercised an option to buy out Huawei's interest in the venture. As 3Com's prospects steadily declined, a leveraged buyout firm, Bain Capital LLC, offered to buy 3Com for $2.2 billion. Huawei was a minority partner in the bid. The deal fell through when a group of eight Republican congressmen charged that it risked giving China access to anti-hacking software produced by a 3Com unit, TippingPoint. The congressmen eventually threatened to pass legislation outlawing the sale.

From Huawei's point of view, the message from the 3Com fiasco was fairly clear: The effort to keep Huawei from competing in the American market had passed from debatable charges of violating intellectual property to one of national patriotism. If you could not compete on price, you could always raise the specter of a threat to national security. One of the most powerful human instincts, the closing of ranks to repel an invader, emerged as the next most powerful marketing tool in the campaign to keep Huawei from entering the American market.

National Security vs. the Outsider

In 2008, when Huawei competed for yet another contract, this time with AT&T, there was no hesitation among opponents about raising the specter of China itself as a potential threat to U.S. security. This time, the contract was worth just over $1 billion. At the last moment in the lengthy negotiations, according to a report by John Pomfret in the *Washington Post*, the U.S. National Security Agency

—the secretive intelligence agency that is responsible for spying on telephone and electronic communications in foreign countries, especially China—had quietly threatened to exclude AT&T from lucrative future U.S. government contracts if it did not pull out of the deal. AT&T protested that it was more than capable of guaranteeing that the equipment would be safe to use, but it then opted for the path of least resistance and gave the contract to Sweden's Ericsson and France's Alcatel-Lucent.

Huawei then turned, in the summer and fall of 2010, to competing for a contract with Sprint Nextel. This contract promised to be much larger and more significant. While some companies were bidding as much as $8 billion for the contract, the word on the street was that Huawei's offer was just over $3 billion.

To help it navigate the intricacies of Washington, Huawei hired Amerilink Telecom Corporation, a lobbying firm created in June 2009 by William Owens, a former vice chairman of the U.S. Defense Department's Joint Chiefs of Staff. Huawei was Amerilink's first and only client, and Owens hoped that his previous position on the Joint Chiefs of Staff would qualify him to guarantee safeguards against China using Huawei to slip spyware into the new system. Owens packed substantial credibility by himself, but he didn't stop there. He subsequently hired James Wolfensohn, the former head of the World Bank, along with Richard Gephardt, the former majority leader of the House of Representatives, to bolster the team. Amerilink's CEO and many of its executives had previously worked for major U.S. telecom companies and especially Sprint.

The investment in hiring Amerilink was enough to get Huawei past the starting gate and on to a final short list of six companies. It was not enough, however, to cross the barrier of suspicion that China's military might try to use the opening to pull a fast one on U.S. defense. The contract ultimately went to Alcatel and Samsung, at a considerably higher cost than Huawei's bid.

Although Huawei was not happy at the outcome, it was not exactly dismayed, either. The company issued a typically bland statement, saying simply, "Huawei has never researched, developed, manufactured, or sold technologies or products for military purposes." The reaction in Beijing was less accommodating: "The U.S. reaction is too irrational and exaggerated the situation," said Tu Xinquan, director of the China WTO Institute at the University of International Business and Economics.

The implicit message for Huawei was clear. In spite of the public rhetoric from the United States about free markets, business with the U.S. government is nearly always intensely political, and the old saying that all is fair in love and war is even truer when it comes to global business. Business at the level the multinationals play it is a no-holds-barred street fight in which anything goes.

It was a lesson that Ren and other Chinese private sector entrepreneurs had learned early on in their struggle to survive in their own domestic market during China's turbulent transition from a politically connected, state-controlled socialist economy to one that was in the truest sense of the term a free market. In the coming struggle for the global telecom market, Ren suspected that he might be better prepared than the U.S. giants, which had themselves grown increasingly dependent on government contracts for their own survival and found themselves pleading more and more for Washington's intervention when their own resources were no longer sufficient to close a deal.

Huawei's Long March

For Ren Zhengfei, the journey that had led him to this point had been a heady one. Ren had begun his career as an officer in the Chinese army and eventually served as director of its Information Engineering Academy, the technical school responsible for the army's telecommunications research. In 1984, at the age of 39, he retired as a colonel and went to work for the state-owned Shenzhen Electronics Corporation. Four years later, he took out a loan for $8.5 million from a state-owned bank and launched Huawei Technologies with a total staff of 14 people.

CHANGES IN CHINA'S APPROACH TO TELECOMMUNICATIONS

Ren's decision to launch Huawei in 1988 coincided with major changes in China's approach to telecommunications. From the period following the Chinese revolution (1949 through 1979), the telephone system was state-financed and state-owned. It was operated by the Bureau of Posts and Telecommunications (BPT), which came under the joint direction of the Ministry of Posts and Telecommunications and the Ministry of Electronics Industry. The goal was to provide telephone service to help the country's overall economic development, not specifically to make money from the service itself. Roughly 90 percent of the funding came from the government and only 10 percent from actual users.

In 1979, private commerce was legally authorized in China, and by 1982, the government began opening up the telecom market. Non–state-owned private companies, which had previously been banned from telecommunications, were invited to compete with the state-owned companies. The industry gradually shifted from a not-for-profit operation to one that was increasingly profit-oriented. In order to guarantee rapid expansion, the government encouraged telecom providers to go into debt, promising to make the operations profitable in the future. To further speed the expansion, it made loans freely available. The result was a race to build telephone networks, and local equipment providers such as Huawei Technologies, Datang Group, and ZTE (Zhongxing Semiconductor Ltd.) emerged as local providers.

From 1990 to 1993, revenues for the industry increased 3.5 times and the number of subscribers more than doubled to 17.3 million. The number of residential subscribers more than quadrupled from less than 2 million to 9.4 million. The number of mobile phone subscribers increased by 354 percent. Internet and e-mail usage also soared. By 1993, China's optical fiber trunk network had been increased to 24,000 miles, a 645 percent increase over 1990.

In order to avoid the high cost of buying foreign equipment, the BPT had established numerous state-owned subsidiary companies to manufacture equipment locally. Many of these companies were badly managed and produced equipment that was unreliable. Half the companies were on the verge of bankruptcy. Given the paternalistic traditions of state-run enterprises, however, the BPT couldn't simply shut them down without facing strong resistance. It could, however, introduce competition from the private sector. In 1993, it opened nine telecom services to domestic private companies, to introduce leading edge technology into the industry. Foreign companies were not allowed to own, manage, or operate domestic telecom systems by themselves unless there was an urgent need to directly purchase foreign technology, to significantly increase China's R&D, or in the case that the collaboration would lead to the introduction of advanced production techniques. The main foreign companies that became involved through partnerships with Chinese companies were Alcatel, Motorola China, Seimens, Nortel, and Ericsson. The largest domestic companies were ZTE, Datang, Wuhan Research Institute, Great Dragon Telecom, and eventually, Huawei.

FROM LOCAL TELEPHONE EXCHANGES
TO ADVANCED NETWORKS

Huawei adopted a two-pronged strategy relying both on sales of foreign equipment and on developing its own technology. To get the business moving, the company began importing telecom switches from Hong Kong and selling them to local networks. It did not take long for the competition to catch up. Ren was soon competing with at least 100 companies in Shenzhen alone.

But Ren realized early on that developing his own technology was the key to creating a sustainable business. From the beginning, Huawei committed more than 10 percent of its revenue to R&D. Within a year, it had designed, manufactured, and was aggressively marketing its own private branch exchange (PBX) products. At the time, roughly 200 domestic companies were producing telephone exchange switches, mostly for hotels, mining operations, and small enterprises. The average switch was capable of handling up to 2,000 connections, and the most reliable models were still being produced by foreign multinationals. Ren wanted to aim higher than that, but Huawei was already strapped for cash as a result of its extraordinary investment in research. To make matters worse, the banks, having suffered through the failures of so many state-owned companies, were reluctant to make loans to a private start-up with no political connections.

Ren nevertheless decided to push ahead. He gambled the company's future by taking out loans on the unofficial "gray market," at a potentially crushing 20 percent interest rate. Plowing the money back into development, he managed to produce the company's first 10,000-port, C&C08 switch, capable of handling five times as many connections, in 1994. Developing the switch cost Ren more than $10 million, but it was worth it. The gamble coincided with a massive government push to expand telecommunications at an even faster pace.

Not satisfied with merely producing switches, Huawei next moved into building signal transfer points (STPs), a critical component of narrow-band telephone systems, which until then had mostly been the preserve of the large multinationals. Since the multinationals, specifically Alcatel and Nortel, had locked up the market for the telephone networks in China's most important cities, Ren decided to focus on the provinces that the major players considered too remote and undeveloped to bother with.

In a sense, Ren was following a strategy familiar to players of the game Go, and also adopted by Mao, of gradually encircling the target before finally closing in and enveloping it. Mao had referred to it as "using the countryside to encircle and then expand to the cities." In Ren's case, it meant counterintuitively focusing on regions that did not seem promising to the major brands. When Ericsson sent three or four salespeople to talk to officials in Heilongjiang Province, Huawei sent more than 200. Huawei also made an extraordinary effort to provide the kind of fast and reliable service that foreign companies were not in a position to deliver. Huawei implemented its first STP equipment in Yinchuan, the capital of Ningxia Province, in 1996. The Ministry of Posts and Telecommunications monitored the implementation of the system carefully, and it provided proof that Huawei's equipment could do the job as well as foreign manufacturers. Before long, nearly all the provinces had signed up to buy STP equipment from Huawei, and by 2005, Huawei had captured a third of the Chinese market.

While many Chinese companies were content to copy Western products and then sell them at reduced prices, Huawei increased its efforts to develop its own technology. When the world telecom market reached a low point in 2002 and most companies were cutting back, Huawei increased its R&D investment to 17 percent of revenues. By June 2005, it had set up ten research institutes and was sharing technical know-how with Texas Instruments, Microsoft, Sun Microsystems, Motorola, IBM, and Intel. Huawei was averaging three new patents a day and giving substantial bonuses to engineers who developed the best ideas. It had soon accumulated more patents than any other company in China.

Ren had clearly targeted the leaders of the global industry, and he not only intended to catch up to them—he wanted to surpass them. At the same time, Ren emphasized the importance of designing products that specifically answered the customer's needs rather than producing technology for its own sake.

Huawei Goes Global

Although Huawei turned out to be extraordinarily successful in its domestic market, Ren sensed that the company needed to continue expanding or it would be in trouble. In fact, one of Ren's most characteristic obsessions was fear that the market would evolve faster than Huawei's ability to keep up with it. Huawei had tentatively begun to sell its products internationally as early as 1996, but this was mostly in developing markets, such as Brazil, South Africa, Ethiopia, and Yugoslavia. Its main focus had continued to be on China, but Ren was increasingly aware that the market in China was becoming saturated.

The biggest foreign client that Huawei had tried to sell to was Russia, but the company encountered the natural skepticism that one country in the Eastern bloc is likely to feel about the technology coming from another. Ren countered Russian doubts by flying potential clients to Beijing, Shenzhen, and Shanghai to see China for themselves. Despite that effort, Huawei's first major foreign sale turned out to be to Yemen and Laos in 1999. Two years later, in 2001, its efforts to impress Moscow paid off. Huawei won a $10 million bid to sell GSM (global system for mobile communications) equipment to the Russian government.

The need to step up its overseas expansion became apparent in 2002, just two years after the worldwide dot-com bust. Huawei's sales in China had risen to $2.2 billion, but its domestic market share was shrinking by 21 percent a year. It was increasingly obvious to everyone that the domestic market now really was becoming saturated. Huawei's international sales were only around $500 million, or roughly 18 percent of its total sales. Ren decided that it was time to make a major effort at going international. By 2004, just two years later, international sales accounted for 40 percent of the company's revenue. The only area that seemed off limits for major contracts was the United States.

HUAWEI'S INTERNATIONAL SUCCESS

Huawei had been cautious about trying to enter the U.S. market, even though it had created an institute in Silicon Valley in 1993 to explore chip production. But its success outside the United States was startling. By 2005, the company was providing telecom and Internet switching equipment to more than 30 of the world's top 50 telecommunications companies. British Telecom had selected it as one of its eight preferred suppliers for its 21st Century Network. Huawei's sales still added up to only 17 percent of those of Cisco, the market leader, but it had clearly marked itself as a global contender.

A major breakthrough in the European market had been Huawei's successful sale of equipment to what later became Neuf Cegetel, which is now owned by SFR, France's largest alternative telecommunications supplier (and second largest telecom supplier) and second largest mobile and fixed-line telephone provider. In 2001, Neuf was on the point of launching a program to provide a competing broadband Internet network for all of France. A final short list of manufacturers had already been decided upon when Huawei asked for a chance to make a last-minute bid. Michel Paulin, Neuf's CEO, was impressed by Huawei's low-cost offer and even more by its determination, but he was also concerned that China was geographically on the other side of the planet, and he was uncertain about Huawei's ability to deliver on time in Europe.

To break the ice, Huawei offered to build part of the network and run it for three months while Neuf's engineers tested it for free. That offer clinched the deal. Huawei won the contract and quickly became an integral part of Neuf's strategy to undercut the pricing of its chief competitor in France, Orange. More important, Huawei had successfully positioned itself to be ahead of other competitors when Neuf inevitably expanded its system from 40 gigabytes to 100 gigabytes.

Neuf had based much of its business strategy on providing the simplest interface possible to French consumers who were likely to be easily confused by computer and mobile phone technology. What impressed Neuf's Paulin the most was Huawei's readiness to listen to Neuf's requirements and then to deliver exactly what was required.

Huawei's flexibility and responsiveness was not an accident. Early on, the company had gone out of its way to hire local talent rather than relying solely on Chinese executives. It outsourced much of its hardware installation and some of its services to local partners. But it also managed to maintain high standards of quality. François Paulus, who headed the network division at Neuf, noted, "When we first saw Huawei, we couldn't believe that a Chinese company could match an occidental one—we were wrong. Their technology was better and they were 30 percent cheaper."

HUAWEI TARGETS THE U.S. MARKET

That kind of attention to detail still hadn't managed to get the company a frontline position as a provider of cutting edge equipment to America's top telecom networks. United States government opposition had effectively killed the Sprint Nextel deal, but Huawei executives did not seem overly upset. Charlie W. Chen, who headed Huawei's U.S. operations, told the *Wall Street Journal* in the days leading up to the final decision about the deal that Huawei was adopting a long-term strategy. "We are not in a hurry to win any significant or big project," he said.

In fact, Ren seemed intent on using the same strategy that he had used to conquer the Chinese market: Go for the smaller players first and gradually encircle the actual prize, until it became apparent to the target that there was nowhere else to turn. Only this time, instead of encircling a city, Huawei was signing up nearly every telecom system outside the United States. If it continued the kind of investment in R&D and innovation that it had done in the past, Huawei figured, even the major players in the United States would eventually have no other option but to open their doors to the best technology.

Ren had developed a number of guiding principles that had helped Huawei to grow while other companies fell by the wayside under the pressure of an increasingly competitive market. His most important insight was to make Huawei develop its own technology. The policy created cash flow problems at different intervals, but it put the company ahead of the technological curve in a fast-changing industry.

As previously stated, in developing his business, Ren applied Mao Zedong's strategy of starting in the countryside and gradually surrounding the cities. With few political connections at the beginning, he dispatched hundreds of sales personnel to China's poor interior provinces, which the established multinationals hadn't thought worth bothering with. As the company grew stronger, he moved into the more established urban areas. Applying the same principle along a different axis, he built a reputation for the company with relatively basic technology, and as the company grew stronger, he moved into increasingly sophisticated areas. Approaching the American market, Huawei established a strong reputation for design and effectiveness of cell phones and other basic consumer electronics and sold its most advanced networking equipment everywhere except America. As Huawei's technology grew stronger, Ren sensed that eventually the American market would either have to open up to him or satisfy itself with paying more money than it needed in order to have second best. Huawei sensed that the market trend was in its favor.

In a sense, Ren, a former army officer, had applied another of Sun Tzu's principles. "Military tactics are like water," Sun Tzu had said. "As water shapes its flow according to the ground, an army wins by relating to the enemy it faces and adapts to the conditions of the environment and modifies its tactics according to the enemy's situations." In Huawei's case, the principle called for paying special attention to forming the company's production to the client's needs, even if it meant hiring engineers who were not necessarily stars but were likely to be more sensitive to the vision of its customers. As Huawei's breakthrough in the French market showed, the company also placed an emphasis on being more flexible and moving more quickly with more innovative proposals than its competitors.

But by far, Huawei's most important advantage was its decision to invest heavily in R&D. As shown in Chapter 4, good management can turn improperly run companies around in a stable environment, but when technology begins to evolve quickly, even the best-run company is likely to find itself in uncharted waters if it is relying on others for its technology.

F O U R

TCL Takes Over Thomson
Li Dongsheng's Normandy*

For China to become a strong nation, we must have our own global companies. We dare to be the first to eat crab. Without the courage to become martyrs, we cannot be pioneers.**

> —Li Dongsheng, Chairman of TCL, on being named one of the top ten economic personalities by China Central Television in 2004

EARLY IN JULY 2006, Li Dongsheng faced one of the toughest decisions in his 24-year career. The chairman of TCL International Holdings had just read a financial assessment by the consulting firm McKinsey & Company of TCL's European affiliate, TTE Europe SAS. TTE Europe had lost €60 million the previous year and was now projected to lose another €200 million. The McKinsey report did not pull its punches:

---

* This title was adapted from a Chinese article: http://www.businesswatch.com.cn/Html/Cover/0782416565541938.html.

** The Chinese saying "the first person to eat crab" means the first person with the courage to try something new.

❖ The sales organization was too big, too expensive, and not efficient for the existing business model.

❖ The supply chain and product lines were not responsive to market changes.

❖ The affiliate was financially bankrupt with continuing losses that were likely to increase.

McKinsey proposed two solutions: Either declare bankruptcy and write off the €100 million invested over the previous two years, or restructure and make an additional cash injection of €100 million just to stay afloat. Li Dongsheng had a tough decision to make.

Li Dongsheng's Personal Rise to Power

During China's Cultural Revolution, when Mao promoted the notion of young people from cities learning from the peasants, Li had been dispatched to an agricultural cooperative in Guangdong Province for three years. He spent his days doing hard manual labor and his nights reading, a habit that he continued throughout his life.

In late October 1977, Deng Xiaoping launched his Open Door Policy. One of his first initiatives was to resume the nationwide university entrance examinations that had been discontinued in 1965. At least 5 million candidates, ranging in age from 13 to 37, took the examination. It was the most competitive scholastic test in modern Chinese history. Fewer than 5 percent of the 5 million who took the exam were admitted to universities. They were widely regarded in China as the best and brightest of that decade. Li was one of them.

Li graduated from Hua Nan Polytechnic University in 1982, with a bachelor of science degree in electrical engineering. He quickly accepted an entry-level job in a small factory assembling tape cassettes. Little more than 20 years later, in 2004, *Fortune* magazine chose Li as its "Asia Businessman of the Year." The relatively anonymous factory that he had joined as a technician had evolved into TCL, one of the largest consumer electronics enterprises in China, and Li was its chairman and CEO.

TCL's ambitions extended beyond the Chinese domestic market. Its operations had gone global, and by 2005, TCL had transformed itself into a conglomerate with three subsidiaries under its umbrella: TCL Corporation, TCL Multimedia Technology, and TCL Communication Technology.

From Humble Beginnings to an Industrial Powerhouse

Huiyang Electronic Industrial Company, the small cassette-tape factory where Li began his career, had been started a year before Li's arrival with a $600 loan from the Huizhou city government. As China's economy began to accelerate, Li and his colleagues decided that the next big thing was likely to be telephones. In 1985, Li was named CEO of TCL Telecommunication Equipment Company Ltd., a joint venture with Hong Kong investors. The TCL trademark was registered in 1986. By 1989, the company had become one of China's biggest phone manufacturers. Over the next two years, it developed a nationwide sales and service network.

TCL produced its first color TV in 1992 through another joint venture, this time with Hong Kong–based Huizhou King Audio Visual Electronics Company Ltd. In 1993, TCL was listed on the Shenzhen Stock Exchange and raised $10 million. The move made TCL the first electronics company to be listed in China, although 80 percent of TCL was still owned by the Huizhou city government. TCL began making international acquisitions in 1996 with the purchase of Luk's Industrial, a Hong Kong–based TV manufacturer. In 1997, TCL restructured and became TCL International Holdings Co. Ltd. Li Dongsheng was named chairman and CEO.

With Li at its helm, TCL embarked on a domestic buying spree. It acquired the Henan Meile Electronic Group in 1997, the Inner Mongolia Rainbow TV Company in 1999, and the Wuxi Hongmei TV factory in 2000. Most of these companies were on the brink of bankruptcy. While TCL itself lacked the core technology of each of the companies it acquired, it was still able to make them profitable by focusing on marketing, distribution, and tight cost control. TCL also showed a flare for gaining public attention. In the winter of 1995–1996, the company spent RMB 4.5 million building a women's volleyball foundation. China had won five consecutive world championships in women's volleyball between 1981 and 1985, and the sport was immensely popular. TCL followed this up by hiring a famous actress to do a TV commercial, which was aired nationally. Within a month, TCL's big screen TVs dominated the market. By 2000, TCL had emerged as one of the largest television producers in China.

To finance its rapid expansion, TCL International Holdings Co. Ltd. raised $128 million in 1999 through an IPO on the Hong Kong Stock Exchange. The next year, TCL ventured into Vietnam and Russia. It also started an OEM (original equipment manufacturer) business, producing for Philips, Thomson, and Panasonic. TV sets under the TCL brand were exported to South Africa, South Asia, and the Middle East.

While TCL was extremely successful in emerging markets, it was effectively barred from the lucrative markets in the United States and Europe because of anti-dumping charges against Chinese TV manufacturers. In 2002, TCL sold an 11 percent stake to 12 strategic investors, including Toshiba and Philips. After failing to acquire Philips's Magnavox brand in 2001, during the following year TCL acquired Schneider, an insolvent German electronics company, including the Dual and Schneider brands, production plants, and distribution networks.

By 2003, TCL was shipping 11.5 million televisions. It had captured 18 percent of the market in China, 14 percent in Vietnam, 8 percent in the Philippines, and significant shares in India and Pakistan.[1] Aggressive expansion through mergers and acquisitions had enabled TCL to balance its phenomenal growth with profitability. It emerged as the only Chinese television manufacturer to be consistently profitable from 1998 to 2003. For the first three quarters of 2003, TCL reported profits of $169 million on sales of $4.2 billion. By then, TCL ranked as China's first television and mobile phone producer and its fourth largest electronics company.

But TCL wanted more. The company's ambition was to become a "world-class enterprise." Li realized that this was not going to happen unless TCL became a genuinely market-oriented company. In January 2004, to fuel further expansion, TCL announced its A-share listing on the Shenzhen Stock Exchange and raised another $330 million. (In addition, the Huizhou city government reduced its ownership to 25 percent. At least 38 percent of the remaining shares were held by the public. Strategic investors held 14 percent, and Li himself 6 percent.) Li realized that if he could make TCL's model work, it would very likely establish a model for other state-owned enterprises. He was beginning to feel the pressure to grow faster with even more profits.

The TV Market in China

The Chinese television market had experienced high demand in 1978, but by 1995, it was turning into a buyer's market. In the early 1980s, the typical Chinese family owned a nine-inch black and white set. Everyone wanted a TV, but to even be able to buy one, you needed to have guanxi (special connections). By 1985, television had switched to color in China, and the number of companies manufacturing sets had skyrocketed. More than 300 television manufacturers competed across the country. Foreign brands, including Toshiba, Sanyo, National, and Philips, captured a significant share of the high-end market.

From 1990 to 1995, Chinese TV manufacturers made enormous strides in cathode ray tube (CRT) technology. Local brands such as Changhong, TCL, Hisense, Skyworth, Konka, Panda, and Haier controlled about 90 percent of China's domestic TV market. But to their chagrin, Chinese brands were still not able to penetrate the U.S., European, or Japanese markets.

By 1999, China's saturated domestic TV market was driving TV manufacturers into cutthroat competition and suicidal price reductions. The situation was further complicated by the fact that many of the TV manufacturers were state-owned enterprises, controlled by local authorities. Political considerations often blocked the consolidation that might have made some of these companies viable. As losses mounted and manufacturers made less on each set sold, the manufacturers focused on trying to get consumers to trade in their old sets for new ones or to buy more sets per household.

In the struggle for survival, manufacturers increasingly looked for expansion outside China. Europe, which purchases 10 million to 15 million sets a year, looked particularly attractive.[2] Entry into the European market was being held back, however, by an investigation into anti-dumping charges against Chinese television makers that the European Union had begun in 1988. In November 1999, the EU imposed a 44.6 percent tariff on China. The United States soon followed Europe, in response to trade union complaints that China was off-loading color TVs in the United States by selling them at cost or below market value.[3] The United States imposed its own tariffs, ranging from 28 percent to 46 percent.

Li Dongsheng was determined to add TCL to the Global 500 list of the world's largest companies within a decade, and that meant he would have to sell ten times more sets than before. The only way to do that was to extend sales beyond China's domestic market. That meant making an alliance with a European manufacturer to gain entry to their market. Li was fully aware that competing with the multinationals on their own ground could be dangerous, but he was equally convinced that unless TCL went global, it would perish. In July 2003, Li met with Charles Dehelly, the CEO of the European electronics company Thomson, to talk about a potential alliance.

Thomson's History

Thomson's history dates back to 1879, when engineer Elihu Thomson and inventor Edwin Houston founded the Thomson-Houston, with headquarters in the United States and subsidiaries in Europe and South America. In 1892, Thomson-Houston merged with Thomas Edison's companies to form General Electric. The next year, the Compagnie Française Thomson-Houston (CFTH) was created in Paris as a sister company to General Electric. CFTH eventually became the modern company Thomson.

Thomson entered the radio and television business in 1929 through the acquisition of the French company Etablissements Ducretet. In 1987, Thomson bought RCA and GE Consumer Electronics from GE. A year later, Thomson Consumer Electronics was formed. It was renamed Thomson Multimedia in 1995 and simply Thomson in 2002. In 2003, the French government privatized Thomson.

Thomson's consumer products division, which reported a $540 million loss in 1996, had been in trouble ever since.[4] The French government tried to sell it to Daewoo for a single symbolic franc. In exchange, it wanted Daewoo to assume Thomson's debt of more than $1 billion. French labor unions sabotaged the sale, and Thomson's worldwide market share continued to slide from 1999 to 2002. In the United States, Thomson's market share dropped from 20 percent to 13 percent. Meanwhile, in Europe, it went from 9 percent to 7.4 percent.[5] In 2003, third-quarter revenue for

Thomson consumer products dropped another 12 percent, down to $859.6 million, compared with $1.1 billion the previous year. In total, Thomson's TV operations lost $130 million in 2003.

The company distributed its products under the Thomson brand in Europe and as RCA in the United States. In Europe, the Thomson brand lagged behind Philips, Sony, Samsung, and LG. Although RCA was still a well-known brand in the United States, it was increasingly typecast as "the TV that only old people watch."[6]

Thomson's aging technology was based largely on 34,000 patents relating to the cathode-ray technology, the kind that went into the bulky television picture tubes that preceded flat screen TVs. The company had placed its future bets on micro-displays, rear pro-jection TVs that used chip-based light engines such as DLP (digital light processing). It had virtually ignored other new technologies such as PDP (plasma display panel), LCD (liquid crystal display), and OLED (organic light-emitting device).

In contrast to Thomson, Japan's leading high-end TV manufac-turers—Sony, Sharp, Matsushita, Toshiba, and Hitachi—were already planning to phase out their CRT television production lines. To get rid of their excess inventory, the Japanese began slashing the prices of their CRT sets worldwide. Thomson, as the oldest CRT television maker, was also looking for an exit, but French unions, highly resist-ant to any change, made finding one particularly difficult.

On November 4, 2003, Thomson signed a memorandum of understanding with TCL to merge the television activities of both companies into TCL-Thomson Electronics (TTE). The market wel-comed the deal, since analysts had been convinced for a long time that both companies needed to find a partner. TCL was especially eager to obtain new technology, as well as brand and sales distribu-tion channels to expand abroad. For its part, Thomson needed a manufacturing base with lower costs—either that, or it needed to get out of the television market altogether. Once the news of the merger broke, Thomson's share price gained 14 percent and closed at a new high for the year. TCL's shares gained 24 percent, closing at a three-year high.

How the Deal Played Out

With Boston Consulting and Morgan Stanley advising TCL and McKinsey and ABN Amro advising Thomson, the $560 million joint venture, TCL Multimedia Technology, would take a majority stake (67 percent) and Thomson Holding would retain the remaining 33 percent. TCL would appoint two-thirds of the board and Thomson one-third. TCL would nominate the CEO, the CFO, and the head of the China business unit, while Thomson would nominate the heads of the European and North American operations and the deputy CFO. Under the agreement, both companies would transfer their respective television assets to TTE.

Thomson would transfer to TTE the majority of its manufacturing and sales of TV sets (including its television-manufacturing facilities in Mexico, Poland, and Thailand and some R&D facilities). This amounted to nearly 60 percent of Thomson's consumer products division. TCL would transfer to TTE its television and DVD manufacturing, R&D, and sales network in China, Germany, and Vietnam. Both companies would also contribute cash—€70 million from Thomson and €140 million from TCL.

Li realized that the plants Thomson was offering him were costly, inefficient, and behind the times, but he decided that the deal would be worth it if it could open European and U.S. markets to TCL's products. The pre-acquisition study showed that sourcing cheap parts from China and tightening up the supply chain would greatly reduce costs. The cloud on the horizon was the deal's enormous complexity when it came to defining the three things Li wanted the most: TTE's access to brands, intellectual property, and Thomson's sales network.

Thomson and TCL would retain ownership of the brands, and TTE would license the brands in order to market televisions in Asia (TCL), Europe (Thomson), and the United States (RCA). According to the 20-year license contract, TTE would not pay license fees during the first two years of operation and would pay 0.25 percent to 2 percent for the remaining years. If TTE could not meet the sales target, Thomson had the right to end the license agreement with one year's notice.

Thomson had focused on CRT technology, which would not be transferred to TTE, and TTE had to negotiate specific contracts for access to intellectual property owned by Thomson. (TTE paid Thomson HK$136 million, HK$284 million, and HK$330 million in 2004, 2005, and 2006, respectively.) New intellectual property rights generated by the joint venture company would have to be licensed to one of the shareholders for use, with royalties being paid back to the joint venture.

Thomson's sales and marketing network would become the exclusive agent for distribution in North America and Europe. TTE would have to pay fees, commissions, and bonuses for sales and marketing and engineering work, with product service and support being provided by Thomson. (The initial arrangement was altered so that Thomson transferred its sales and marketing network to TTE in 2005. TTE paid HK$100 million for the change.)

Within TCL, there was some hesitation over the fact that for the previous five years, Thomson had been desperately searching for an exit from the TV-manufacturing business. Everyone knew that its technology lagged behind its competitors. TCL's consultants were especially aware of these weaknesses. The strongest objections, however, centered on the difficulties of integrating two companies with very different cultures. TCL had neither the experience nor the professional management capability to accomplish an integration of this scale. The risk was huge.

In the low-margin TV manufacturing business, scale is a key factor. Li was well aware of the role that size was likely to play in TCL's future. He reasoned that being bigger would not necessarily make his company stronger, but he also knew that unless he could become bigger, he would never have any hope at all of becoming stronger. Size was a prerequisite for survival. After listening to both sides, Li became increasingly uneasy about the joint venture's future. Thomson reported €130 million in losses in 2003, mainly in its North American operations. In the same period, TCL's sales of TV sets earned a $73 million profit.

The feasibility study suggested that with aggressive marketing, relentless cost control, low-cost sourcing, and supply chain optimization, combined with the Thomson brand, R&D, and marketing support, TTE's North American and European operations could be profitable within a year. The approach was similar to the one that TCL had used to turn around the failing Chinese companies it had acquired early in its history.

Li was also highly aware of the fact that since China had entered the World Trade Organization in 2001, the China market was in the process of becoming a global market, and TCL would soon be forced to compete with global players in its domestic market. To survive, TCL would have to go global itself. Li decided that he didn't really have any other option. He received the board's approval to move ahead. The goal was for TTE to break even in 18 months.

The Deal Goes Through

TTE was officially established on July 29, 2004. Zhao Zhongyao, its first CEO, was dutifully optimistic. "Through scale economy, cost control, shared R&D capacities, lowered sourcing cost," he said, "our management team has full confidence."[7]

TTE now had more than 20,000 sales outlets, 29,000 employees (9,000 from Thomson), 10 TV plants, and five R&D centers around the world. It projected sales of $3.5 billion and planned to sell more than 18.5 million TV sets a year. The deal made TTE the world's largest TV manufacturer in 2004. TCL was hailed as the first Chinese company to acquire the majority share of a well-established global business.

TTE quickly created five profit centers: China, Europe, North America, Emerging Markets, and Strategic OEM. Two committees were assembled to coordinate the transformation process. One committee, led by a Korean executive who was formerly deputy CEO and COO at LG Philips Display, was devoted to cost containment in sourcing, manufacturing, and supply chain operations. The other committee, led by a longtime Thomson veteran, focused on value creation. Its role was to develop new products and market opportunities to improve sales.

Focus on North America

Management efforts centered heavily on North American operations, which had suffered $100 million losses on $1 billion sales in 2003. The immediate goal was to turn the North American division around and to stop the bleeding.

A year-long investigation, identifying several weaknesses in the North American market, was launched immediately after the signing of the memorandum of understanding. Thomson had been spending considerably more for components than its competitors. Three of its Mexican factories had large capacity but were mostly idle. Worse, the TV main circuit board design that Thomson had adopted was both extremely expensive and required two years of lead time to manufacture compared to the industry standard of seven months.

At the end of 2004, TTE launched its TCAT program, which put a TCL main circuit board into a Thomson box. Several smaller programs were initiated to cut costs, including Component

Chinalization, BIC (Best in Cost), NAV (North American Value), and NAC (North American Cost Down). At first, these initiatives were resisted. Thomson was accustomed to buying parts from expensive suppliers in Europe, Japan, and Korea, and Chinese parts were criticized as "low price, low quality." TCL fought back, reasoning that components from China were subjected to the same quality engineering tests that the Europeans and Japanese used, and that the 20 percent price difference was significant.

Within six months, TTE's material costs had been slashed by 10 percent, saving $80 million. Nearly 50 percent of CRT, LCD, PDP, and DLP components were manufactured in China, but the agreement forced TTE North America to continue purchasing some of its components from Thomson's other plants in Marion, Indiana, and Mexicali, Mexico. The design of the TV main circuit boards was shifted to China. The U.S. engineers were left with the responsibility for industrial design, which required final fine-tuning to fit the local market.

TTE progressively consolidated its manufacturing. The three factories in Mexico were merged into one MASA factory, located just 30 miles from the U.S. border. The new production line reduced the number of employees from 4,000 to 2,500, delivering the same output as before without compromising quality. This alone saved TTE $20 million a year. More than 90 percent of the components were shipped to the United States via container, which again lowered costs.

But while cost containment was succeeding, the sales side was doing less well. The RCA brand, suffering from years of neglect, was continuing its downward slide. The market shift from old-fashioned picture tubes and bulky sets to sleeker models with flat screens was also having an impact on TTE's North American sales.

TTE soon realized that subcontracting sales and services to Thomson was not working. Expenses related to sales were 23 percent of the revenue, which was 4 percent higher than the industry average, and after-sales costs were running at 1.5 percent higher than the industry average. It was becoming increasingly apparent that the turnaround was not going to work unless TTE gained full control of the sales and services network. After months of negotiations in 2005, Thomson sold the entire sales network, including Europe and North America, to TTE for $12.87 million. The turnaround team then decided to focus on the largest U.S. clients. The total number was reduced from 300 to 25. The restructuring created a sales organization of 80 people, down from 160 a year earlier. By the end of 2005, the total loss of the U.S. operations had been slashed in half to $45 million.

TTE in Europe

The European Union market that had been positive in 2002 experienced a loss of €3 million in 2003. Compared to what was happening in North America, the European losses looked like a drop in the ocean. "We put all our effort into turning the North American division around," Li recalled. "We left the Thomson management team intact in Paris, although we did send an HR manager to coordinate." (TCL called them "interface," a cost-effective solution to facilitate communication with local management.) Li really did not have much choice. Its shortage of international managers meant that TCL Multimedia Technology could not afford to initiate another restructuring in Europe.

The European business incurred more losses in 2004, but it had projected an €8 million profit for 2005. This was based on plans to launch 25 models (including three different flat screen technologies—LCD, plasma, and DLP) simultaneously, as well as continuing production of the old-fashioned CRT TVs that had previously formed the bulk of the company's product line. As it turned out, the strategy was too little and too late. European customers had already switched to flat screen TVs in early 2005, and sales of the bulky CRT TVs dropped precipitously. TTE's president for Europe, a French manager who had been transferred from Thomson to the new company, assured Li that things would be better in the second half of the year. In retrospect, Li would have been much better off taking charge himself and keeping a tighter reign on the situation, but he really didn't have much choice. He was overextended. By the time he realized the seriousness of the situation, it was already too late.

TTE had gradually become aware of the fact that the market was changing, and it frantically tried to increase the number of its LCD products in Europe. But the company's senior managers soon learned that only a handful of companies manufactured the LCD screens that were the major component in each set. LG Philips LCD and Samsung Electronics had a 45 percent share of the worldwide market. These companies made their own televisions, which gave them a strong competitive advantage since their most advanced LCD televisions were on the market long before competing manufacturers could incorporate the screens into their models. It took six to nine months for TTE to buy the panels, integrate them into the new TV design, and manufacture the sets. By the time TTE products hit the market, the prices of the market leaders' existing models were already being discounted to make room for newer models. Television manufacturers that couldn't make their own LCDs were always going to be behind the curve. As with IT products, manufacturers of flat screen televisions were likely to be forced into slashing their prices by 5 percent to 10 percent a quarter.

To make matters worse, TTE was forced to pay panel manufacturers in advance. Prices were dropping so fast that when TTE received payment from customers three to six months later, the payments often failed to cover the original price of the panel. Before long, lagging cash flow delays threatened the company's survival. To compound the situation, TTE's sales representatives, whose commissions and bonuses were based on gross sales, had allowed customers to trade old models in for new ones without factoring in the cost of product returns.

There was also an initial disconnect between production and sales because of the fact that the sales organization belonged to Thomson, not TTE. When TTE took over Thomson's sales and marketing operations in September 2005, at least two-thirds of TTE's new 600-strong European sales organization consisted of former Thomson sales agents who had spent as much time selling audio, video, and other consumer electronics products as they had televisions. With CRT TVs losing market share and flat screen TVs losing money, the sales organization that TTE had inherited from Thomson was simply too large and costly to keep on board. The multilayered sales structure based in major countries and oriented toward CRTs was too hierarchical to adjust to the sudden transition to LCD televisions.

At the end of 2005, instead of its projected profit, TTE Europe registered a €60 million loss. With TTE's limited R&D capabilities, the launch of new products had been delayed two months, and the company missed out on the critically important 2005 fall buying season. As a result, it was drowning in inventory. A TTE inspection team, headed by COO Shi Wanwen, arrived in Paris in February 2006. The team soon discovered that the CRT TV market share had nose-dived in 2005 from 88.8 percent to 70.9 percent. The decline was much faster in Europe than in any other market. It was projected to decline to 40 percent in 2006.

If that wasn't bad enough, TTE Europe was hit a few months later by European legislation requiring televisions and computer hardware to be "RoHS-compliant"—referring to "Restriction of Hazardous Substances"—by July 1, 2006. (The banned substances were cadmium, mercury, hexavalent chromium, polybrominated biphenyls, polybrominated diphenyl ether, and lead.) There was a rush to dump any product containing the outlawed materials before the deadline on future sales went into effect and, as a result, all the companies had to slash their prices in an effort to empty their inventories. With losses mounting, Li dispatched TCL's CFO to Paris in May 2006 and hired a local team from McKinsey to help assess the situation.

At a board meeting in June 2006, Li took over control as the interim CEO of TTE. A month later, he received McKinsey's report that TTE Europe SAS was very close to insolvency. As TCL's share of the worldwide TV manufacturing market dropped another two points from 11.2 percent to 9 percent, it became clear that as far as manufacturing TVs went, TCL was now in third place. It had been overtaken by LG Electronics and Samsung.

The easy way out was to cut the company's losses and declare bankruptcy, but from Li's point of view, the original reasons for engaging in the merger with Thomson were still valid. On the other hand, if TTE continued its spiral downward, it would need the injection of another €100 million just to stay afloat. Li knew that his current business model was not sustainable, and he looked for another alternative.

Restructuring

Because it was the first joint venture of its size involving a Chinese company, TTE had symbolic importance—something that Li had to take into account. Its collapse might have political implications. Rumors were already beginning to circulate that the joint venture was a failure. The Chinese government preferred not to interfere, but its concern was evident. Thomson also had reasons to hope that TTE Europe would not declare bankruptcy: Thierry Breton, the French minister of Economy, Finance and Industry, had been chairman and CEO of Thomson from 1997 to 2002.

Li was also concerned about the longer term implications. He was worried about a Chinese company being labeled as socially irresponsible, about being excluded from the European market permanently, and about the risk of prolonged litigation. In August 2006, TCL and Thomson arrived at a restructuring plan: Thomson would pay €20 million in cash and TCL would contribute €25 million by selling some of TTE's assets for the restructuring. All that was necessary was for Li to convince TCL's creditors (mainly Chinese banks) that the plan had a chance.

In October 2006, TCL announced a €45 million restructuring plan that called for closing down most of TTE's European TV business. The government and employees were at the top of the list to be repaid. After that came suppliers and customers. The sales force would be reduced. The plan made sense, but it had not taken into account resistance from the unions. Negotiations quickly reached a deadlock. The unions demanded job priority for workers who were unlikely to be taken on anywhere else. TTE wanted to retain its high-performing salespeople and to get rid of the rest. The negotiations continued for three months and, during that period, TTE was locked into continuing to pay everyone's salaries. "We seriously underestimated the difficulties and costs of restructuring the European operations," Li later admitted. "We planned to pay several million euros to make the system more efficient, but the cost was far more than that."

Ultimately, TTE was forced to pay a €100,000 severance package to each of the remaining TTE Europe employees. There was not enough to pay off suppliers and customers, and by May 2007, despite extensive negotiations, TTE Europe had failed to find a way out. TTE Europe SAS filed for bankruptcy.

Rising from the Ashes

Despite its failed venture with Thomson, TCL was reluctant to abandon the European market. The task of rebuilding TCL's presence in

Europe was entrusted to Dr. Yan Fei, a native Chinese man with French citizenship, who spoke impeccable French. Yan had been sent to Belgium to do a PhD in engineering in 1984 as part of a Chinese government–sponsored program. After completing his PhD, he worked in various positions for the oilfield services company Schlumberger and the construction products company Saint-Gobain. In 1999, Saint-Gobain sent him to head its Beijing office. In June 2004, he joined TTE.

After the bankruptcy, Yan decided to create a new legal entity through TCL Macau. Since the old business model was clearly unsustainable, he needed a new one. The question was which one. A quick survey of the worldwide TV manufacturing industry indicated that most operations were now either completely unprofitable or possibly making a meager profit if the company ran a really tight ship from the supply chain, through manufacturing, to sales. But Yan noticed two significant changes in the market. First, the technology of LCD flat screens was maturing. More and more companies, other than South Korean manufacturers, were now able to produce flat screens of comparable quality at competitive prices. Second, the European anti-dumping duties covering TV sets were scheduled to end in August 2007. As in Sun Tzu's *The Art of War*, timing was likely to be the deciding factor. Yan had first noticed the trend in June 2006. Now, he needed to come up with a business plan to present to the TCL board.

A New Model

The new business entity that Yan proposed to the board, TCL Overseas Marketing (Macau Commercial Offshore) Ltd., was created under the TCL Multimedia Technology division. As Yan (now the VP of TCL Multimedia Technology) had noted earlier, the 44.6 percent anti-dumping duty on imports of color televisions that had been imposed on August 30, 2002, was set to expire on August 30,

2007. Yan assumed from the start that the old business model—with R&D, manufacturing, warehousing, and support functions clustered in Europe—was unsustainable. With short product life cycles and declining sales, holding on to inventory was too risky and too expensive. The practice of maintaining large inventories in multiple warehouses clearly had to end. Yan proposed a hybrid model that integrated build-to-forecast and build-to-order into a borderless centralized organization. The board quickly approved his business plan, which now targeted profitability rather than market share.

In February 2007, Yan hired 30 employees who had previously worked for TTE Europe and added about ten additional staff from outside the company. The 40 employees were mainly involved in sales, but Yan added two extra criteria to the selection process: cultural flexibility and the ability to work as a member of a team. "You don't need to like Chinese people or Chinese food, " Yan told his recruits, "but you should be open-minded, objective, and have little disposition for racial prejudice."

TTE Europe had previously maintained separate HR, finance, and IT teams in each European country. The support functions were now centralized with a staff of around 40 employees who were based in Shenzhen. Employees based in Europe could contact their counterparts in Shenzhen via videoconference, e-mail, voice mail, and frequent face-to-face meetings. Yan called this "borderless and centralized organization." The operating expenses of the new organization were only 3 percent of sales, among the lowest in the business.

To make the model work, Yan had to focus on major customers that could function with a system based on rolling forecast-based orders. He decided to eliminate dealing directly with any of the old customers that were dependent on point-to-point delivery. The company's largest customers had developed their own distribution channels and generally preferred handling delivery themselves.

They often consolidated different goods in their own warehouses so they could transport them more efficiently to their retail outlets. To the other customers, Yan suggested establishing relationships with wholesalers capable of handling logistics on their own. TTE Europe had previously served 1,000 clients, about half of them small stores. The new entity had 60 customers by the end of 2007, with more than 80 percent of sales concentrated in only 15.

The model required three- to six-month rolling forecasts with no obligation necessary from customers during the first phase. This would be followed by a firm order one month in advance of delivery. Rolling forecasts made it possible to order LCDs (three months in advance) and chip sets (four and a half months in advance) and to transport main circuit boards and other components to Poland. (TCL had bought the Poland plant long before TTE's bankruptcy.) Filling a firm order required two weeks of production time. As a buffer for last-minute order changes, TCL kept five days' worth of inventory in Poland. The cost saving was huge compared to the old model, which had maintained inventories of televisions in warehouses across Europe. The key to making the model work was close coordination between sales, production, and suppliers.

In addition to lowering inventory costs and reducing obsolescence, the elimination of warehouses across Europe had other benefits. TTE Europe had been swamped with 10 percent product returns in 2006 because its retail customers could easily get to warehouses that were located near them in order to trade old models for new ones. With only a single warehouse in Poland, product returns were practically eliminated. The business model still offered a 24-month warranty, the same as the market leaders, but now, if products were reported faulty or damaged, after-sales representatives contacted the contracted local service repair providers to fix the problem. If the problem could not be fixed, TCL would provide a refund and leave it to the customer to dispose of the faulty item. If the customer balked at doing that, TCL could ask its repair partner to dismantle the item for spare parts.

Though anti-dumping duties were no longer in force, LCD products imported into Europe were still subject to a 14 percent custom duty. Producing in Poland would save the company money. Countries with no custom duty, such as Russia and other Central European countries, would import finished products (branded as TCL) directly from China. In Europe, 80 percent of the company's televisions were sold under the Thomson brand.

The new business was launched in August 2007. One month later, TCL's new European division was profitable and continued to be so, with the factory in Poland producing 100,000 sets monthly. Li's gamble had paid off. Both he and his company had come a long way from the small factory manufacturing tape cassettes that had only needed a $600 municipal loan to get started.

NOTES

1. Economist Intelligence Unit, February 16, 2004.

2. "Chinese TV Manufacturers Face Up to Anti-Dumping Charges," *People's Daily Online*, August 13, 2000.

3. "U.S. Commerce Dept. Slaps Anti-Dumping Duties on Chinese Color TVs," *Working Life*, December 18, 2003, www.workinglife.org.

4. TCL-Thomson Electronics Corporation, ICFAI, 306-414-1.

5. TCL-Thomson Electronics Corporation, ICFAI, 306-414-1.

6. Matthew Forney, "Li Dongsheng," *Time Canada*, December 20, 2004.

7. Chang Tianle and Zhan Lisheng, "TTE Vows to Become TV Industry Leader," China Daily.com, July 30, 2004, www.chinadaily.com.

FIVE

Lenovo
IBM Lends a Hand

When was the last time you saw a successful acquisition or merger in the computer industry?
—Michael Dell, founder and CEO of Dell, Inc.

ON DECEMBER 7, 2004, Lenovo, China's top computer company, astonished the world with the announcement that it was acquiring IBM's personal computer division for $1.75 billion. It appeared to be an exceptionally bold move for a relatively young Chinese company and a sign of its determination to extend its global reach. Fang Xingdong, the chairman of Blogchina.com and a well-known pundit on information technology issues, called it "a magnificent acquisition." He added, "The new Lenovo becomes a major global player in the PC industry overnight." Fang predicted that Lenovo would be getting "IBM's first-rate products, technology, brands, market, channels and management." [1]

A little more than four years later, on February 5, 2009, Lenovo seemed to be hovering on the edge of catastrophe. The company announced a quarterly loss of $96.7 million, and it confirmed the departure of CEO William Amelio, a former Dell executive who had taken the job only three years earlier. Lenovo's chairman, Yang Yuanqing, replaced Amelio with the company's founder, Liu Chuanzhi, who took over the duties of chairman. Yang and Liu both concentrated their efforts on stabilizing the company, and Liu had to be asking himself whether Michael Dell didn't have a point: Mergers in the computer industry can turn out to be far more complex and unpredictable than they first appear.

Only a year after its dramatic quarterly loss, Lenovo recorded an $80 million profit for the same quarter and was back on track as the world's fastest-growing computer company and fourth largest manufacturer of PCs. Turning Lenovo around, however, had required abandoning IBM's vision of the industry and effectively abandoning the American market approach for a model that was specifically Chinese. For Liu Chuanzhi, Lenovo's journey to becoming a major player on the global technology scene had been a dizzyingly informative ride.

Written in the Stars

In Chinese astrology, 12 animals symbolize the zodiac. The first is the rat, known for its intelligence, nimbleness, cunning, and aggressively entrepreneurial spirit. It may have been a coincidence, but in 1984, a year of the rat, the world witnessed the launch of a group of extraordinarily enterprising Chinese companies, including Haier, TCL, Chint, Vanke, and Lenovo.

The company that was to become Lenovo got its start on November 1, 1984, when the Computer Technology Institute of the Chinese Academy of Sciences authorized about $25,000 for its 11 computer scientists to set up a private company calling itself the

New Technology Developer, Inc. Liu Chuanzhi, who had just turned 40, was one of the original founders. Born in Shanghai and raised in Beijing, Liu graduated with an engineering degree from Xian Military Communication Engineering College in 1966. During the Cultural Revolution, he was sent to a state farm to do manual labor, but within two years, he had managed to join the Computer Technology Institute.

His work focused on magnetic storage. At the time, it was hard to see much of a commercial future in China in such an esoteric field. There were no products or markets for the designs he was working on, and the Cultural Revolution had cut investment in research and development to a minimum. Liu recalled:

> No new houses had been built since the Cultural Revolu-tion, so people just crammed into buildings as the popula-tion grew. Three other colleagues, scientists who were ten years older than I was, lived with me in a 12-square-meter room the size of a bicycle shed. I can't even call it a house. The walls were just a single layer of brick. It was impossible to stay warm.

In 1984, China had just begun to engage in market reforms, and a new emphasis was put on turning R&D into useful products. The new venture that Liu helped found was given a mandate to com-mercialize the Computer Technology Institute's research and hope-fully to generate enough money to improve living conditions for its scientists. If possible, it would also help to pay for improving the Institute's scientific research.

Liu soon found himself riding a bicycle across Beijing, looking for promising business opportunities. To finance the salaries for its employees, the new company experimented with selling electric watches, roller skates, sportswear, and refrigerators. On one occasion,

Liu put up $17,500 in a deal to buy color TVs, which turned out to be a scam. The fraud briefly shook Liu's confidence and nearly sank the struggling company, but soon afterward, Liu's luck improved. IBM asked the company to represent it in China, and as it turned out, IBM was a hot product. The sales from IBM alone generated enough revenue to keep the fledgling company afloat.

The Institute's own software soon provided an even bigger windfall. Ten years earlier, the Institute had started working on an innovative computer circuit designed to translate a computer's English text into Chinese characters. The scientists who had worked on the project were assigned to the new company. They developed a prototype on a card that could easily be plugged into a computer's main circuit board. In April 1985, the company launched its invention on the commercial market as the Legend Chinese Character Card. The name *Legend* means "association" in Chinese, and one of the card's most attractive features was its ability to immediately come up with Chinese characters relating to anything typed on a keyboard. The program would then suggest multiple choices as possible translations. The Legend Card was an instant hit and became an essential add-on for PCs imported into China. It was soon bundled with most new PCs entering the market. The company generated substantial sales, and the card's success made New Technology Developer the distributor of choice for anyone importing computers into China. In 1989, the company changed its name to Legend.

Growing Pains

In 1990, Legend introduced its own branded PC in China and became a computer producer as well as a distributor of foreign imports. The initial focus was on business clients, but Legend soon found that its lack of financial backing made it difficult to compete head-on with foreign PC makers. In 1994, the stress of trying to keep Legend afloat led to Liu being hospitalized. As it turned out, the forced vacation gave Liu an opportunity to rethink Legend's strategy. When he left the hospital, Liu decided that in addition to having the company focus on the office market, he would create a consumer PC division, targeting individuals who wanted computers for personal use. Liu pioneered the home PC concept in China to the Chinese market. PC 1+1 stood for "one home, one computer" or "one child, one computer." The idea was that the computer was something you could use for your own amusement and enrichment, and that it was not a machine limited to office work. The separate division was headed by Yang Yuanqing, who was 29 years old at the time and had joined the company as a salesman in 1988.

Taking the Lead

Chinese PCs were usually a generation behind the West, and Liu decided to change that. Teaming up with Intel, Legend launched its first Intel Pentium PC in China just as Pentium PCs were going on the market in North America. Legend was soon able to boost its sales volume dramatically by selling Pentium-chip–powered PCs at much lower prices than the competition. Before long, the company began overtaking foreign brands in China. By 1996, it was clearly a market leader. In addition, Legend had previously focused on desktop computers, but it introduced its first laptop in 1996. The company was beginning to show a knack for balancing innovation and cost. Ease of use was another advantage. One of Legend's cheapest models allowed inexperienced users to get on the Internet by just pushing a button.

By 1999, Legend was ahead of its competition with a 21 percent share of the market in China and 8.5 percent of the Asian market. In 2000, Liu decided to spin off his distribution business for imported PCs and services. The new company was called Digital

China. In 2001, Yang Yuanqing, who had headed the consumer division, was appointed CEO of the entire company. By then, it controlled 30 percent of China's PC market.

In 2000, however, the consumer market was beginning to reach saturation. Legend's growth, which had been compounded at 30 percent over the previous six years, also flattened out. Domestic PC makers found themselves caught in price wars, while foreign PC makers, including Dell, were gaining ground against domestic players. The growth potential in China was beginning to look limited. Yang was still determined to make Legend a top Fortune 500 company within the next ten years, but consumer PC sales, which had been driving the company's growth, remained static. In an effort to continue growing, the company tried to diversify.

Diversification Fails

By the year 2000, more than 100 million Chinese were using the Internet, which created a vast range of new business opportunities. From 2000 to 2003, Legend was swept up in the dot-com fever and invested heavily in Internet companies. In August 2001, Legend spent $35.37 million to acquire 40 percent of the outstanding shares of Yestock Information Technology Co. Ltd. It hoped to cash in on e-commerce trading in securities over the Internet. In December 2001, it invested in New Oriental Education & Technology Group, Inc., a company focusing on providing online training. In partnership with AOL Time Warner, it invested in an Internet company called FM365. The total investment in Internet businesses exceeded $100 million.

Legend also briefly explored moving into IT services. The technology research firm Gartner predicted that the IT services business in China would increase 3000 percent from 2000 to 2007. The forecast was based mainly on the expectation that all levels of government would eventually need to go online to increase services and transparency. In 2000, China had initiated a program to encourage business enterprises to set up corporate websites. As demand increased, Legend added IT services to its diversified portfolio, although its total investment in IT services added up to only around $13 million.

In 2001, the penetration rate of Chinese mobile phone usage was 11.2 percent, less than half of the standard rate in Western countries. Legend saw the potential and invested nearly US $11 million in a joint venture formed with Xoceco to manufacture and sell cell phones.

When the Internet bubble finally burst in 2003, Legend's investment in Yestock decreased to 90 percent of its former value, and its ventures into online training and FM365 had to be closed with losses. The company had spent $25 million on FM365. IT services also continued to lose money. By the end of 2004, the company's share in China's PC market had dropped to 24 percent, a significant decline from the 30 percent it had held just three years earlier. The diversification strategy had obviously been a failure. Noncore businesses including the Internet and IT services were spun off. Legend determined to return to its core business: personal computers.

An International Strategy Proves Problematic

In an interview with McKinsey in 2001, Liu Chuanzhi appeared undecided over whether to sell under his own brand or take the OEM approach. Legend's past performance in China had been driven by the company's ability to leverage competitive advantages, but once the company was selling overseas, the advantages offered by the market in China would no longer be relevant. Liu felt that the situation called for caution.

Taiwan, which already had considerable experience in electronics manufacturing, had tried to break into western markets for computers using its own brand names and had failed to compete successfully with established foreign brands, and Liu was afraid that Legend would run into the same kind of resistance. The safer approach might be to remain an original equipment manufacturer or to team up with a Taiwanese company and try to build a brand together.

While Liu was deciding whether to adopt the OEM approach or form an alliance with a Taiwanese company, he had begun selling PCs in Hong Kong under the Legend brand. To test the international waters, the company had arranged in September 2001 to sell its PCs through more than 50 outlets owned by Fortress, Hong Kong's largest consumer electronics and household appliances retailer. Hong Kong had traditionally been dominated by international brands such as IBM, Compaq, and Dell. Legend did not have much impact on the market. The next year, Legend tried to expand into Spain and a few other regional markets. The loss of market share in China forced Legend to make a strategic retreat from its efforts at foreign expansion.

When the company tried to establish its brand overseas, it soon became apparent that other companies had already registered the name "Legend." Something needed to be done. "We needed to have an English brand name that could be used without restriction in all countries, " Yang explained. Although still focused on the China market, Yang realized that the IT business would eventually have to go global, and going global required building a brand name that could be used everywhere.

In 2003, Legend changed its name to Lenovo. The new name combined the first two letters of *Legend* with the Latin word novo, meaning "new." The idea was to reflect both the spirit of innovation and novelty. In April 2004, Lenovo formally changed its name to Lenovo Group Limited. "The board of directors believed the alignment of the English brand name and the company name would help to raise the recognition and popularity of the brand,"

Yang explained. (The name in Chinese remained unchanged.) However, despite the hopes it had pinned to its international strategy, international sales dropped to less than 2 percent of total revenue in 2003. Then an acquisition that promised to be a game-changer suddenly appeared on Lenovo's radar at precisely the moment when it needed it the most. The target was nothing less than IBM's PC division.

IBM Reinvents Itself

IBM had introduced its first personal computer for business in 1981, which quickly became known as the PC. Computers in business had until then tended to be massive machines tightly controlled by technicians under the watchful eye of a company's headquarters. The introduction of the Apple 2 computer and the Radio Shack Model 1 had interested amateurs at first, but it soon became apparent that a small computer could be useful for businesses at the corporate level as well as to individuals in their daily lives. As the market for personal computers expanded, IBM's decision to put its own desktop computer on the market effectively legitimized the personal computer for business. The IBM PC was largely assembled from off-the-shelf components bought from other manufacturers. But for most business executives, the IBM brand name was all it took to make the desktop computer a credible business machine. Few executives knew much about computers at the time, but everyone knew that IBM had a solid reputation. For corporations, investing in hundreds or thousands of computers, choosing IBM was a no-brainer. Even if equivalent computers made by other manufacturers were cheaper or performed slightly better, IBM would still be there tomorrow, and that counted for a lot.

To make its new computers work, IBM turned to a youthful Harvard dropout named Bill Gates and his pal, Paul Allen, who cobbled together an operating system based on some work that they had bought from another programmer. The original system was called QDOS, for "Quick and Dirty Operating System." Apple soon equipped its operating system with a graphic user interface that allowed folders and files to be visually organized on a screen. Apple had based its system on work being done by Xerox's Palo Alto Research Center. Xerox never pushed the concept itself, but when Apple incorporated it into its Macintosh computers, the graphic interface became an instant hit. Microsoft, the company founded by Gates and Allen, modified their system, renamed Windows, to give it a visual interface as well. Because most people in business wanted an IBM PC, Microsoft Windows ended up dominating the market. Computers that could run Windows and its accompanying programs became known as IBM-compatible PCs.

In contrast to Apple, which designed its chips and operating system exclusively for its own computers, Microsoft's Windows could run on any Intel-based computer chip that followed the same architecture as an IBM PC. As copycat vendors, led by Compaq, began to sell their own IBM-compatible PCs, an entire industry developed. Chip makers such as Intel and AMD and software companies such as Microsoft and Lotus drove remarkable growth of PC usage both in business and at home. However, the real money in the PC industry moved to software and the chips or integrated circuits that made the PCs run.

IBM was itself assembling parts bought from other manufacturers. The difference was that IBM's machines usually cost more than the competition's and often underperformed competing computers that sold in their price range. Assembled PCs were gradually becoming a commodity. The transition helped Dell, which offered to tailor its computers to the no-frills, basic needs of each of its customers. By eliminating the extras that might make a computer more versatile but were likely to go unused in most offices, Dell thrived at operating on razor-thin margins. It generally sold its computers directly to

customers on order. Because it could eliminate superfluous components, it was able to undercut most of the competition, and it soon
became the market leader in PC business sales. IBM was either
unwilling or unable to match the Dell model, and it incurred losses
that were becoming a drag on its other businesses.

GETTING OUT OF THE PC BUSINESS?

After several attempts at restructuring failed, IBM considered getting rid of its PC business altogether. Lou Gerstner, who headed
IBM at the time, remarked that nothing was unthinkable at Big
Blue. IBM had dumped a number of businesses when their profitability was threatened by market erosion. These included various
timekeeping devices, card-sorting machines, videodiscs, typewrit-
ers, and printers. As management professor Mark J. Zbaracki put it,
"IBM's strength historically has been reinventing itself."

IBM had sensed early on that the global IT industry was moving into a new phase, and the company's strategists predicted that
the emphasis would soon shift to software. Profits from hardware
manufacturing would decline from 58 percent in 2000 to 42 percent
in 2005, while profits from software development would increase
from 29 percent to 41 percent. In this period, IBM sold its hard-
drive business to Toshiba and its disk-drive business to Hitachi. The
company also shed its display and network processor businesses. In
2002, IBM acquired PriceWaterhouseCoopers's services. By adding
other software companies such as Tivoli, Rational, and Informix,
IBM successfully transformed itself into a services, software, and
consulting company. IBM's PC business was put up for sale.

IBM TRIES TO MAKE THE SALE

In 2000, shortly after Samuel J. Palmisano was named IBM's president and CEO, IBM's efforts to find a way out of the PC business
took on a new urgency. IBM approached a number of PC makers in

hopes of selling the company's ailing unit. The price sought by IBM was a major obstacle. IBM wanted $3 billion to $4 billion, and it had difficulty finding anyone willing to pay that amount for a business that was already in trouble and had a questionable future. In 2001, IBM approached Legend for the first time.

IBM's then CFO, John Joyce, went to Beijing to discuss a potential sale in 2002, but Legend rejected the offer. IBM's PC business had lost nearly $400 million the previous year. That added up to almost four times Legend's total profits for the entire year. To make its offer more attractive, IBM performed radical surgery on its PC division, slashing costs and outsourcing manufacturing.

In July 2003, before beginning formal talks with Legend, Palmisano arranged a private meeting with a senior Chinese government official in charge of economic and technology policy. Palmisano explained that IBM was interested in helping Legend create a global enterprise. IBM would contribute its expertise in technology, management, marketing, and distribution. Building a truly international Chinese-owned company would demonstrate China's desire to invest abroad instead of merely serving as a manufacturing hub for the rest of the world.[2] The Chinese official replied that this was exactly where China wanted to go, but unfortunately, times had changed. Chinese authorities might have orchestrated such talks a few years earlier, but they were now reduced to the status of observers. IBM needed to negotiate with Legend on its own. IBM never really knew whether the official had interceded on its behalf or not, but the discussions resumed with Legend suddenly expressing a renewed enthusiasm for going global.

THE TALKS CONTINUE

Liu was now open to a deal, but he still insisted on caution. Mary Ma, Legend's CFO, flew to New York to follow through on the discussions, but Liu warned her not to fall in love with the deal. As it

turned out, Ma was very impressed with IBM's radical restructuring of its PC business. She returned as an enthusiastic supporter.

During the summer of 2004, at secret talks in Raleigh, North
Carolina, Yang and Palmisano agreed to go beyond the idea of a
simple sale and purchase of assets. Instead, the two companies
would form a strategic alliance. Legend—which would now be
known as Lenovo—would become the preferred supplier of PCs to
IBM and would be allowed to use the IBM brand name for five
years. IBM would continue to sell Lenovo PCs through its sales
force and distribution network. Big Blue would also provide marketing, services, and financing for Lenovo PCs.

In an interview in *Fortune* magazine, Liu said that he had
finally come to see the IBM offer in a different light. He explained:

> We gained confidence that many of the risks we'd feared
> could be distributed or controlled. We worried about los-
> ing customers, so we worked out an agreement that
> would allow us to continue using the IBM brand, to keep
> the IBM salespeople, and even to keep the top IBM exec-
> utive as CEO. That gave us confidence we could give cus-
> tomers the same level of service and quality after the
> acquisition.[3]

What Lenovo Bought

On December 8, 2004, Lenovo announced that it would acquire
IBM's PC division for $1.75 billion. Lenovo would pay roughly
$650 million in cash and $600 million in securities and would
assume debt of an extra $500 million. According to the terms, IBM
would get an 18.9 percent stake in Lenovo. The new company
would have an annual sales volume of 11.9 million units and sales
of $12 billion, based on the two company's 2003 sales. The deal

instantly transformed Lenovo, which had been a distant ninth-place contender, into the world's third-largest PC maker.

It also quadrupled Lenovo's PC business, which turned Lenovo's dream of globalization into a reality. Now, Lenovo had sales volume and could also continue to use the IBM logo on its products for five years. IBM's famous ThinkPad laptop and ThinkCentre desktop brands would belong to Lenovo forever. Together with sales channels, management, R&D capabilities, and global corporate clients, it would have been hard to imagine an arrangement more favorable to Lenovo. The mystery was why IBM had been willing to agree to half its original asking price, especially since its cost cutting had begun to make the PC unit more profitable.

IBM's Interest in China

IBM had, in fact, received attractive offers from other interested bidders, including an American company, the Texas Pacific Group. But from the very beginning, Lenovo was the only option that IBM pursued seriously. "There were simpler transactions that we could have done," Palmisano admitted. "What we wanted was not a divestiture, but this strategic relationship with Lenovo and China." The *New York Times* reported that IBM had decided to play its "China card":

> The sale of I.B.M.'s personal computer business to Lenovo for $1.75 billion . . . is "a three-dimensional deal," according to Mr. Palmisano. The sale provides I.B.M. with a path to leave a business that is large but not profitable. It is also the latest step in I.B.M.'s shift toward services, software and specialized hardware technology from mainframes to microprocessors for computer game consoles, all of which promise higher profits than the fiercely competitive PC business.

Yet the most intriguing, and potentially most important, dimension of the deal for the company is that it is I.B.M.'s China card. The new Lenovo, folding in the I.B.M. personal computer business, will be China's fifth-largest company, with $12.5 billion in sales in 2003, and the Chinese government will remain a big shareholder. I.B.M. is eager to help China with its industrial policy of moving up the economic ladder, by building the high-technology engine rooms to power modern corporations and government institutions with I.B.M. services and software.[4]

The real reason that IBM wanted the deal with Lenovo was that IBM wanted a way into China. Palmisano saw it as building a bridge to China's future. To IBM, the payoff would come when closer ties materialized with the Chinese government and the Chinese public. As Palmisano explained:

We don't have any special deal with the Chinese government or any other government really. It's a much more subtle, more sophisticated approach. It is that if you become ingrained in their agenda and become truly local and help them advance, then your opportunities are enlarged. You become part of their strategy.[5]

Echoing that line of reasoning, IBM announced in March 2005 that it intended to develop its Chinese business as a "China IBM" rather than an "IBM China," and that it was planning to provide integrated solutions for China's healthcare system. This came to fruition on May 1, 2009, when IBM announced the opening of a Healthcare Industry Solution Lab in Beijing. IBM would work with hospitals and rural medical cooperatives to make healthcare "smarter." The healthcare reform initiated by the Chinese government called for a $124 billion investment by 2011, to make health-care services safer and more affordable for China's 1.3 billion citizens. IBM would provide part of the solution.[6]

Integrating Very Different Cultures

IBM was keen to make the transaction work in order to demonstrate the company's long-term commitment to China's growth. However, integration required creative solutions because the companies were very different:

- ❖ IBM's PC business had higher overhead, while Lenovo was lean.

- ❖ IBM's PC business was three times larger than all of Lenovo.

- ❖ IBM's PC business had higher production costs, while Lenovo's labor costs were $3 per desktop PC, the lowest possible.

- ❖ IBM's PC was a strong global business, while Lenovo was the No. 1 player in China.

- ❖ IBM excelled with high-end corporate clients, while Lenovo did well with retail customers and small businesses.

- ❖ IBM had the best notebook technology, while Lenovo had great desktop technology.

Given the drastically different but complementary cultures and business practices of the two companies, it was unlikely that Lenovo's management could handle the integration on its own. To make the transition smoother, IBM decided to keep an 18.9

percent stake in the new company and retain executives to run the combined company. Besides allowing Lenovo to use the IBM brand, IBM continued to sell Lenovo PCs through its sales force and distribution network. In doing so, IBM risked its brand image and prestige and made a substantial commitment in human resources. It was an impressive demonstration of the company's confidence in Lenovo.

IBM volunteered Stephen M. Ward Jr., the head of the former PC division, to be the CEO of the newly combined company. Lenovo's outgoing CEO, Yang Yuanqing, would become chairman. Initially, Yang wanted dual headquarters, in New York and Beijing, but Ward preferred to have a single one in New York. After a few days, Yang came around to Ward's point of view. "Steve made a lot of sense," Yang said. "Putting the headquarters in New York told our global customers that we're a global company." Later, it was decided that the headquarters did not need to be in any specific city. Senior leadership meetings were held in various cities around the world, depending on which location made the most sense at a particular moment in time. Board directors and executives evolved into a true blend of East and West.

Ward's task was to ensure a smooth transition and integration of the merged business following the acquisition. He spent most of his time on customer retention and integrating the organization. The accomplishments following the merger in May 2005 were impressive on all points:

* *Customer Retention.* Lenovo shipped record volume and had nearly even market share compared with Lenovo and IBM's combined pre-acquisition shares.

* *Profitability Growth.* EPS (earnings per share) grew by 1 percent quarter-over-quarter, and Lenovo succeeded in

turning the IBM PC division from a loss-maker to profitability compared with its prior year's performance.

❖ *Strong Cash Position.* Lenovo had nearly $964 million in
net cash reserve as of September 30, 2005.

❖ *Successful Integration.* Lenovo had managed successful
integration into a global organization, and it was on
track to successfully meet its target for integrating both
organizations.

With integration accomplished, Lenovo accelerated its strategy for the next phase: expanding profits. In 2005, Lenovo had a
net profit rate of less than 2 percent, while its direct competitor,
Dell, had a much higher rate of 6 percent. To improve profitability, the company had to improve efficiency and cut costs. Ward's
background at IBM made him hesitant to launch into a drastic
reform. To increase its growth rate, IBM would need to expand
into emerging countries and the consumer market, and Ward
lacked experience running a business in an emerging market.
With retirement approaching, Ward and the Lenovo board agreed
that it was time for him to step aside. On December 20, 2005,
Lenovo announced that William Amelio would be appointed the
new CEO, effective immediately.

Yang had only praise for Ward's handling of the integration of
the two companies:

Steve Ward successfully helped to create a single, global
PC company from two distinct organizations. As a result,
we have created significant value for our shareholders
over the past year, and Lenovo is in a strong position to
make continually better progress against our goals. We

appreciate Steve's contributions to Lenovo and his continuing support.

When Lenovo approached him for the job, Amelio was Dell's senior vice president for the Asia-Pacific and Japan regions. Before Dell, Amelio had worked in senior management for NCR and AlliedSignal from 1979 to 1997. He had held a number of senior positions with IBM, including general manager of worldwide operations for its PC business. Amelio had sales experience in the emerging market and seemed to be an ideal candidate for the top job.

In January 2006, Amelio unveiled his strategy for Lenovo:

We must first keep a laser sharp focus on our cost and expense structure to continue to drive operating efficiency. Second, we must drive product competitiveness with innovative, high quality, appropriately priced products that address key growth areas. Third, we must leverage our success in China and the success of the dual transaction/relationship model in support of our products. I'm looking forward to building on the strong momentum Lenovo has delivered to date.[7]

Following the IBM PC acquisition, Lenovo divided its sales system according to two functions: relationship and transaction. The relationship model, based on the Think brands that had been acquired from IBM, targeted large corporate customers that needed tailored solutions, fast delivery, and quick responses to service demands. The transaction model, based on Lenovo's successful practice in China, targeted small and medium businesses and individual consumers. For the transaction model, the selling points would be a large distribution network, service, and low pricing.

Lenovo believed that it had developed a successful model in China that could now be duplicated in other parts of the world.

Expanding into emerging countries was a necessity. According to International Data Corporation (IDC), in 2006, Lenovo PC shipments in Europe declined by 12 percent, and in the United States, its growth was 5.3 percent below the industry average of 6.7 percent. The growth was almost all in China, which was getting 30 percent more shipments than anywhere else. As a first step in its effort to replicate its success in China, Lenovo chose Germany and India to test its transaction model in both mature and emerging markets. The experiment worked in both markets and produced significantly higher growth in 2006.

Amelio did a great in job integrating, streamlining, and improving IBM's former PC business, but when the economic crisis hit hard and fast in 2008, Lenovo's profits went into a tailspin, leaving Amelio very little time to refocus on China, the emerging markets, or consumer products.

What Went Wrong?

In May 2006, when Lenovo's results for 2005–2006 were announced, Amelio declared:

> Lenovo is a great business with innovative products and a disciplined operating plan. We are sharply focused on taking the steps now that we believe will make us successful and more profitable over the long term: improving our operating efficiency, building brand awareness, and expanding our dual business model.[8]

The statement raised questions about the coherence of Amelio's long-term strategy. The mystery is why the company had decided to change its primary focus from innovative product offerings to one that concentrated instead on brand awareness. The shift marked a departure from Lenovo's initial strategy, and it posed a dilemma: Where would growth come from without innovative products? The dual business model stayed in the third place.

In 2007, Amelio removed the IBM logo from ThinkPad laptops. The market's reaction was less than enthusiastic. To promote the Lenovo brand, Amelio began pouring money into marketing. He clinched an advertising deal with a soccer star, Ronaldinho, who had previously played for Brazil and Barcelona. Ronaldinho became a Lenovo Worldwide Brand Ambassador in 2006. To that questionable coup, Amelio added sponsorship of the Winter Olympics in Turin in 2006, sponsorship of the AT&T Williams Formula One racing team in 2007, and sponsorship of the Beijing Olympics in 2008. Amelio concluded his three-year tenure at Lenovo on an optimistic note in a press release:

> Over the past three years, we've implemented a successful international strategy. Lenovo has joined the ranks of the top global PC companies. Our brand is recognized around the world. We have developed a solid reputation for quality and innovation, and our customer service is second to none. I'm pleased with what we have accomplished as a team.

In a 2007 interview, Amelio reconfirmed his priorities:

> Improving supply-chain efficiency outside China is one of Lenovo's four strategic objectives, along with moving away from IBM's business model of selling mostly to large corporations; cutting prices and improving performance in

PC manufacturing outside of China; and lastly, building a Lenovo brand that is not in IBM's shadow.[9]

Amelio's intention was to move away from the relationship model, which focused on corporate customers, but he had failed to build an international transaction/consumer model. Compared to Lenovo's 5,000 stores, which the company referred to as "touch points" in China, Lenovo's distribution network outside China was too weak to boost sales of entry-level laptops, which had become increasingly important in the market. Worse, product launches for the new laptops were experiencing potentially fatal delays.

Innovative product offerings were not high on Amelio's list of priorities. During his tenure, the PC market turned increasingly to laptops, not the expensive models favored by corporate clients but entry-level models, priced to appeal to individual consumers on tight budgets.

It took until 2007 for Yang Yuanqing to lose patience and decide to personally create a global consumer business group to push for consumer models. In March 2008, Lenovo introduced a new line of PCs linked to the word *Idea* as a brand concept. These included IdeaPad laptops and IdeaCentre desktops. Lenovo had its first global consumer-oriented PC, and the initial impulse to build it had not come from Amelio.

It was also becoming increasingly apparent that there were no innovative products and no appropriate channels that could possibly benefit from Amelio's costly marketing hype. It was too late for Lenovo to play catch-up with Acer and HP and other competitors that were already responding to market trends with ultra low-priced netbooks. Acer's market share rose from 9.4 percent to 11.8 percent, and HP's increased another 3.1 percent to 19.6 percent in 2008.

With the global recession, corporate customers were cutting back on spending. Computer makers like Dell and Lenovo that had depended heavily on corporate customers for sales were losing market share. Lenovo's global PC market share fell to 7.2 percent in 2008 from 7.5 percent a year earlier. In the fiscal quarter ending on December 31, 2008, Lenovo reported a loss of $97 million, down from a net profit of $172 million during the fourth quarter a year earlier. Sales dropped 20 percent from $4.49 billion a year earlier to $3.59 billion.

Amelio's effort to turn Lenovo into a globally recognized brand had seemed like a good idea at the time. What was lacking was a compelling product line to justify the market hype: With uncompetitive products and an inadequate sales presence at the local level, the money spent on branding simply increased costs without adding to sales.

Lessons Learned

The fact that Lenovo went back to relying on Chinese managers and shifted its focus back to China, emerging markets, and individual customers does not mean that the original acquisition was a bad idea. Legend had wanted to go global in 1988, but it only considered being serious about it in 2003, when it had become clear that diversification had failed and that there was not enough room for continued growth in China. Everyone knew that going global would require considerable time, and the IBM deal still looks like an ideal choice. The deal gave Lenovo everything the company needed to be a global enterprise: brands, customers, executives, R&D, channels, and a global sales force. IBM was straightforward and highly sophisticated in building the relationship with Lenovo and China. The payoff for IBM was not the onetime deal with Lenovo but the ever enlarging software, consulting, and services business in China itself.

The integration of the IBM PC business and Lenovo still rates as a success despite the decision to change the CEO and chairman. The management shakeup at the beginning of 2009 was driven at least in part by the global economic crisis and the company's dependence on corporate customers.

It is fair to say, though, that if Lenovo had stayed focused on its original strategy and executed it well, the company might not have experienced as much stress as it did during the crisis, which helped to emphasize the challenge of integrating two drastically different corporate cultures. Executing a new strategy is far more difficult when time-consuming cultural issues constantly need to be dealt with.

Looking to the Future

In January 2009, Lenovo announced that it was cutting its workforce by 11 percent, or about 2,500 employees, worldwide during the first quarter. The company sought to reduce expenses in support and staff functions, such as finance, human resources, and marketing. Executive compensation would be reduced by 30 to 50 percent, including merit pay, long-term incentives, and performance payments. The cuts produced savings of approximately $300 million. Lenovo also relocated its call center operations from Toronto, Ontario, to Morrisville, North Carolina, which produced additional savings.

As part of the reorganization, the company consolidated its China, Asia Pacific, and Russia divisions into a single business unit. The Asia-Pacific headquarters moved from Singapore to Beijing. Chen Shaopeng, the senior vice president and president for Greater China, was picked to lead the new organization.

In February 2009, Lenovo announced the departure of CEO Amelio, with Yang Yuanqing taking over as CEO, and Liu Chuanzhi returning as chairman. The new management team was given the mandate to put the company back on track and make it profitable.

Liu said, "So right now, we should emphasize China and emerging markets, and consumer customers."

In March 2009, Yang created two business units, Mature Markets and Emerging Markets, and two product groups, Think and Idea. The Mature Markets unit included business in Western Europe, the United States, Canada, Japan, Australia, New Zealand, and Global Accounts, including large enterprises, SMEs, and relevant consumer products. The Emerging Markets unit, headed by Chen Shaopeng, was composed of business in China, the rest of Asia, the Middle East, and Africa, including large enterprises, SMEs, and relevant consumers. Lenovo's Latin America group, including Mexico, was to report to Rory Read, the president and COO.

The Think Product Group, led by Frances K. O'Sullivan, took worldwide responsibility for all Think-branded desktops, notebooks, workstations, displays, peripherals, and software. The Think group focused on commercial customers, Lenovo's relationship business model, and the premium end of the transactional small/medium business market. The Idea Product Group, led by Liu Jun, oversaw product development and portfolio management for the Idea product line. The group focused on consumer and commercial SME transactional business in emerging and mature markets and entry-level products.

More recently, Lenovo launched its own tablet computer, LePad, and shifted its focus toward the emerging markets, especially India. The emphasis shifted from the top of the line toward computers that were more affordable for the potentially huge market emerging in the developing world.

Lenovo had reorganized itself based on lessons learned in a few short years after biting off a dynamic portion of one of the world's top multinationals. The gamble seemed to be paying off. In the third quarter of 2011, Lenovo shipped 12.5 million units, surpassing Dell to become the world's second largest PC maker, surpassed only by Hewlett Packard, which briefly considered getting out of the PC business. Lenovo's sales were up 14.5 percent over the previous quarter, while global computer sales increased only 5.5 percent during that period. The increase gave Lenovo a global 13.9 percent market share. Analysts attributed Lenovo's increased sales to China's booming PC market, while the economic slowdown in the West and the growing interest in smartphones and tablet computers had depressed PC sales from U.S. and European competitors.

NOTES

1. The IBM/Lenovo Deal: Victory for China? http://knowledge.wharton. upenn.edu/article.cfm?articleid=1106.

2. Steve Lohr, "I.B.M. Sought a China Partnership, Not Just a Sale," *New York Times*, December 13, 2004.

3. *Fortune*, "The Man Who Bought IBM," December 27, 2004, http://money.cnn.com/magazines/fortune/fortune_archive/2004/12/27/8 217968/index.htm.

4. *New York Times*, December 13, 2004.

5. *New York Times*, December 13, 2004.

6. "IBM Collaborates with China in Steps to Healthcare Reform," May 1, 2009, www.healthcareitnews.com.

7. "Lenovo Reports Third Quarter FY 2005/06 Results," January 26, 2006, www.lenovo.com.

8. "Lenovo Reports Fourth Quarter and Full Year 2005/06 Results," May 25, 2006.

9. "Bill Amelio: The Boss Who's Breaking Free of a Big Blue Shadow," *The Independent*, April 1, 2007.

S I X

Kangnai, Haili, and Li Ning
Moving Up the Value Chain

It doesn't make sense to have our people run in foreign clothes, with foreign ads on their backs.

—Li Ning, China's greatest Olympic athlete

The Kangnai Group Builds a Brand

WENZHOU DISCOVERS THE LIMITS OF LOW-COST PRODUCTION

ZHENG XIUKANG began working as a shoe-making apprentice in 1979. He was living in Wenzhou, the port providing access to the sea to the mountainous interior of southeastern Zhejiang Province. The first official license to an individual to engage in private enterprise thanks to Deng Xiaoping's economic reforms was issued in Wenzhou in November 1979, and the city was eager to embrace the tidal wave of entrepreneurialism that was about to sweep through

China. But Zheng's key priority was personal survival. He had a daytime job as a machine worker, but he couldn't make enough money to support his wife and two children, and he needed to earn more. He was 33 years old, well beyond the age when most people learn how to make shoes.

"We were poor and we were desperate," Zheng recalls. He had two options: Learn how to make shoes or learn how to make sofas. With a family of four crammed into a tiny space that measured barely 90 square feet, Zheng realized that there was not enough room to make sofas. Shoes won the day. Zheng's experience was in machinery, so he naturally relied on calipers to make precise measurements for his shoes. When they began outselling most of the competition, he quit his day job and went into shoe-making full time.

A major advantage of the shoe business in Wenzhou was that it required a relatively small investment and generated a fast return. It was the ultimate low-cost, low-end manufacturing venture. The trouble was that just about everyone in Wenzhou seemed to have the same idea. At one point, more than 4,000 shoe-making enterprises in Wenzhou generated roughly $20 billion in sales per year. But as competition mushroomed, it put pressure on the shoemakers to make more shoes faster and at a lower cost. Many of these shoes were made so poorly and fell apart so quickly that they began to be referred to as "shoes for a week" and further down the line as "shoes for a day." It became an embarrassment to be seen wearing them. Wenzhou had created a negative brand that soon promised to be disaster by association.

On August 8, 1987, authorities in Hangzhou, a city in the north of Zhejiang Province, publicly burned more than 5,000 pairs of poor-quality Wenzhou shoes. Other cities followed the Hangzhou example and began staging similar burnings. Shopping malls refused to sell Wenzhou footwear, and some even posted advertisements stating, "No products made in Wenzhou in the mall." The shoemakers in Wenzhou felt humiliated. Roughly half quit the business altogether.

THE KANGNAI GROUP IS BORN

Zheng Xiukang refused to be discouraged, though. In 1988, he traveled around China, investigating shoe factories. He quickly realized that none of the shoemakers he met had any idea of what an assembly line was, and they knew nothing of modern technology. Zheng decided to take a look at what was happening in Taiwan and Italy. He was shocked by what he discovered. Modern factories, geared toward quality production, were clearly the answer. Since China still lacked venture capital financing, Zheng borrowed from friends and relatives. None of them had cash on hand, but Zheng got them to put up their houses as collateral for bank loans.

"The pile of title deeds was a foot thick," Zheng recalls. After borrowing $800,000, Zheng established his first assembly line, which put 280 people to work making a single pair of shoes that previously would have been turned out by two shoemakers operating on their own. The assembly line was less likely to take short cuts than individual cobblers, and it produced more shoes in a fraction of the time. The quality was more consistent and much easier to monitor.

Zheng changed his trademark to Kangnai, which translates into Chinese as "I pursue healthy development and what can they do to me?" It did not take long for Kangnai to become one of China's best-known brands of footwear.

Kangnai, which subsequently became known as the Kangnai Group, invested heavily in updating its craftsmanship and technology, and it soon became ISO 9002 and ISO 14001 certified. Today, its Italian design team introduces original models each season, and its 15,000 employees produce 8 million pairs of leather shoes a year.

The company's R&D team works with doctors to design shoes that are healthy to wear, and it also works directly with fashion consultants on aesthetic trends and the culture of footwear. Kangnai's corporate literature states its dual goals as customer satisfaction and the pursuit of excellence.

The Kangnai Group put a major focus on developing its own brand. Beginning in 1996, the group began pulling back from the wholesale market and started building a franchise network in chain stores across China. By the end of 2007, it had franchised more than 2,500 outlets in China and another 100 stores in ten countries, including the United States, France, Italy, Spain, Portugal, Belgium, and Greece. Kangnai was the first of China's shoemakers to establish its own brand in an overseas market.

MOVING UP THE VALUE CHAIN

The Kangnai experience illustrates an ongoing phenomenon in the China market. The shoemakers in Wenzhou, including Zheng, rushed into the business because shoes are a simple product that is relatively easy for anyone to make, and the business promised a quick return.

But as the competition intensified, the shoemakers felt compelled to lower their prices, reducing their profit. That meant that they had to turn out more shoes faster, just to stay in business. Ultimately, they reached a limit and the market went into revolt. The problem with competing solely on price, the shoemakers discovered, is that you find yourself increasingly squeezed until the exercise is no longer worth it. The solution is either to increase productivity through automation and streamlined processes or to move up the value chain and produce more complex goods that either fit a limited niche or are simply more difficult to copy. The alternative when selling a commodity product that is difficult to differentiate from the competition based on price or superior quality is to establish a brand that makes the public perceive a difference, even if it is mostly in the imagination.

China's Advantage

Until recently, China's biggest advantage in trying to break into the world's global economy has been its nearly inexhaustible supply of cheap labor. According to Chinese census statistics, by 2006, more than 200 million rural farmers had flooded into China's cities to become industrial workers, constituting one of the largest human migrations in history. The phenomenon is not over yet. Another 740 million farmers remain on farms scattered across China's immense territory. The continuing population explosion, combined with limited land resources, virtually guarantees that more people will crowd into the cities in search of work.

Until now, the average wage earned by these newly industrialized workers usually ranged from $63 to $125 a month, or roughly one-30th of that demanded by workers in the West. The average workday is anywhere from ten to 16 hours, and despite the economic boom, wages continue to grow at a slower rate than China's GDP.

A spate of worker suicides in 2010 at Foxconn, which manufactures the Apple iPad, drew attention to the strain that China's hyper-heated economy is placing on many workers. In Foxconn's case, the company promptly responded with salary hikes and worker improvements, but the Foxconn experience served as a warning that China needs to base its competitiveness on more than low-cost production.

As more people flow in from the countryside, however, China is going to have access to workers willing to be hired at low wages for the foreseeable future. As China moves into more complex manufacturing, these workers will force the nation to put more and more of its resources into education and training, and that effort is likely to give China an even greater advantage over

Western countries that are tempted to skimp on education as their business opportunities diminish.

Many emerging markets face the dilemma of having to rely on an unsophisticated workforce. China's advantage is that it is already well advanced in investing in its human capital. Not everyone is highly educated and productive, but enough of the citizens are to produce impressive results. As George Feldenkreis—the CEO of Perry Ellis International, Inc.—stated in 2004 at the Wharton School's China Business Forum, China's low labor costs and high productivity gives the country an advantage over industrialized countries and emerging markets. He said:

> While U.S. workers, for example, may be more productive and technologically sophisticated, they are also more expensive. Likewise, people in places such as the Dominican Republic and Romania may be willing to work just as cheaply as workers in China, but they are not as productive.[1]

While wages are rising in China's industrial areas, roughly a third of the country's population still depends on agriculture, compared to less than 2 percent in the United States or 6 percent in South Korea. Another 30 percent of the labor force in China is composed of migrants, whose wages increase by only 4 to 6 percent a year in real terms. An analysis by Goldman Sachs noted that the role labor costs play in overall manufacturing costs is actually lower now than it was in 2001.

China's cost advantage is augmented by other factors that are already in place, such as available real estate dedicated to industrial use, integrated transportation, energy, and machinery.

How the West also Benefits from Cheap Chinese Labor

The advantages for Western consumers are lower prices for consumer goods and an effective counterweight to inflation. *Global Insight* reports that as a result, real apparel prices are as low now as they were in 1990. Price reductions are likely to continue for some time, although at a more moderate rate.

China has become the world's top producer of clothes, shoes, toys, socks, pens, neckties, lighters, and many other labor-intensive products. Back in 2003, Chinese garments and textiles constituted only 17 percent of the global market. When global textile quotas were eliminated on January 1, 2005, the demand for China's garments and textiles increased dramatically. China's garments and textiles were expected to grow by at least 50 percent in 2008, with $83.85 billion worth of exports in the first six months of the year. Every year, China exports 22 billion toys to the United States—roughly 80 percent of the U.S. toy market. China also produces more than 10 billion pairs of shoes every year—50 percent more than the amount needed to supply one pair for every human being on earth. China's low-cost, labor-intensive, and export-oriented light industries have been largely responsible for keeping worldwide inflation under control during the first decade of the 21st century.

When China began reforming its economy and opening itself to the worldwide market, most foreign direct investment flowed into primary-processing and export-oriented industries. China's government showed that it was ready to sacrifice its environment, resources, energy, and even the welfare of its own workers to jumpstart the economy.

While the strategy turned China into an industrial powerhouse in record time, it also became increasingly clear that growth based on low cost, low quality, and relatively primitive technology would not be sustainable over the long run. What the Chinese make up for in volume they lose in pricing. An example is the watch industry. China produces 1.2 billion watches a year, while Switzerland produces 26 million, yet when seen in dollar terms, Switzerland accounts for 60 percent of the world market since the average Chinese watch sells wholesale for $2, while the average Swiss watch sells for more than $500.

The production of low-cost textiles and shoes will inevitably migrate elsewhere in search of even less expensive labor, just as the industry previously migrated from Japan to South Korea, to Taiwan, to Southeast Asia, and then to China.

The Downside to Outsourcing Manufacturing

Multinationals initially went to China to manufacture their products because of their own relentless efforts to drive down costs. The transfer of so many manufacturing jobs was painful to workers in countries that lost the jobs, but it has also exacted a heavy price in China in terms of damage to its environment, air quality, and supply of fresh water. The emphasis on low wages and long working hours meant that workers received relatively few benefits, and until China could develop its own middle class with domestic buying power, China was condemned to remain overly dependent on exports. That, in turn, meant that its economy was at the mercy of forces and events beyond its control.

Today, increases in raw material and energy prices are putting pressure on China's low-end manufacturing. Consumers who buy Chinese products are beginning to see the downside as poor quality or even dangerous materials are introduced into production lines in the interest of pushing costs down even farther.

DONGGUAN FUAN TEXTILES: A CAUTIONARY TALE

The negligence of some factory owners who felt that they had received a green light to increase production regardless of the environmental costs has bordered on the criminal, especially when it comes to the disposal of dangerous toxic waste. In one example, Chinese environmental officials were alarmed in 2007 to discover that a local river had turned dark red and become clogged with thousands of dead fish. The culprit was the 230-acre Dongguan Fuan Textiles factory—the largest knit cotton manu- facturer in the world, responsible for about 6 percent of the global supply of knit cotton, with a huge volume going to the United States. In June 2006, Chinese environmental-protection officials discovered that a pipe buried underneath the factory floor was dumping roughly 22,000 tons of chemically contaminated water into the river daily.[2]

The textile producers had decided that it was worth risking a violation of China's antipollution laws in order to cut the cost of disposing of the toxic waste. They were wrong. The amount saved was roughly 13 cents a metric ton, so that over the course of a year, the cost reduction might add up to a few hundred thousand dollars. The final cost to the plant's owner, Hong Kong–based Fountain Set Group, was roughly $1.5 million in fines. The company subse- quently had to spend $2.7 million to upgrade its water-treatment facilities. The crackdown was part of an aggressive Chinese govern- ment campaign to curb environmental damage, intended to serve as a warning to factory owners that the early days without limits were now over.

TEXTILES: A DOUBLE-EDGED SQUEEZE

Today, Chinese textile producers are experiencing a double-edged squeeze: Western retailers demand even lower prices, while cotton producers want more for their crops. More cotton is produced in China than anywhere else, but production demands have grown so intense that China is increasingly forced to import cotton from the United States and other countries. The textiles industry in China increased its demand for cotton by 42 percent in 2005 alone, and China will need 12 million tons a year by 2014. The price of cotton more than doubled in just six years, from $0.3 per pound in 2001 to $0.7 in 2007. It is expected to double again over the next few years. China imports more U.S. cotton than anyone else but, as a result, it is simultaneously blamed for driving up prices for American cotton and at the same time for dumping textile goods in the United States.

Labor-intensive manufacturing companies in China typically operate on razor-thin margins. Even a slight rise in costs or an unexpected decrease in foreign demand can force a factory to close. Migrant workers from the countryside have often been exploited, abused, or even enslaved and then cast aside as a result of market fluctuations beyond their control. Because China's economic advantage is based on keeping costs at a minimum, there has been very little up to now in the way of a social safety net.

Three decades of rapid industrial expansion have also sparked trade friction and antidumping charges, and China's accelerating hunt for raw materials in other developing countries has not helped the country's image abroad. Weighing costs against benefits, China's government has an increasing incentive to move away from low-end manufacturing and to place a greater emphasis on value-added high-tech industries. The new direction is outlined in the "Catalogue for the Guidance of Foreign Invested Enterprises," released by the National Development and Reform Commission (NDRC), which became effective on December 1, 2007. In the rush to build China's economy, government leaders were prepared to assign a lower priority to the rights of individuals, labor conditions, and the environment. As the cost of neglecting these issues becomes more apparent, government priorities are beginning to show signs of change. The new Labor Contract Law provides improved protection for workers, stricter environmental controls, and a tighter approval process for applications. The export licenses of shoddy toy makers are being revoked, and industries that were previously subsidized now face higher taxes.

New Rules of the Game

The NDRC dramatically revised China's foreign investment strategy when it issued the "Catalogue for the Guidance of Foreign Invested Enterprises." This guidance shifted the goalposts from quantity to quality production. The Catalogue divided foreign investment into three categories: "encouraged," "restricted," and "prohibited." Foreign investment in advanced technology, modern manufacturing, sustainable resources, and environmental protection was to be encouraged; foreign investment in traditional enterprises or export-oriented enterprises continued to be allowed; and foreign investment in enterprises that were energy-intensive, relied heavily on natural resources, and produced high levels of pollution were either restricted or prohibited entirely. The shift in policy has been a hard awakening for labor-intensive, primary-products–processing, and export-oriented enterprises.

China's LCL, which went into effect on January 1, 2008, made hiring more difficult and may turn out to be the proverbial straw that breaks the camel's back when it comes to cheap manufacturing. It is likely to force some industries that rely on cheap labor to find other locations where wages continue to be low. Together with the appreciation of the RMB, rising trade friction, lower demand, lower tax rebates, and rising raw material prices, Chinese export-oriented, labor-intensive companies are beginning to realize that their razor-thin margins are no longer enough to keep them afloat. A few have moved from the coast to interior provincial cities where labor costs are cheaper. Others have shifted their manufacturing to Indonesia, Bangladesh, Vietnam, and Cambodia.

The multinationals, interested in China mainly as a low-cost manufacturing platform, may eventually pull out altogether. According to "China Manufacturing Competitiveness 2007–2008,"—a study by the American Chamber of Commerce and Booz Allen Hamilton—roughly 17 percent of the companies surveyed said that they plan to move their operations out of China. The reasons cited were the appreciation of the RMB, inflation in prices for components and materials, wage increases, and poor employee retention. About 90 percent of these companies said that they had originally been drawn to China by lower labor costs, but now they are finding that other countries (India and Vietnam currently head the list) offer cheaper labor and better tax benefits. Many Chinese companies are also following the trend and either relocating to interior provinces or simply moving their manufacturing to other countries.

According to the study, the major reason for staying in China is access to its vast domestic market. Those companies that want to remain in China say they are beginning to focus on the new business model, based on quality, brand building, and moving their products to the higher end of the value chain. Chinese companies like the Kangnai Group are experiencing the same pressures. In some cases, the answer is to leave the initial business altogether or to take a momentary hiatus before returning to it with a different approach.

Haili Weathers the Storm

The story of Haili Toys also illustrates how acute sensitivity to market circumstances and timing can lead businesses in unexpected directions, which ultimately result in profitable synergies.

China's toy exports slowed dramatically in 2008, hurt by higher costs, a stronger home currency, and safety concerns. Chinese toy companies have always been driven by fierce competition that forced the industry to operate on extremely thin margins. A toy sword, for example, that sells for $7 in a store in California is likely to net the manufacturer in China around .0016 cents, or less than a penny. Unless a manufacturer has its own brand, impressive technology, added value, and creativity, it is likely to find itself caught in the trap typical of most OEM models. The manufacturer will eventually find itself squeezed between the rising cost of raw materials and its customers' relentless search to get the same product at a lower price. Chinese export-oriented toy companies suffered an additional blow when a series of product recalls involving toxic paint and other safety hazards made customers suspicious of Chinese products.

In August 2007, the Chinese government started a nationwide crackdown on faulty products. At least 700 toy-export licenses were revoked on the grounds that the companies involved violated safety standards. Despite these daunting setbacks in the industry, Haili Toys, a privately owned toy maker in Zhejiang Province, boasted $110 million in sales in 2007. Haili's profit margin was five times higher than its competition.

Fang Guangming, a self-made millionaire, was one of the company's founders. Fang built his first toy factory in Haiyan in 1992. He was 25 years old at the time and he used his family's entire savings of $4,000 to launch the company. Haiyan is a city of around 300,000 people about 60 miles from both Shanghai and Hangzhou. Since the toy business is a labor-intensive industry, it has a very low investment entry threshold, and the designs are easy to copy. In Haiyan, the number of toy companies increased ten-fold in just a few years. Fang's toy business soon faced fierce local competition. With increasingly low margins, he and his company had to struggle to survive.

FROM FINISHED TOYS TO THE FIBER INSIDE AND BEYOND

Most of the local toy manufacturers responded to the competition by putting pressure on their employees to work harder and faster. Fang was convinced that this approach could go only so far. He decided instead to focus on reducing the cost of a key component of stuffed toys—the synthetic fiber used for stuffing, which accounts for about a third of the toys' production cost. In the 1990s, toy companies in China had to pay high prices for imported fibers, and Fang was convinced that replacing the imported fiber with a domestic product would save money. He acquired a local fiber company and set up a joint venture with a South Korean company that provided the technology and equipment to produce the polypropylene fiber used to fill stuffed animals. Fang found that he could lower the cost of the stuffing by more than $800 per ton. The savings gave him a significant cost advantage over the competition.

The advantage proved short-lived, however. Within three years, the other local toy manufacturers were copying his idea. By 1998, Fang's toy business again faced declining profits. He began to look for more attractive business opportunities.

THE MATTER OF FREQUENCY CONVERTERS

In analyzing his costs, Fang realized that an unexpected expense resulted from the fact that the frequency converters that controlled the automatic textile production line kept breaking down. The effect was to stop the entire assembly line, and if Fang couldn't find someone to repair the equipment immediately, he had to pay for factory time during which nothing was being produced. Fang noted that the frequency converters were expensive and costly to repair, and he realized that this might be a new business opportunity. He knew that the Haiyan city government was ready to help local companies move into high technology. With a few partners, Fang founded a new company, Holip, to manufacture and service locally assembled and serviced frequency converters.

Manufacturing converters and repairing them were clearly two very different businesses. Holip started by reverse-engineering Japanese mainstream products. With limited R&D and design capabilities, Holip was anxious not to overdesign its products, and it outsourced some of the more capital-intensive parts of the manufacturing process, such as printing circuit boards, to local contractors so that its own role was largely limited to final assembly and testing. Even basic converters were assembled from about 1,000 components, half of which were sourced internationally. Fang believed that the key to success was selecting the right components and maintaining high quality during the assembly process. In the first year, nine out of ten converters the company produced either failed or were returned because of faulty components or mistakes in the assembly process. That year, Holip suffered a net loss of $84,550 on sales of $241,572.

The management team was appalled at the losses, especially since the repair and maintenance side of the business had always been profitable. Fang remained adamant about making the idea work. "To become an industry leader," he told his management team, "we need to be a pioneer. Innovation doesn't come cheaply."

The team soon realized that if it could not improve the quality of the converters, Holip was going to go under. In 2002, Fang hired a Taiwanese consultant to help with new product development and quality control. It worked, and the improved quality—combined with prices that were 40 percent lower than the competition's—helped to boost sales to $966,533 for 2002. Holip was able to break even on its 30 percent net margin, thanks to its low-cost structure. Sales reached $2,416,334 in 2003, with $845,717 in net profits. In 2004, sales quadrupled to $10,270,041, and net profit hit

$3,141,424. Holip became one of the leading domestic producers of frequency converters with a 2 percent market share.

Holip's founders had lofty ambitions. The company not only wanted to capture the segment of the market for purchasers that were easily satisfied with "good enough" converters—it also wanted to capture the high end of the market occupied by the products considered to be the best available anywhere. With a limited internal R&D capability, the company turned to the universities to develop new technology and products. In 2004, in conjunction with a professor at Tsinghua University, Holip embarked on a $241,648 project to develop frequency converters capable of generating higher torque. When the project failed, Holip's management team realized that its lack of the right technology was a significant roadblock to future growth. As Fang put it, "Now we know how deep the water is."

To develop or acquire the technology it needed, Holip required additional funding. It hired PriceWaterhouseCoopers to help prepare an IPO to raise money and to release some of the initial investors' funds. The urge to cash out was strong among some of the shareholders. Fang needed extra funds to increase the scale of his toy business and upgrade his online toy business model. He had several other ventures in mind, many of which required significant initial funding, and he also saw an advantage in cashing out rather than proceeding with an IPO.

In November 2004, Holip's senior management met with a team headed by Erhardt Jessen, a vice president of the Motion Controls division of Danfoss China. After a detailed analysis of what both companies had to offer, Holip reached the conclusion that selling the company to Danfoss would be a better alternative than resorting to an IPO. In addition, tapping into Danfoss's technology would enable Holip to upgrade its product line, and it might then be able to expand into new markets. In November 2005, Danfoss Motion Controls purchased Holip.

THE WEBKINZ WORLD

Fang Guangming considered himself wiser for the experience. "As an entrepreneur," he explained, "you need to realize what you can change, and what you cannot change. You need to be brave and decide to push forward or pull back. Innovation is not limited to technology, and creative ideas are the soul of innovation."

In 2004, Haili Toys entered into a partnership with the Canadian company Ganz to sell stuffed animals online. Ganz invested $20 million to build the website, and Haili supplied all the cute and cuddly toys. On April 29, 2005, the company released its most innovative new idea for stuffed toy pets. They were called Webkinz, and according to the company's promotional literature, they were lovable plush pets that each came with a unique secret code. If you had the secret code, you could enter Webkinz World online, where you cared for your virtual pet, answered trivia questions, earned KinzCash (the Webkinz World's "currency"), and played the best kids' games on the Net.

Webkinz became an instant, overwhelming hit. The Webkinz World was presented as an online play area where kids could create an online identity for their pets, adopt them, feed and dress them, and even furnish rooms for them. Kids could also earn KinzCash by adopting new pets, playing online games, doing small jobs, and answering questions. The Webkinz World was actually educational in that kids could theoretically learn to grow with their pets, play games, and expand their knowledge.

The success of Webkinz in the overseas market engendered explosive growth for Haili Toys. In 2008, Haili Toys licensed the website from Ganz to recreate the concept in China. Combining traditional toy making with the Internet upgraded Haili's business model, added more value to the products, and paved new paths for growth in a very competitive industry.

Lessons Learned

In the cases of both Kangnai and Haili, it was unlikely that a low-cost business model would be able to keep up with market changes for very long. Moving factories out of China to find cheaper labor might have worked for a while, but it made more sense to move up the value chain. The Kangnai Group survived precisely because its products established brand recognition for their reliability at a time when price competition was driving the competition out of business. As more of its competitors were driven into bankruptcy, Kangnai was able to capture market share and absorb the assets of its competitors.

As for Haili Toys, instead of blindly trying to produce a greater quantity with thinner resources, the company analyzed its own processes and detected market opportunities. It moved into these new market areas at a time when it was possible to maximize profits, and it pulled out of them at precisely the moment of diminishing returns. As a result, Haili's capital resources increased to the point where the company was able to take advantage of new opportunities and strengthen its overall market position.

In the cases of both companies, innovation was the key to survival for what had at first appeared to be a simple, low-cost, labor-intensive industry.

Li Ning Builds a Purely Chinese Brand Based on Celebrity

The difference between one athletic shoe and another tends to be more emotional than physical, but athletics are about pushing the limits, and sports enthusiasts look for anything that will give them even a slight edge. Even for those who aren't champions but want to be, wearing a brand name can establish an emotional connection to a winner. When it comes to sports apparel and footwear,

endorsements by sports champions often make a decisive difference. Brand names like Nike and Adidas have pushed the business a
long way beyond the 4,000 shoemakers in Wenzhou, who found
themselves squeezed into creating a negative brand. When you wear
a Nike shoe, with its distinctive "swoosh" logo, or an Adidas, you
get the feeling—rightly or wrongly—that somehow you are in the
same club as the Olympic champion who also wears that shoe. For
a manufacturer trying to sell a shirt, a pair of sports pants, or a shoe
that almost any manufacturer can produce, this identification adds
powerful value to an otherwise indistinguishable product.

The main problem that Nike and Adidas face in trying to establish that magical connection in China is that they are not Chinese.
The advantage that Li Ning Company Ltd. has is that it is Chinese,
at least to a certain point. While Li Ning's sports apparel and running shoes are manufactured in China, the company has made a
major effort to sign up leading American sports stars, including
NBA players Shaquille O'Neal and Evan Turner. A number of market analysts have speculated that the foreign athletes provide credibility that counters a residue of distrust of local production that still
lingers in the minds of many Chinese consumers. The endorsement
of a Chinese brand by an American or international star athlete
goes a long way toward convincing the average Chinese consumer
that the brand meets international standards despite the fact that it
is home-grown. According to that logic, signing up American sports
stars is aimed more at boosting sales in China's own market than
internationally. That is not to say that Li Ning lacks global ambitions, despite the fact that only 2 percent of its sales are actually
made outside China.

THE COMPANY IS BORN

The company was founded as Guangdong Li Ning Company Ltd. in
1989, almost as an afterthought, when the sports star Li Ning

retired from competition and put his energy into creating a first-class training facility for Chinese gymnasts. "We can do nothing without money," observed Li, so he started a sports equipment company in order to raise the funds needed to promote athleticism in China.

At the time, Li was not only China's greatest sports hero but an international star as well. He was named by an international jury in 1999 as one of the greatest all-time athletes of the 20th century. His accomplishments put him in a select group of world stars that includes Muhammad Ali, Pele, and Michael Jordan.

Over a 19-year career, Li Ning, who was born in 1963 in Liuzhou in China's southern Guangxi Province, won a total of 106 medals in gymnastics. During the 1982 World Cup gymnastics competition in Zagreb, he earned the title "prince of gymnastics" after carrying away six of the seven gold medals open to men. In the 1984 Los Angeles Olympics, he won more medals than any other participant and walked off with three gold medals, two silvers, and a bronze. He was also both World Amateur Champion and Asia Games Amateur Athletic Champion. Li was injured during the 1988 Seoul Olympics and retired shortly after, although he had already begun to participate in the Athletic Commission of the Interna-tional Olympics Committee.

Looking for a new career, Li decided to dedicate himself to addressing the critical shortages in equipment and facilities that he felt were hindering the training of young Chinese athletes. He noted that China's best soccer players had had to learn the game by play-ing on city streets and roads. China's vaunted table tennis champi-ons had been forced to learn the game on tables that were actually slabs of concrete.

In 1989, Li—who had already gained management experience working as a special assistant to the general manager of the Jianlibao Group in Guangdong—learned that bids were being accepted to provide sports equipment for the Asian Games torch relay, slated to take place in Beijing in 1990. A number of established foreign sports apparel companies had bid on providing the clothing for the Asian Games, but Li argued that it made no sense to have foreigners advertising their companies on the backs of Asians participating in the games, and he won the contract to provide 10,000 athletic suits for the event. Li decided to use his own name as the brand for the clothing, reasoning that his popularity as a sports star would be a powerful selling point.

Having succeeded at the Asian Games, Li moved his company to Beijing and decided to focus on providing clothing and equipment to other sports enthusiasts. On June 28, 2004, the company was listed on the Hong Kong Stock Exchange. The IPO raised $70.54 million, which enabled it to evolve into a professionally managed corporation. At the same time, the company established an R&D center in Hong Kong. The idea was to be in touch with global trends, provide new designs, and make Li Ning's products internationally competitive.

GROWTH AND DEVELOPMENT

In 2003, Li Ning was still trailing behind foreign brands like Nike and Adidas, but it was already producing more than half of the sports apparel and footwear sold by Chinese companies in China. From 2004 to 2008, the company added around 800 stores a year. By August 2010, there were more than 7,000 outlets across China, 11 flagship stores in major cities, and new stores opening at a rapid clip. The vast majority of the outlets were franchises supplied by 130 distributors. The company was also introducing 600 new shoe models a year. The flagship stores were intended to build brand recognition and credibility. Li Ning was actively talking about plans to have more than 9,000 stores by 2013. At the same time, it announced plans to consolidate or drop some 600 stores that were not doing well, replacing them with others in more promising locations.

By the summer of 2010, Li Ning had 14.2 percent of China's market share for sports gear. It was still trailing behind Nike, which had 16.7 percent, but it had managed to pass Adidas, which had dropped slightly to 13.9 percent. Li Ning's gross profit margin was running at 46 to 47 percent, and it meant to maintain that despite a 7 percent drop in its sales of sports apparel and an 8 percent drop in footwear. Li Ning's strategy was to go for second- and third-tier cities in China's rural areas, which were now beginning to have enough spendable income to invest in sports.

Li Ning had early on adopted a logo that resembled a stylized liquid L that bore a striking resemblance to the famous Nike swoosh, except that it was red. In addition, the company's original motto, "Anything is possible," recalled Adidas's slogan, "Impossible is nothing." By the summer of 2010, the company announced that it was adopting a new logo, essentially separating the L at its base so that it resembled the Chinese character for "people." A new company slogan, "Make the change," was introduced. The message was clear: From now on, Li Ning intended to compete on its own merits and wanted to distinguish itself from its leading foreign competitors, Nike and Adidas. It no longer wanted to be seen as a pale copy. In general, Li Ning's quality was considered close to that of Nike, Adidas, and Reebok, while the price was significantly less. Li Ning's product line was much better than that of any of its domestic competitors.

THE INTERNATIONAL STRATEGY AND FOREIGN COMPETITION

Li Ning had been pondering an international expansion since 1999, but as of 2008, 98.8 percent of its revenues were still coming from sales in China. Some of the company's board members expressed concern that spending money on international stores risked starving Li Ning's China operations for cash at a time when it was encountering increased foreign competition. In 2007, the company opened a store in Maastricht, Netherlands, mostly at the suggestion of two Dutch entrepreneurs. The company was still not fully committed to selling in Europe. Disputes among the company's senior management resulted in the Maastricht store not being outfitted with European sizes. After a year, the store closed.

Although Li Ning was the biggest player in the China market, it was not certain how long it could continue to hold that position. It was running into mounting competition from domestic companies, and both Nike and Adidas were beginning to look at the China market with new interest. Nike had previously divided the world into four regions. China was lumped together with Japan and other Asian countries spread across the Asia-Pacific region. By the time the Beijing Olympics took place in 2008, Nike had already reorganized itself into six regions, assigning "greater China" to a region by itself. Nike, which had nearly 40 percent of the China market, suggested that China might well become its largest market. The prospect of a surge in foreign competition seemed to energize Li Ning. To avoid taking on the multinationals in territory that they already dominated, Li Ning opened a flagship store in Singapore and planned to open up to 100 outlets across southeast Asia, mostly in Indonesia, Singapore, and Malaysia. In December 2009, Li Ning opened a flagship store in Hong Kong. A month later, it opened its first store in the United States, in Portland, Oregon—less than a mile from Nike's own flagship store.

This time, the international strategy served two purposes. It provided a tentative venture into a potentially lucrative market as yet untapped by the company, but more than that, it also served to give Li Ning the kind of international credibility that it felt it needed to compete with Nike, Adidas, and Reebok in the China market. If Li Ning could actually cut into Nike's and Adidas's market share in their home territories by providing comparative or better quality at an affordable price, so much the better.

The company had scored a major coup for the China market during the Beijing Olympics. During the opening ceremony, Li Ning was chosen to light the Olympic torch. In a remarkable piece of showmanship, he was lifted high into the air by wires attached to a harness. He seemed to be running through the air as a spotlight followed him around the walls of the stadium until he finally lit the torch for all athletes around the world. Following that, the company set out to secure endorsements from a wide range of international sports stars. Signing on Shaquille O'Neal and Evan Turner was considered a major coup, but the company also signed a contract with NBA properties to ensure that its ads would appear at NBA games and that NBA stars would endorse its products. In addition, Li Ning became an official apparel sponsor for the U.S. Diving Team through 2012, and it also sponsored the U.S. Table Tennis Team (clearly an endorsement that meant more to the Chinese public than to most Americans).

To get its message across to a wider audience, the company developed a series of slick television commercials. One shows three inchworms, sporting logos from Nike, Adidas, and Li Ning, slowly moving across a white expanse. Suddenly, sneakers with the Li Ning label rain down on them. The camera pulls back to show an endless formation of Li Ning sneakers stamping on the ground.

The question remains, of course, whether Li Ning can grow big enough and fast enough not only to tap into the markets outside China but also to survive against stiff foreign competition on its own purely Chinese turf. To increase its chances, it dramatically stepped up its advertising budget and increased its ad spending in the United States by $10 million. American sales, handled through Foot Locker, had lagged, partly because the company was still trying to sell shoes that had been designed and manufactured for Chinese customers, not American. To get over that hurdle, the company announced that it was hiring 20 product designers to specifically target foreign markets. Li Ning's executives declared boldly that they intended to be one of the top five sporting brands in the world by 2018. It is a long shot, but not an impossible one.

NOTES

1. "Sourcing: How China Compares with the Rest of the World," September 8, 2004, www.wharton.universia.net.

2. "China Pays Steep Price as Textile Exports Boom," August 22, 2007, online.wsj.com.

SEVEN

CHINT Switches on China's Electricity

Share the wealth, and people are committed. —CHINT's philosophy

Nan Cunhui, Wenzhou, and the Founding of CHINT

NAN CUNHUI, THE FUTURE FOUNDER, CEO, and chairman of the CHINT Group, was born in Yueqing County, Wenzhou, in July 1963, three years before the start of the Cultural Revolution. From the beginning, Nan's education tended toward practicality rather than theory. To help his family make ends meet during the chaos and economic disarray that characterized the Cultural Revolution, he began selling eggs and rice bran in Wenzhou's streets at the age of six. Child labor was one way of getting around the restrictions against private enterprise. While street peddling was forbidden and adults risked going to jail, children were usually exempt from prison, although they risked having their goods confiscated.

Like other children his age, Nan attended school while his father scratched out a living repairing shoes. But when his father had an accident that made it impossible for him to continue working, Nan—at age 13 and only 17 days from graduating middle school—dropped out and took up his father's job. Armed with his father's toolbox, he began scouring the streets of Wenzhou, looking for customers. Often, he worked from early morning until late at night. Although he earned at most a few dollars a day, he was more successful than many of his competitors. As Nan explains it, "I earned more money than other shoe repairers because I did the work fast and carefully." Nan not only learned about shoe repair— he also learned to be on constant lookout for police patrols from the government office against "smuggling and speculation," who were likely to arrest anyone working at an unofficial job.

As it did for millions of Chinese, economic reform changed Nan's life dramatically. Many people in Wenzhou left to find work elsewhere; others began peddling in the streets of Wenzhou. The ongoing ban on "smuggling and speculation" was increasingly ignored. In January 1982, though, the authorities cracked down on the Wenzhou businessmen known as the Eight Magnates, who were famous for "speculation." The "Nail Magnate," who collected used nails and sold them to factories in Shanghai, was thrown in jail along with six other magnates and a scattering of entrepreneurs. The crackdown was so effective that many Wenzhou entrepreneurs fled the town, shops closed, and the local economy stalled.

Within a year, Wenzhou's economy was half of what it had been. Under growing public pressure, local officials reversed themselves and decided to free Wenzhou's imprisoned entrepreneurs.

To mark the event, the officials offered to issue certificates of approval finally authorizing the entrepreneurs to engage in business. (Most of the entrepreneurs decided that it was safer not to show up for the ceremony.) Although caution reigned, change was clearly in the air. Nan, among others, identified electrical parts and components as both a major gap and a promising economic opportunity. With little to go on and even less to lose, he founded CHINT. Nan's initial idea was simple enough: Disassemble a few electrical parts, copy them, and then sell the parts to the local market.

By 2008, the CHINT Group, the descendant of a tiny enterprise that Nan founded in Wenzhou a quarter of a century earlier, had grown to become China's largest manufacturer of low-voltage electrical products, including power transmission and distribution equipment, meters for measuring, instruments, and solar products. In 2006, *Forbes* ranked it 15th among the top 100 Chinese companies. CHINT's 2,000 retail outlets in China and 80 general agents abroad generated sales of more than €2 billion a year by 2006. Its trademark was recognized by the State Administration of Industry and Commerce as a "Top National Trademark," one of China's most prestigious honors for outstanding enterprises.

Nan, who was already a billionaire, was elected as a delegate to the 9th, 10th, and 11th National People's Congresses. He had come a long way from his humble beginnings as a cobbler doing shoe repairs.

The Qiujing Switch Factory

Nan had had two options when he started his electrical parts and components business: He could either set up his own workshop or work as a salesman. Neither was easy. He had no technical knowledge, and he had even less sales experience. He had never even been away from his hometown.

Ultimately, he decided to set up a workshop with three friends. The first step was to buy some simple switches, take them apart, and trace the outlines of the pieces on paper in order to understand how they worked. The group of four worked hard, and in their first month, they managed to clear a total of about $10 after deducting costs. The sum was equivalent to one month's salary for one worker, and there were four of them. Nan's partners became depressed and abandoned the project, but Nan's reaction was the exact opposite. He was delighted that the project had produced any money at all, and he decided to forge onward despite the fact that even his parents could see no future in it. They advised him to close the workshop and go back to repairing shoes. At least that way he could count on an income of $3 to $6 per day.

In July 1984, Nan teamed up with Hu Chengzhong, a childhood friend, to create a new venture called Qiujing Switches. Nan and Hu each invested RMB$6,465 to keep Qiujing Switches going. As it turned out, the two friends had skills that complemented each other: Nan knew about production and management, and Hu was experienced in sales. The two partners agreed that quality and brand identity were the keys to success, even though the industry at that time was loosely regulated.

Because they knew next to nothing about technology, Nan and Hu went to Shanghai to seek help from retired technicians at a state-owned factory that produced switches. The two partners didn't have enough money to stay in a hotel, so they slept on the floors of the homes of the technicians they were trying to recruit. Several of the technicians who made the trip to Wenzhou to see Nan and Hu's facility left after taking a quick look at the company's shabby sur-roundings. A few decided to stay. They had been impressed not by the company's physical plant but by the boundless enthusiasm of the two young men.

In the 1980s, as China's economic boom was gaining speed, Nan's intuition about the industry was proved right. Demand outstripped supply for almost all electrical products. Buyers began flooding into Wenzhou's electrical flea market, known as the "City of Electrics." Everything was for sale, regardless of whether it worked or not. There was no standard for quality, and product testing was almost unheard of. Local competitors used flimsy plastic or cheated on the amount of silver in the contacts for the switches. Some even substituted bronze, which corroded almost immediately. Nan and Hu decided against compromising quality even though that meant charging higher prices in a competitive market. Nan had already decided on the philosophy that would characterize his career. "We are not going to earn money," he said, "by cheating in a business that has an impact on human life." As frustration with faulty products surged, customers were increasingly ready to pay a premium for better quality. Qiujing Switches began to attract a larger customer base, and the company made a net profit of roughly $3,000 in 1986.

To improve quality further and obtain a formal government license, one of Qiujing's technicians suggested setting up a test lab at a cost of $86,886. Since Qiujing's total assets were less than $28,962, the proposal seemed outrageously expensive, but Nan and Hu decided to go for it anyway. They borrowed money and set up the first thermal overload relay test lab in the region. The company had to pay 2.5 percent interest per month on private loans, and they used their family homes as collateral. As a result, they had to rent space to live in. With the test lab, however, the State Electrical and Mechanical Department awarded Qiujing the first production permit for mechanical and electrical products in Wenzhou in 1988.

Not long afterward, Wenzhou experienced a long overdue crisis as a result of the failure of many of its small businesses to institute quality control. In 1990, an explosion in a coal mine resulted from a spark from a substandard electrical switch. A team, composed of representatives of eight state ministries, was sent to Wenzhou to crack down on electrical producers that lacked certification. The five-month crackdown was dramatic: 1,267 shops selling low-voltage products and 1,544 family workshops were forced to close, and 359 business licenses were revoked. Only 20 percent of the manufacturers, including Qiujing Switches, survived. Qiujing Switches, which had already distinguished itself as a reliable manufacturer, expanded its market share at the expense of the substandard producers.

In 1990, Nan Cunhui and Hu Chengzhong decided to split the company. Each of the original partners received $209,065 of the company's assets. Hu founded Delixi, which eventually competed with CHINT in the production of power transmission and distribution switches and Nan went on to create CHINT.

CHINT's Expansion

To encourage foreign direct investment, Wenzhou's local government offered concessions (real estate, water, electricity, etc.) to foreign joint ventures. Many of Wenzhou's leading entrepreneurs decided to take advantage of the new policy. In September 1990, Nan established Wenzhou CHINT Electrical Co. Ltd., a Sino-American joint venture. He brought his younger brother and brother-in-law into the new company, a practice that is more or less common for family businesses in China. Nan's share of the company fell from 100 to 60 percent. Each of the company's original nine employees was a shareholder in the company.

CHINT's low-voltage business took off. The company upgraded its production lines and built new factories at a cost of $1.7 million. It also invested in an enterprise resource planning (ERP) system to control expanding production, sales, accounting, and human resources. In 1994, CHINT spent $463,972, acquiring what at the time was the most advanced test facility in China and the largest low-voltage electrical test lab ever established by a Chinese private enterprise.

Rapid Growth and Reorganization

The investment and the government permit from the State Electrical and Mechanical Department, which CHINT had acquired after investing in its test lab in 1988, soon paid off. When stricter regulations were introduced, the local electric manufacturers, which were not allowed to operate without a permit, rushed to CHINT, anxious to operate under the umbrella of CHINT's brand. In exchange, CHINT collected a royalty and management fee. By early 1994, more than 40 enterprises were affiliated with CHINT.

Taking over so many small enterprises enabled CHINT to expand rapidly, but it also had a downside. Managing so many enterprises turned out to be much more complicated than running a centralized company. Quality control was especially difficult to maintain. To tighten CHINT's control over the expanding network, Nan overrode the objections of several members of his family and initiated a stock split in 1994. The maneuver left CHINT in control of 48 enterprises. There were different levels of participation: 100 percent ownership, controlling share of more than 50 percent, single largest share between 20 percent and 50 percent, and participation with less than a 20 percent share. CHINT's shareholders increased to 40. Nan's share in the company fell to 40 percent, but the exchange of shares increased CHINT's net assets from $463,972 to $5,799,656. Nan's personal assets increased 20-fold over the next three years.

Having accomplished the stock reallocation, Nan initiated a series of structural changes within the group. He expanded the core business, weeded out the low-quality producers, and focused on those enterprises with the greatest growth potential.

Building a Sales Network

When Qiujing Switches had split into two companies in 1990, Hu Chengzhong kept the original sales team and its resources. Sales for Nan's new company (CHINT) suffered in the short term, and CHINT immediately set about reestablishing a new sales network across major cities in China. Luckily, an abundant supply of Wenzhou salespeople was available to help out. The sales network was to become a major factor in CHINT's future success.

While the multinationals were mostly present in the first- and second-tier markets, CHINT's salespeople hit all the tiers. Wenzhou sales personnel were accustomed to travel and were not particularly bothered by hardships on the road. When reforms began in China in the late 1970s, the salespeople had covered thousands of miles, carrying their samples on their shoulders. It was not unusual for a salesperson to walk ten hours a day on muddy country roads in order to visit remote villages. If a salesperson had a chance to share a hotel room with 20 other people for only $0.23 per night, he would consider it a luxury. With this kind of determination from its salespeople in the 1990s, CHINT soon established a sales network that provided in-depth coverage of far-flung cities and villages. Multinational companies lacked the staffing and the resources to keep up.

Until 1995, Wenzhou salespeople regularly visited customers and then returned to the head office with orders. Between 1995 and 2000, however, CHINT created ten sales offices in major cities. These offices began hiring agents to reach smaller cities and counties through their own outlets or through small shops. From 2000 to 2005, CHINT transformed the ten sales offices into ten distribution centers. The goal was to reinforce sales, marketing, and after-sales service and reduce delivery time.

After 15 years of rapid expansion, CHINT began to realize the need to optimize the sales channels. Most of its agencies had been created and managed by Wenzhou salespeople who sold directly to customers after traveling to their location. Many of the salespeople settled in the areas where they worked. But as CHINT transformed itself from a family business to a more modern enterprise, the company needed outlets to make more sales, provide better service, and use its resources more efficiently.

CHINT solved the problem by setting up a tiered distribution system. Preferred agents (or distributors) with higher sales volumes, better technical competence, and reliable after-sales service received greater discounts. Core distributors were treated with more favorable conditions, and weak distributors were replaced if they were unable to meet sales and performance targets. The three-year transformation process proved painful since it required changing the rules for a network that had been based on established relationships. Nevertheless, by 2008, CHINT had ten distribution centers, seven sales companies, 900 major distributors, and 2,000 smaller distributors.

Sharing Equity with Employees Critical to the Enterprise

Although restructuring was a challenge, Nan decided to heed an old Chinese proverb: "Hoard wealth, and people are detached; share wealth, and people are committed." The challenge for most businesses is to recruit and retain the best people. Added responsibility and above-average pay works to a certain extent, but the most effective approach is to share ownership of the company. After considerable deliberation, Nan decided to reward key employees with shares, an unusual approach in China. Starting from 1998, the number of shareholders steadily increased from 40 to 100 in 2008, and Nan's ownership in the company fell from 40 percent to 20 percent. Each year, CHINT created a number of millionaires by awarding shares in the company. Nan's philosophy held that sharing was more than generosity. It made good business sense.

As the number of shareholders grew, CHINT established a board of directors with some external directors and a supervisory board. The modern ownership and management system began to unlock CHINT's growth potential and paved the way for CHINT to go public.

Focusing on Quality

The CHINT Group made quality a top priority to an extent that at times surprised its customers. In 1995, a dealer in Greece was astonished when his order arrived by airfreight. The transportation costs had already wiped out CHINT's profits on the order, so why had airfreight been used? When the order had originally reached the ocean freight forwarder, a quality controller had noticed a minor problem with some of the items. They were fine according to domestic standards, but not according to those set by CHINT. Nan inspected the products himself and decided not to ship any more orders until a thorough test had been carried out. Realizing that quality is an essential ingredient in the life of a brand, he preferred to lose money than to lose his credibility. After missing the ocean shipping deadline, Nan then spent more than $60,000 to send the products by air in order to make sure that they arrived on time. "I would rather spend millions of dollars," he explained, "than have even one substandard product leave our factory."

Starting in 1995, CHINT chose the month of May as its "quality month." In addition, to guarantee quality control, all products had to be signed for by a quality manager before shipping. One quality control manager was so tough that she ended up making a number of enemies in the company. When Nan heard about it, he promoted her to be a company shareholder.

Over the years, CHINT developed an effective quality assurance system that included factory automation, product testing, inspection, and a quality hotline for employees to report problems. Evolving from a labor-intensive manufacturing process to one that was technology-intensive also improved product quality substantially. In 2004, CHINT received China's National Quality Award, the country's highest quality award and the first made to a private enterprise in the low-voltage business.

Investing in R&D

Many small businesses in China begin by reverse-engineering existing products to see how they are made. When the business scales up, most entrepreneurs realize the importance of developing their own technology. Nan believed that CHINT could grow only through vigorous innovation. A major emphasis was placed on researching and developing new technology to update its products. From 1996, CHINT committed 3 to 5 percent of yearly sales to R&D and established research centers in Silicon Valley in the United States, in Europe, and across China. Out of CHINT's 20,000 employees, 20 percent were engaged in technology. Since 1998, CHINT has introduced more than 100 new products, most of them with independent intellectual property rights.

Nan's success made others anxious to copy even his minor innovations. For example, a week after CHINT added a red dot to the *I* in its logo, a score of companies introduced red dots in their logos as well. Even CHINT's meeting room layout was copied by other companies. From products to sales channels, there were no secrets: Everything could be imitated. Nan didn't seem overly upset. "The followers copy fast," he said. "That pushes us to be more innovative. We would be in trouble if nobody copied us." Nan acknowledged that when it came to technology, CHINT still had a long way to go compared to the multinationals.

Nan's Challenges

The low-voltage market is divided into four segments, M1 through M4, based on price. M1 is at the top of the market, and M4 at the inexpensive, low end. Many small Chinese local companies served the M4 market through flea markets in which product quality was not guaranteed and prices were very low. These manufacturers tended to engage in small-scale production, focus on a narrow product range, and have a regional presence.

The M3 market is served by large domestic manufacturers that provide a wide range of quality low-voltage products. They benefit from economies of scale and some even have their own distribution networks, although coverage and service levels of these networks vary greatly. About 70 percent of products are sold through distributors and roughly 30 percent through design centers. The distribution network plays an important role in reaching a diverse customer base. Prices are extremely competitive.

The M2 market is generally served by domestic niche players such as Changshu Switchgear and Tebian Electric Apparatus. These companies usually trace their roots to state-owned enterprises with long track records. Specializing in certain product categories, they invest heavily in niche markets and work directly with system designers and integrators. They have good reputations. They are knowledgeable about their field and maintain high quality in the categories in which they specialize. In the same product category, some multinational companies offer standard products (often produced in Chinese factories) and advanced products (with more sophisticated features incorporating the newest technology, often imported from factories in developed countries). Generally speaking, their standard products could be grouped in the M2 market.

The M1 market is served by multinationals marketing their most advanced products. Quality and reliability are very high. In China, these multinationals mainly serve other multinationals and the big utility companies. They usually dominate their sector when it comes to projects that are considered critically important. The price they ask is usually very high. For example, if a simple electric component is priced below RMB 1.2 in M4, it would be in the range of $0.19 to $0.23 in M3, $0.22 to $0.28 in M2, and $0.31 to $0.47 in M1.

CHINT was the unquestioned leader in the M3 market, but it faced challenges from below and from above. It also had to deal with the fact that the distinction between the mid-tier M2 and M3 segments is often not very clear-cut.

THE MULTINATIONALS BEGIN MOVING INTO THE MID-TIER MARKETS

Multinationals such as ABB, Siemens, and Schneider Electric have shown themselves to be formidable competitors in the China market. When they first entered the market, they focused on the M1 segment and avoided direct competition with the domestic players. Gradually, they began to move into the mid-tier segments. Given their deep pockets and technical knowledge and the high quality of their products, Nan felt that he had good reason to be concerned about future competition. Schneider Electric highlighted the threat when it acquired 15 companies in the 1990s. Its share of the low-voltage market in China suddenly increased to 15 percent, and its sales in 2008 were estimated at well above $1.5 billion.

In 1994, Schneider offered to buy an 80 percent interest in CHINT, but Nan declined the offer. A year later, Schneider sued

CHINT in Hangzhou for intellectual property infringement. The suit was amicably settled out of court. In 1998, Schneider offered to buy a 51 percent share of CHINT. Nan turned Schneider down again, and the next year, Schneider took CHINT to court again for intellectual property infringement, this time in Beijing. The court decided that Schneider's patents were no longer valid. Once again, in 2004, Schneider offered a hefty sum to acquire 50 percent of CHINT's equity. Nan said, "I was quite tempted as I probably won't make so much money in generations." But he decided not to sell.

Meanwhile, the lawsuits continued. Since 1993, Schneider has filed 24 suits against CHINT. Internationally, Schneider took CHINT to court in France, Germany, Italy, and other countries. CHINT had "CHINT" registered as its English trademark in 1998. Schneider then registered "CHINT" as a trademark in 1999 in France, Russia, Brazil, and other countries. In 2005, Schneider filed a lawsuit against CHINT for patent violation, this time in a German court; CHINT countered that the Schneider patent had expired. After two years' investigation, the Federal Patent Court found the Schneider patent no longer valid, and Schneider withdrew the case.

In August 2006, CHINT decided to take Schneider to court, alleging that Schneider had encroached on a CHINT utility model patent. On April 15, 2009, Schneider and CHINT agreed to settle ten minutes before the case was scheduled to start, with Schneider paying just over $23 million (half of the original sum CHINT was asking for). The two companies also reached a global compromise on patent infringement cases.

In 2007, Schneider bought 50 percent of Delixi, CHINT's direct competitor, which was started by Nan's friend Hu Chengzhong after the decision to divide Qiujing Switches. CHINT and Delixi had been competing for the top position ever since 1990, when Nan and Hu had gone their separate ways. CHINT had gradually edged into the No. 1 slot, and by 2008, Delixi was half the size of CHINT.

With its investment in Delixi, Schneider was able to effectively compete directly with CHINT in the M3 market.

But Nan was not only concerned about competition from Schneider. Other multinationals were also moving into the mid-tier markets. The competition promised to be fierce.

COMPETITION FROM LOCAL PLAYERS

In Wenzhou alone, CHINT faced competition from Tengen and from People Electrical Apparatus Group, and across China, from a multitude of niche players. These companies were managing to improve the quality of their products while remaining competitive on pricing. Some had even placed advertising billboards in front of CHINT's factories.

By the beginning of 2009, CHINT was beginning to feel pressure from the multinationals in the top tier as well as from local manufacturers that were moving up from the lower-tier markets into CHINT's M3 territory. It was beginning to look as though the days of CHINT's leadership in China's low-voltage business might be numbered.

MOVING UP TO THE PREMIUM SEGMENTS

As Nan saw it, a solution was to move up to the premium segments of the market. As CHINT gained more knowledge about the market and improved its products, processes, and technology, it was natural for it to begin looking toward the M2 or even M1 markets. Customers in the M1 and M2 markets, however, are very different from those in M3.

In M3, customers tend to be small and medium-size companies serving local markets and individual consumers. They were mainly served by CHINT's regional distributors. Some local utility companies and real estate developers also buy large quantities from distributors. The customers in M1 and M2 are mostly foreign multinationals, big Chinese state utility companies, and high-end real estate developers. The products are often used in big projects. Professional designers and systems integrators choose which products to include.

If CHINT entered M1 and M2, it would have to compete directly with multinationals with strong reputations, technology, and a broad range of products, as well as with branded niche players that had long track records. None of CHINT's attempts to move up the value chain had been successful before.

Launching the N-Series

In 1998, CHINT launched its low-voltage N-series products with energy-saving features and a more aesthetically appealing look. The N-series added desirable features and accommodated clients' needs. For example, when a client suggested smoothing the plastic edges on a product so that it could be repaired without scratching one's hands, CHINT was prepared to change its design to accommodate them.

The N-series greatly improved CHINT's image by introducing innovative design features and technology, some of which was patented. However, the CHINT brand continued to be known best for its mid- and low-tier pricing, and clients were likely to choose other brands if the product quality and design were roughly similar. From the customer's perspective, the N-series was not perceived to be clearly positioned. After ten years, the N-series had some success, but it failed to reach the sales level CHINT had hoped for.

A Joint Venture with GE

In February 2005, CHINT and General Electric entered a joint venture (GE 51 percent and CHINT 49 percent) in Wenzhou, producing a circuit breaker sold under the GE brand. GE was responsible for management and production, and CHINT was in charge of selling via its channels. The circuit breaker was priced at $1.99 to $2.11, much higher than CHINT's original pricing of $0.87 per piece. The product improvement over CHINT's existing product was not perceived to be significant enough by the customers. The product line was also too narrow, so clients had to complement their purchases with other brands. The circuit breaker did not sell as well as expected, and after a two-year trial, management decided to pull the plug on the joint venture.

Outsiders observed that cultural collisions between the two companies might have been the source of the early termination. Others suspected that CHINT's distributors had no experience handling more expensive products with recognizable brands.

Attempting the Acquisition Route

In 2007, the Moeller Group, a German supplier of electrical components for commercial and residential buildings, was up for sale. Based in Bonn, the company sold its products primarily to customers in Western and Eastern Europe and Asia-Pacific. It had annual sales of about €1 billion and had 8,700 employees.

CHINT was interested in acquiring the company, but Moeller was too big and the deal fell through, partly because CHINT did not want to settle for only part of Moeller's assets. Eventually, the Moeller Group was acquired by Eaton Electric Systems, a company based in the United States, at the end of 2007 for €1.55 billion.

Creating a Brand

In 2007, the profit margins in the mid-tier market continued to be eroded, and the pressure to expand was becoming intense. CHINT decided to go ahead with a €100 million expansion. Lily Zhang, a 32-year-old general manager at CHINT, was delegated to manage the expansion. Zhang had joined CHINT in 1998 and had worked in various departments within the company, including finance, accounting, and strategy. In 2002, at the age of 27, she became the general manager in charge of global sales for CHINT's low-voltage business.

Zhang hired a team of consultants from A.T. Kearney to design a strategy for entering the M2 market. The recommendation was to launch a new brand called Noark that could easily be distinguished from the N-series.

Going Global

Another avenue in response to the competition was to go global. In 1994, CHINT exhibited its products at the Canton Fair, which opened the company to international markets. Exports soon reached €1 million in annual sales, but they were limited to a few countries such as Argentina and Greece. All exports were sold under distributors' brands in the relevant country.

In 1998, CHINT registered its trademark in 66 countries worldwide. International sales surged, with annual growth of more than 70 percent. Most products were sold under CHINT's brand. CHINT had set up an international sales network, comprising eight international offices, 30 sole agents, and more than 80 local partners who were Chinese by origin but living in foreign countries. CHINT had three ways to reach global markets: contract manufacturing, exports to dealers, and direct exports.

CHINT also manufactured electric meters and instruments and other products for international companies based on their specifications. In these relationships, CHINT's main role was to handle manufacturing. In 1994, CHINT was working with 30 OEMs; by 2008, the number had declined to five OEMs.

CHINT had set up long-term relationships with local dealers in other countries. In 1999, CHINT started to sell products abroad under its own brand name. The company helped dealers with promotions and by attending trade exhibitions. In 2007, at the Hanover Fair in Germany, CHINT was the only independent exhibitor from

China, and it had a stand of some 2,000 square feet. Thanks to yet another dispute with Schneider, CHINT was barred from entering the Belgian market and had to rely on dealers in Spain and Greece to tap into the neighboring countries.

About 70 percent of CHINT's international sales were made through exports to local dealers. This had slowed down in recent years, and CHINT noticed that the main drawback of working with local dealers was that they supplied almost no information about customers, channels, and pricing. There was no transparency. CHINT had no control over this channel, and feedback usually came too late to be of any use. It was hard to tell whether the dealers were protecting their own interests or simply being driven by market conditions. By some estimates, the dealers were able to make as much as 100 percent profit, leaving CHINT with only 10 percent of the wholesale price that it had charged the dealers. CHINT realized that it needed a new approach.

Direct Export

One answer was to begin establishing strategic partnerships with China's big machinery import and export companies, international engineering contractors, and energy companies. CHINT could join them as bidding partners for energy projects in international markets. In 2006, CHINT outbid established foreign rivals, including Schneider and ABB, to supply €60 million worth of equipment to Italy's national electricity company. CHINT also won energy contracts in Saudi Arabia, Cuba, Kenya, and Greece.

While CHINT's international sales had increased steadily, they were still only a small portion of its total sales. Beginning in 1995, CHINT started to establish international offices in Spain, the United States, Greece, and other countries. To expand its own sales forces abroad, CHINT needed to decide whether it really wanted to have its own exclusive sales force and, if so, how to staff it. On the one hand, it could send its own salespeople abroad to staff the sales offices. The advantage of this approach was that these people would know the products and could be counted on to be loyal to the company. The overseas sales offices would be an integral part of CHINT. On the other hand, it was difficult to find salespeople who were proficient in a foreign language, and even more difficult to find people who knew the local culture well enough to develop a sales channel. Hiring local professionals already working in the field promised to solve the language and cultural issues but proved to be very expensive. An even greater challenge was how to manage, coordinate, and work with these people. Would they be receptive to the Chinese way of working? After all, CHINT was a Chinese company. The third option was to hire overseas Chinese, including Chinese nationals studying abroad. These people could understand Chinese culture, but they lacked technical knowledge. They might not be as familiar with the local market and local laws as the local professionals. A minor issue was their legal status working in a foreign country. In the end, the company decided on a mixture of these options. It expanded its product line and expanded into the international market, hiring the best qualified people it could find. Today the company has clients in 70 countries and 2,000 worldwide distribution points.

Moving Down to Related Products

Another way for CHINT to deal with the growing competition was to extend the company's product line. In 2000, CHINT became the largest producer of low-voltage electrical products in China, claiming about 30 percent of market share. Low-voltage products made in Wenzhou accounted for more than 50 percent of total sales in China. CHINT would have to win market share from local companies to grow further. The most likely scenario would be a price war, which would drive the already thin margin into negative territory for all the players.

Nan faced a dilemma: Should he diversify into other lucrative businesses, such as real estate and pharmaceuticals, or should he upgrade his product line to medium- and high-voltage electrical products?

In 2003, CHINT finally made the decision to expand from low-voltage products to the whole range of electrical products, including power transmission and distribution (T&D). The same year, an opportunity presented itself. Shenyang Transformer Works, a state-owned enterprise with a long history of producing medium- and high-voltage transformers, was for sale. CHINT wanted to acquire it but was outbid by Tebian Electric Apparatus.

CHINT decided on a different line of attack. In July, it invested nearly $423 million in launching a T&D project in Shanghai to produce power transformers, power wires and cables, and power automation equipment. The creation of CHINT T&D made it clear that the company intended to transform itself from a low-voltage equipment producer to a company that could also manufacture medium- and high-voltage products, as well as providing related electrical engineering and installation.

The power T&D business differed greatly from CHINT's traditional market. While CHINT's low-voltage products were sold through its 2,000 distributors, power transformers and equipment were sold mainly through electrical design centers or direct sales to customers. Initially, the company had some success domestically selling transformers to small and regional utility companies and some industrial users for whom price was important. At an international level, CHINT's manufacturing flexibility—with lead times of six to 12 months—stood it in good stead. Although well-known global brands were often the preferred choice as transformer suppliers, demand for their products far exceeded supply. Many companies had a backlog of 18 to 24 months, which was simply too long for most projects. As a result, CHINT got some of these contracts. By 2006, its T&D sales amounted to RMB 1.7 billion, increasing to RMB 2.7 billion the following year. CHINT T&D was ranked first in the Power Transmission & Distribution and Controlling Devices Sector at the China Machinery Summit in 2008.

In order to expand to the next level, CHINT needed to attract larger clients. Some of the big state-owned utility companies handled very big projects and qualified as perfect candidates. For these potential customers, price was important but not the major concern. Instead, they needed to be sure that the high-voltage equipment they purchased would not fail, and so their managers preferred to rely on the top global brands in order to avoid blame if things went wrong. On the international stage, in order to ensure quality, larger utility companies normally required a five-year track record for the relevant product before buying from a manufacturer. They might also insist on certification of the production process and final assembly, as well as of suppliers of critical components. CHINT also needed to decide whether domestic customers and international customers should be approached differently.

Lessons Learned

Private enterprises such as CHINT received little government support and grew through tough competition in both domestic and international markets. The experience turned the survivors into formidable competitors. One of the advantages of growing up in China's fast evolving economy is that the notion of change and the need for flexibility as well as sensitivity and quick adaptation to customers' demands are literally built into the DNA of these companies. China's cultural history also helped guide Nan to the right decisions—first to insist on quality in his company's products, and then to sense the importance of making his employees feel that they also were owners of the enterprise. In the end, Nan realized that survival ultimately required confronting the global market. The experience and insights that Nan had obtained in China's overheated, highly competitive domestic market promised to make CHINT a formidable competitor on the global stage.

Ping An Brings Modern Finance to China

If you think changing the mindset of Chinese consumers is difficult, imagine train-ing the insurance agents, who do not even know what life insurance is. . . .
—Dominic Leung, former CEO of Ping An Life

UNTIL CHINA OPENED ITSELF to private industry, there did not seem to be any real need for life insurance. The state pro-vided China's social safety net and was expected to take care of each citizen's needs from birth until death. Since the state was the biggest player by default, it was hard to see how anyone else could do any better. More than that, the Chinese by their nature tend to be pragmatic optimists, and until recently they saw little value in investing in a future that by definition they would not be allowed to enjoy. Put more simply, there seemed to be little advantage to expending energy contemplating one's death or per-manent disability. The rise of privately owned industries outside the government umbrella, and particularly those controlled by foreigners, changed all that.

Today, insurance is an integral part of China's service industries. Since the initiation of economic reform and the Open Door Policy, this sector has been expanding at a rate of 10 percent annually. In 1979, services accounted for only 21.6 percent of the GDP. By 2007, the service industry's share of the GDP had risen to 40.1 percent. Since 1978, the service industry has provided China with 200 million additional jobs and accounted for 32.4 percent of the country's total employment.

Ping An Gets the Ball Rolling

The rising star in this story was the Ping An (Peace) Insurance Company. Initially limited to Shenzhen's Special Economic Zone (SEZ), the company was launched by Peter Ma in 1988.

Ma had been a local government official in Guangdong Province. In 1983, he decided to move to Shekou, an industrial town about 15 miles from Shenzhen. As it turned out, Shekou was included in China's first SEZ, and its workers discovered to their dismay that under the new rules for a free market economy, the government was no longer prepared to guarantee them accident protection or lifetime employment. To fill the gap, China's first social security company was created in 1985, and Peter Ma—then age 31—became a manager. The company required foreign corporations to make payments on behalf of their workers to cover their accident benefits and pensions.

In 1986, Ma began lobbying the People's Bank of China, which governed the insurance and banking industries, to set up a private insurance company. Ma pointed out that since China was opening its doors to foreign investment, foreign investors had a right to demand an alternative insurance provider to the state-owned PICC (People's Insurance Company of China). Ma's argument coincided with a significant anniversary. The year 1986 marked the 100th anniversary of China's first private insurer, the Ren Gi He Insurance Company, which had been established during the Ching dynasty and was later abolished in the 1930s. Ma argued that the private insurance industry constituted a national heritage that should be restored. The People's Bank of China turned down the idea the first time he suggested it, but Ma continued to lobby relentlessly, and his application was finally approved on March 21, 1988. The Ping An Insurance Company became a legal entity, at least on paper.

At the time, China was still very much a planned economy. The concept of a free market appeared foreign to most officials, and attempts to make a profit outside the government sector were treated with suspicion. Deng Xiaoping's celebrated declaration that "to get rich is glorious" hadn't penetrated most local bureaucracies yet. Ping An, the country's first joint stock company, found the going particularly difficult. With only 13 employees, it had a limited authorization to sell property, transport, freight, and liability insurance products, but nothing more. Even that was a stretch. When Ping An tried to sell third-party liability insurance, the local Shenzhen police department refused to recognize the policies. The company's authorization from the National State Council was initially ignored. Ma later recalled:

> At that time, people still thought that insurance was a state-owned entity, not a commercial product. It was nearly impossible for them to imagine having another insurer under the communist regime. The police chief asked me a rhetorical question: "If there are two police departments, who is supposed to control whom?" I could not give him an answer.

After continued lobbying, the local police department finally recognized Ma's right to offer insurance. It had taken him a year to communicate the idea and have it accepted.

Facing the Competition

Ping An began its operations at a time when it had virtually no competition. Foreign insurers were not allowed to operate in China. Throughout the 1980s, though, foreign investment had started pouring into China, most of it concentrated on manufacturing goods for export. Foreign companies had to buy property insurance both to cover the value of manufactured goods and to obtain loans from foreign banks. Early regulations required foreign companies to buy their insurance in China from a state-owned monopoly, the PICC. There was little choice about the products offered and no flexibility in pricing. As government regulations gradually eased, Ping An became one of the first privately owned companies to offer a more flexible alternative.

By 1993, Ping An had nationwide operations with 38 sales branches (equivalent to an agency branch today). The following year, it entered the life insurance market and began using commission-based agents to sell its policies.

In 1992, the National State Council had decided to allow foreign competition to enter the insurance industry via joint ventures, and it picked Shanghai to be the first pilot city. Since most Chinese had seen no need for life insurance until then, domestic insurers had not considered life insurance products to be viable. Competition in the field was virtually nonexistent before 1994, and there was very little expertise concerning how to package the idea. The exception was Shanghai, where American International Group (AIG) had created a subsidiary, American Insurance Assurance (AIA). AIG had years of international experience, and its subsidiary dominated China's existing life insurance market.

As competition between foreign and domestic insurers gradually picked up speed, the insurance industry and relevant legislation began to evolve as well. In 1995, the government made a legal distinction between property and life insurance, and in 1998, it created the China Insurance Regulatory Commission (CIRC) as a separate body. With these reforms in place, the market for life insurance in China began to expand more rapidly. In 2000, the total annual insurance premium revenue in China was $19.3 billion, with $7.2 billion coming from property insurance premiums and $12.1 billion from life insurance.

After China joined the World Trade Organization in 2001, the Chinese insurance industry went through a series of policy reforms affecting the industry's business scope and geographical requirements. Foreign companies could now extend their reach beyond the major cities and no longer needed to establish a joint venture as a prerequisite to doing business. Competition intensified. Big national banks, including the Bank of China and the China Construction Bank, applied for licenses to offer insurance, while the Bank of Communications, China's fifth largest bank, applied for permission to offer insurance on a trial basis. Hoping to tap into the future growth of the financial services industry, leading international financial institutions—including Citigroup, Goldman Sachs, and HSBC—made significant investments in China's national banks. By the end of 2004, China had a total of 64 insurance companies. At least 40 were foreign-funded. In 2004, the annual insurance premium reached $58 billion, an increase rate of 31 percent. The insurance depth, measured by the proportion of insurance income to the percentage of GDP, had increased from 1.57 percent in 1998 to 3.7 percent in 2004.

As Ping An grew in size and diversified its product portfolio, Ma realized the importance of recruiting expatriates to the management team. By 2006, more than 60 of Ping An's top 100 managers had experience in international finance and with financial service companies such as Citigroup, HSBC, Goldman Sachs, and Prudential. An example is Hoi Tung, who became the chairman and CEO of Ping An Trust in 2004. With degrees from Oxford and the international business school INSEAD, Hoi had already worked as an executive director of Goldman Sachs Asia before joining Ping An.

By 2006, Ping An had grown to become China's second largest life insurance company and third largest property and casualty insurance company. By then, the company was serving 33 million customers, with 40,000 employees and 200,000 insurance sales agents. It began expanding into banking, securities, trust, annuity, health, and asset management. In 2004, the group companies earned more than $7.7 billion, with a total market capitalization of more than $10 billion.

Although its growth was dazzling, it still faced challenges. When China joined the WTO in 2001, competition intensified in the financial and insurance industries. Along with new foreign and domestic competitors, banks joined what appeared to be a gold rush. To meet the competition head-on, Ma set a goal of turning Ping An into a leading integrated financial services group within ten years. To achieve this, Ma was convinced that the company needed to evolve from a product-driven organization to one that was customer-centric. It needed to provide a full package of financial products through multiple channels. And at the same time, it needed to maintain consistency while raising its operating standards.

Growing the Business: Expanding into Life Insurance

During the early 1990s, only four domestic insurers operated in China: PICC, Ping An, China Pacific, and Tian An. The bulk of their sales were for products that had nothing to do with life insurance.

The only foreign insurer that knew about life insurance—AIA—was restricted to Shanghai.

From 1988 to 1993, Ping An's total income from P&C (property and casualty) insurance premiums experienced a 35 percent compound annual growth rate. But Ma realized that to succeed the company needed to broaden its product portfolio. Life insurance looked like the way to go.

While he was on a visit to Taipei in 1992, Ma learned that companies in Taiwan had successfully sold life insurance. Until then, most insurers in mainland China had regarded life insurance as a taboo subject because of cultural superstitions about death. (Ma had received the first business permit ever granted to visit Taiwan in order to look into a $4 million cargo shipment insured by Ping An that had accidentally become stranded there. At the time, tensions between Beijing and Taipei meant that even a quick business trip to Taipei was controversial.) To his surprise, Ma discovered that the life insurance industry was flourishing in Taiwan. He became firmly convinced that it could be introduced to China.

Despite Ma's enthusiasm, Ping An's first attempt to introduce life insurance in 1993 fell flat. The company lacked the key insights needed to make life insurance convincing in a Chinese culture. With some difficulty, Ma succeeded in bringing a number of professionals in from Taiwan to provide training for his staff. He relaunched the life insurance product a year later, this time using Taiwan's approach.

But life insurance was such an alien concept in China that Ping An had to educate both its customers and its sales agents. Dominic Leung, the former Group Vice-President and Head of Insurance Business at Ping An, noted, "If you think changing the mindset of Chinese consumers is difficult, imagine training the insurance agents, who do not even know what life insurance is, and expecting them to sell life insurance products and educate consumers!"

Ping An had to redesign its products completely and tailor them to a Chinese market. Western models wouldn't work. The Chinese don't like to talk about death, and they place a strong emphasis on saving for the future. Leung explained:

> I have not met a single Chinese who is not keen on saving. It doesn't matter if they are in Hong Kong, Singapore, or mainland China. They all save like they were going to live to 1,000 years. Chinese don't even want to talk about protection. They like to talk about living benefits, such as pension and medical benefits, but they hate death benefits.

To change the perception that insurance was just "a piece of paper," Ping An changed its life insurance products to contain more of a savings component—sometimes as much as 80 percent—providing customers with monthly statements similar to a savings account.

Ping An quickly expanded its life insurance operations and in 1994, it became the first Chinese insurer to implement an agent-based sales system for individual life policies. Following the example set by AIA in 1992, which greatly boosted the life insurance market in China, agents were paid on commission, not salary. Recalling AIA's success, Lee Yuansiong, who was promoted to chairman of Ping An Life and became Ping An's chief insurance officer in November 2011, commented, "AIA was very successful with the agency model, and quickly grew its sales force to 5,000. It was an eye-opener, a shock to the Chinese life insurance companies."

In 1997, Ping An's individual life insurance premiums exceeded group insurance premiums for the first time and became the company's principal line of business. By the end of 1999, Ping An had more than 120,000 individual life insurance agents and more than

1,000 branch offices throughout China. Individual life insurance premium income reached more than $600 million in 1999. Only five years earlier, it had been nonexistent.

Internationalization

As the life insurance business developed, Ping An began to establish international connections. Three significant events marked its gradual transformation—foreign investment, the hiring of McKinsey & Company, and international recruitment.

FOREIGN INVESTMENT

In 1994, Ping An brought in Morgan Stanley and Goldman Sachs as strategic investors to help provide the capital it needed to maintain the regulatory reserve limit. The deal made Ping An the first Chinese insurer with foreign shareholders, and it marked one of the first private equity investments in a Chinese company. In 1994 and 1996, the two U.S. investment banks purchased a combined stake of approximately 13 percent in Ping An for less than $70 million.

Since no precedent existed for a foreign investment of this kind, and since Chinese regulations did not allow foreign management on corporate boards, Morgan Stanley and Goldman Sachs decided to show up at the GATT summit in 1993 and negotiate a special "observer" status for themselves on Ping An's board. The investment was a bold move for Morgan Stanley and Goldman Sachs. They had no voting rights and were taking a risk, but it paid off handsomely. A decade later, the value of their original investment had increased 14 times.

The foreign investors brought not only the capital injection that Ping An needed to expand its operations but also insights into the value of Western corporate governance. As a result, Ping An established a risk control committee and an investment committee.

MCKINSEY ENTERS THE PICTURE

In 1997, Ping An hired McKinsey & Company to implement a series of high-impact programs aimed at improving its operational skills and management expertise. With both life and non-life businesses booming, Ping An felt it could no longer afford to operate on a decentralized entrepreneurial model. McKinsey introduced key performance indicators (KPIs) for assessing staff performance, and value-based management became Ping An's operating policy.

Hiring McKinsey was a bold move. At the time, China's domestic companies rarely hired international consulting firms. Even more controversial, Ping An paid more than $1.2 million for McKinsey's services. Peter Ma faced pressure regarding McKinsey on two fronts. Internally, some of Ping An's managers warned that the enormous fees might cause cash flow problems for the company. Outside the company, provincial newspapers criticized Ma for following Western trends and suggested that bribery might have been involved. Ma justified his decision by pointing out that the consultancy had more than paid for itself through cost savings. McKinsey had analyzed Ping An's asset management and discovered both high capital risk and inefficiency. It recommended pooling assets scattered across China to buy government bonds at a 12 percent coupon rate. This move alone generated more than $12 million of annual interest income for Ping An, and it far outweighed the fee paid to McKinsey.

INTERNATIONAL RECRUITMENT

In 2000, Ping An hired several head-hunting firms, including the premier Swiss executive search firm Egon Zehnder International, to start adding expatriates to its senior management team. The new hires added international experience and experience in foreign practices, such as asset-liability management and policy persistency rate. They proved crucial to Ping An's growth.

New Products and Lines of Business

To meet the increasing financial needs of its customers, Ping An introduced several innovative products and new lines of business, including investment-linked products, regular premium products, and bancassurance (the sale of insurance through a bank).

INVESTMENT-LINKED PRODUCTS

In the late 1990s, Prudential obtained a license to introduce investment-linked products in China. The introduction was hugely successful, and it established a market presence for the company in China. Eager to learn from Prudential's success and diversify investment risk, Ping An approached Prudential for help. Surprisingly, Prudential agreed to train Ping An staff at its regional headquarters in Singapore. Ping An became the first domestic insurer to launch investment-linked products in China in 1999.

REGULAR PREMIUM PRODUCTS

Although regular premium products—paid for in yearly, half-yearly, or quarterly installments—were widely available in the West, China for the most part still required the premium to be paid in a lump sum. Ping An was the first Chinese insurer to develop regular premium products in 2000. This soon became the principal line of its individual life business. In 2005, regular premium products accounted for more than 90 percent of Ping An's total individual life premium income—a significant change, considering that in 2003 more than 90 percent of the premium income of Ping An's major competitor was derived from single premium products.

BANCASSURANCE

In 2001, Ping An became the first company in China to introduce the concept of bancassurance (i.e., selling insurance through a bank's established distribution channels). Although the returns from bancassurance were significantly reduced by the commission paid to the bank, the increased volume made bancassurance the third most important business for Ping An, surpassed only by individual life and group life insurance. By 2004, bancassurance accounted for 10.8 percent of the company's life insurance premium income.

Developing a Company Culture

Although Ping An was quick to adapt the leading modern international business concepts, it was also careful to maintain its own culture, which is profoundly Chinese. Every morning at 8:30 A.M., Ping An's staff and sales agents across the country begin the day by singing the company anthem: "Within the four seas, with our hands on our hearts, we sincerely wish that there is ping an (peace)." After the morning song, the sales agents discuss their targets for the day, and team leaders critique strategy and provide guidance to new recruits. By 10:30 A.M., the agents are ready to hit the streets, spending most of their time demonstrating and selling insurance products.

In 1988, Ping An's culture could be characterized as "entrepreneurial spirit." The main focus was on establishing the company as a national franchise capable of competing with the state-owned PICC. Ma created a company that was very different from the "iron rice bowl" mindset, seen in most Chinese businesses, that promised lifetime employment regardless of performance. Ping An made it clear that merit counted more than seniority. A sense of achievement was fostered through continual job training and development. Ma promoted a philosophy of three possibilities, known as the "3 cans": Employees can come and go; rank can go up or down; salary can increase or decrease. He emphasized that the growth of the organization at this stage was crucial, and he expected employees to make it happen regardless of their rank.

In 1992, Ping An's culture evolved into what could be described as "Confucian ideology." The workforce had gone through a period of rapid growth, with people from all walks of life. There was also a societal trend to "make big bucks and then leave." The result was high turnover. Ma turned to the Confucian principles of Li, Yi, and Ren, which placed a high emphasis on respect and courtesy toward colleagues and the avoidance of conflicts of interest.

VALUE-BASED MANAGEMENT

The opening up of the insurance industry in 1992 helped drive the Chinese market, but it also attracted new competitors. To prepare Ping An for the anticipated competition by expanding its business operations and building its internal capabilities, Ma drafted the "3 Foreigns" rule: Foreign capital (represented by Goldman Sachs and Morgan Stanley), foreign organization (corporate governance, risk control committee, and other procedures common in Western business), and foreign knowledge (management team with international experience).

As the company grew, the focus tended to be on scale rather than quality, so Ma felt the need to pay more attention to value-based management, emphasizing the importance of a value-driven culture as the operating policy for Ping An and as the bridge between personal and professional conduct. There were three principles in value-based management: (1) profitability as the key measurement of performance; (2) people-based management relying on competition, reward, and motivation; and (3) accountability to shareholders, customers, employees, and society.

DEVELOPING THE CULTURE

In 1999, Ping An published a 143-page book called *Ping An: New Management Culture and Values.* It detailed the history of the company's culture and provided guidelines on its values. Ping An culture was represented by three concentric layers, as shown in Figure 8–1. The outer layer covered rituals and provided instructions for Ping An traditions, such as the morning song. It was to be used to influence others to adopt these customs. The middle layer referred to the standardization and enforcement of management policies. The innermost layer encapsulated Ping An's management culture. All of Ping An's managers had to pass a written exam on this section.

A training video was available to teach Ping An's rituals to new recruits. Detailed demonstrations explained the proper way to bow, for example, when greeting colleagues or guests. There were three types of bow, each expressing a different degree of respect: The head bow was for greeting colleagues, the 15-degree bow was for greeting guests, and the 30-degree bow was for a chairperson addressing an audience before the start of a session.

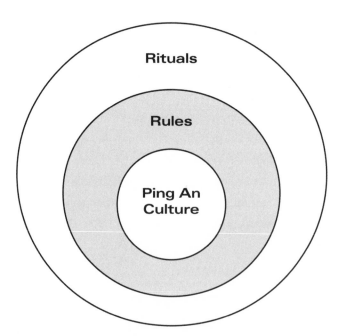

Figure 8–1. The three layers of Ping An's culture.

From Market Share to Profitable Growth

Between 2002 and 2005, China experienced tremendous growth, with GDP increasing by around 10 percent a year. The sustained economic growth stimulated household income and savings. Peter Ma continued with his efforts to build Ping An into a world-class organization capable of competing with leading domestic and international financial services providers by expanding into banking, asset management, health insurance, and annuity businesses. Three major events occurred during this period.

HSBC INVESTS

In October 2002, HSBC purchased a 10 percent equity stake in Ping An for $600 million. The move doubled Ping An's capital base. Three years later, HSBC doubled its ownership stake to 19.9 percent by purchasing the 9.9 percent share owned by Goldman Sachs and Morgan Stanley for $1.1 billion. At the time, it was the largest foreign investment made in a Chinese insurer.

HBSC JOINS PING AN'S BOARD OF DIRECTORS

In addition to capital, HSBC, as the largest shareholder, brought continual improvement to Ping An's corporate governance structure. HSBC added three members to Ping An's board of directors, which helped ensure fairness in the decision-making process. The board members oversaw the newly created special management committees and supervisory committees, including the audit committee, the compensation committee, and the nomination committee. In addition, the KPI system was extended to the heads and executive directors of each subsidiary, ensuring full accountability.

Ping An's reform efforts earned it the award for "Asia's Best Managed Companies 2005—Best at Insurance" from *Euromoney* magazine. Ping An's corporate restructuring had placed it in line with international standards, but it had been a steep learning curve.

PING AN RESTRUCTURES

In 2002, Ping An restructured itself as the Ping An Insurance (Group) Company, Ping An Life Insurance Company, and Ping An P&C Insurance Company. The idea was to align the company with the international practice of separating life and property insurance operations. It also helped position the organization for sustained growth.

Competition in the insurance industry in China had traditionally emphasized market share over profitability. To secure market share, Ping An offered a broad range of products such as dividend participation, investment-linked products, and universal life products. Investment-linked products peaked in 2001 as world and domestic equity markets boomed. In 2002, however, the U.S. economic downturn seriously affected the return from equity markets worldwide, and products linked to investments began to take losses. Ping An contacted its 4 million customers with these policies to explain the situation, and then it made the difficult decision to stop selling new unit-linked products. The downturn damaged Ping An's reputation and forced the company to shift its focus from quantity to quality.

To help the organization transform its operating principles, Ping An adopted a 16-Chinese-character operating policy, shown in Figure 8–2, which was ingrained in its employees.

To adhere to this vision, Ping An restructured its business portfolio to emphasize higher margin products such as individual life policies; it cut back on bancassurance and group insurance, which were proving to be less profitable. It also cut its agent sales force from 350,000 to 200,000. These measures initially had a limited negative impact on market share and revenues for both the life insurance and P&C insurance businesses. In 2004, the life insurance market share dropped to 17.2 percent from 19.6 percent, and the P&C market share dropped slightly to 9.5 percent from 9.7 percent.

品質優先, 利潤導向, 遵紀守法, 重在執行

Quality as the First Priority	Profit Oriented	Law Compliant	Focus on Execution

Figure 8–2. Ping An's 16-Chinese-character operating policy.

By 2005, however, Ping An had become one of the most profitable Chinese insurers. The group's net profit increased 47.3 percent in the six months ending on June 30, 2005, compared to the same period the previous year.

Although restructuring its business portfolio had slowed Ping An's growth in the short term, it actually strengthened the organization over the long haul by creating a solid foundation for long-term growth. It also improved Ping An's position for a public listing on an international stock exchange, which promised to increase confidence in the company and bring in new capital. It was something that many Chinese companies only dreamed of.

Going Public

On June 24, 2004, Ping An was successfully listed on the Hong Kong Stock Exchange, raising $1.66 billion. It was the biggest IPO in Hong Kong in 2004—69 million shares on offer and oversubscribed 58 times. *Investor Relations* magazine crowed that Ping An had had the "Best Investor Relations for an IPO in Asia."

A few key factors were behind the decision to go public. The global insurance industry possessed 40 percent of global assets and needed a huge amount of capital to satisfy the regulatory reserve requirements. Often, insurance companies went public to expand their capital base. Today, 60 to 70 percent of insurance companies in the top 500 worldwide are publicly listed.

Under China's policy of opening up its economy, access to funds in international capital markets had become a major objective for most domestic insurers. The strategy was in tune with the government's policy of encouraging Chinese insurers to become bigger and stronger in order to compete with international players. In December 2003, PICC, the largest property insurer in China, went public, raising $800 million in Hong Kong. China Life, the largest life insurer in China, soon followed suit with its $2.5 billion listing in New York. China Life became the world's largest IPO in 2003.

Ping An's Four Pillars of Growth

As part of the strategy to transform Ping An into an integrated financial services group, Peter Ma adopted a "Four Pillars" model in early 2000. The four pillars were based on:

1. A customer-centric model

2. Rules-based operations

3. Market-based performance management

4. Information and IT management

THE CUSTOMER-CENTRIC MODEL

The customer-centric approach was intended to shift Ping An from its traditional product-driven perspective to a more responsive and customer-oriented model. By doing so, Ping An hoped to leverage its resources, maximize cross-selling opportunities, and be more responsive to customers' financial needs across multiple channels.

In 2003, relying on the group's integrated financial structure, Dominic Leung began using the 200,000 sales agents who had formerly sold mainly life insurance products to sell a wide range of Ping An's products, including P&C insurance. This led to a number of challenges. Conflicts in the distribution channels had to be managed, and rules on compensation had to be redesigned. Pro - motion and demotions followed, but the efforts eventually paid off. In 2004, the premium income generated through cross-selling activities amounted to roughly $65.2 million.

It was important to develop new channels in order to serve customers' increasing financial needs. In 2005, Ping An established a new channel development team in Shanghai to start experimenting with new distribution channels, such as telesales and Internet direct sales. The aim was to start mainly with auto insurance policies with the goal of eventually selling all Ping An financial products. The new channels provided customized financial solutions for specifically targeted personal and corporate customers.

Goh Yethun, the head of the new channel development team, explained the early challenge of setting up the telesales team. "China is a vast country with 11 major dialects, ranging from Mandarin to Hakka," he said. "To ensure consistent quality and service, we had to recruit 250 people for the telemarketing team from all over the country and place them under one roof."

The preliminary results were positive, with double-digit conversion rates from cold-calling alone. There were plans to analyze existing customer databases to create different packages tailored to customers' needs.

The direct channel over the Internet sold simple products, such as auto insurance and travel and accident insurance. It also generated leads and let customers activate their coverage online. Ping An also looked into selling more complex products, such as life insurance, over the Internet.

Although the telesales and direct sales operations were relatively small, they represented a radical departure from the traditional Chinese insurance industry, which tended to be dominated by insurance agents who were convinced that it was the middleman that counted. Goh observed, "Many traditional companies were held hostage by traditional channels. Ma made it clear to the sales force that channel conflict was inevitable, and the segmented channel competition was encouraged."

MANAGEMENT BASED ON RULES

On a typical business day in 2004, Ping An might issue more than 34,000 policies and respond to 42,000 calls. It was likely to pay out roughly $4.2 million in commissions and claims. The breadth and depth of daily operations exposed Ping An to increasing operational risk and made it difficult to maintain consistency and quality. Setting rules for operations management was therefore critical to ensure long-term success.

In 2004 alone, Ping An established nearly 600 department rules at the group level, wrote management manuals for regional/secondary subsidiaries of the life business, centralized the claims system in the P&C business, and completed internal control rules in the securities, trust, and banking businesses. Dominic Leung explained the significance of these measures for the life business: "New products are naturally prone to mis-selling."

Ping An also implemented stringent rules for its insurance products. For example, the person taking out insurance first had to sign the proposal, then the contract, and after that confirm through the call center that he or she understood the small print. Each step was closely monitored according to the rules.

The company rules were also designed to satisfy regulatory requirements of government authorities. For example, as part of the government's effort to enforce mandatory third-party liability insurance, CIRC required annual data on all auto insurance policy holders from the Ping An P&C Insurance Company. The data set had to include detailed and accurate personal information, such as the client's legal name, valid address, and phone number. The sales procedure required following the rules carefully when entering the insured driver's personal information.

Ping An developed an online management manual as a systematic internal control, accessible to all Ping An staff. This website contained working instruction manuals and documents outlining the detailed positions and responsibilities for headquarters and second- and third-tier branches.

MARKET-BASED PERFORMANCE MANAGEMENT

In a market as competitive as the insurance industry, attracting and retaining top talent was always a challenge. Ping An HR adopted a policy of compensating the top 20 to 30 percent of employees more highly than the industry average. Ping An also paid market prices for the senior management team, relying on Egon Zehnder and other executive search firms for advice. In 2005, 41 percent of Ping An employees had a bachelor's degree or above, and 36 percent had worked for at least five years before joining Ping An.

Performance Measurement Systems. To compensate its employees appropriately, Ping An implemented the KPI system introduced by McKinsey in 1997. Every year, employees together with their line managers were required to set annual goals and action plans, with the KPIs and KPI tasks clearly identified. Employees were given monthly and quarterly reviews; biannual and annual appraisals determined the rewards or punishments (including dismissal if an employee failed to meet the three-year rolling target). Ping An was in the process of rolling out a management accountability system in order to develop a "results-oriented, full accountability" appraisal system.

Employee Retention. In 2004, Ping An's overall attrition rate was 13 percent, comfortably lower than the 15 to 16 percent industry average. As part of its continued effort to retain employees, Ping An maintained a policy of organic development by nurturing talents internally, or "bringing young people to the top," according to Allen Ku, Ping An's senior vice president and chief HR officer. Through the performance appraisal system, Ping An identified top performers and placed them in a "Talent Pool," from where they might be short-listed for the "Successors" pool in preparation for joining the management team.

Financial Training Institute. Ping An started building the Ping An Financial Training Institute near Shenzhen in 2003 to provide training courses for its employees. The institute was designed by Takashi Okamoto of Nikken Sekkei Ltd., Japan's largest independent architectural and planning consulting firm. It was completed in January 2006, and included an extensive library, complete with e-books and electronic periodicals.

The institute occupied more than 2 million square feet, with a capacity of up to 900 participants per day. Facilities included auditoriums, classrooms, a 500-room hotel, dining rooms, a nine-hole golf course, a driving range, a swimming pool, and a tennis court. The institute had three main objectives: (1) to transform knowledge into value, (2) to become a communication channel with clients, and (3) to enhance the company brand.

INFORMATION AND IT MANAGEMENT

IT and information management were important to Ping An for two main reasons: (1) to achieve a lower cost base and (2) to underpin the other three pillars. Since the profit margin in the Chinese insurance industry was significantly lower than in developed countries, it was essential for Ping An's long-term success to leverage economies of scale through IT to achieve a lower cost base.

The computer costs in China were 30 percent higher and telecom costs 250 times higher than in the United States. On top of that, the company made only around $12.50 profit per customer, less than one-tenth of the profit in the United States or Europe. Ping An was left with very little room for inefficiency and error.

As the foundation for the other three pillars, the information and IT management pillar provided infrastructure to support centralized back-office operations for 33 million customers, as well as daily performance monitoring systems for 40,000 employees and 200,000 sales agents. Operating an integrated financial institution relied heavily on strong information and IT management and usage.

Like other entrepreneurial start-ups, Ping An did not have a formal IT team during its early growth phase. It decided to introduce IT systems and form a dedicated team when the life insurance business started taking off in the 1990s.

Contrary to the trend at the time, Ping An IT made a conscious decision to implement open technology as opposed to the popular IBM AS/400 technology. It proved to be a wise decision. There was no historical baggage, no tie-up to a single vendor, and the company had more choices compared to competitors that were full IBM houses. The open technology approach allowed most Ping An IT systems to be developed in-house with functionalities tailored to internal business requirements. These were driven by business-oriented people, not IT staff. To ensure uniformity of service quality, Ping An used the same version of its business applications nationwide and shared them across business lines and distribution channels.

Ping An did not shy away from adopting state-of-the-art technologies as long as it could maintain its first-mover advantage. For example, Ping An developed a strong partnership with major vendors, such as HP, Microsoft, and Intel, and was a beta test partner for the latest technology. In 2004, to boost Ping An's sales agents' productivity in the field, Intel partnered with Ping An to support insurance selling activities on personal digital assistants

(PDAs). In addition, Ping An IT continued to optimize its processes by standardizing development processes based on SEI-CMM and ITIL standards.

Centralization. Ping An's centralization initiative started in 1999. With its life and P&C businesses booming, the organization grew rapidly. Managing the information from all the branches across China became an enormous challenge. Around the same time, the network infrastructure in China started to take shape. Ping An started rolling out client-server technology to remotely link the operations from its third- and fourth-tier branches in 1999 and started to centralize its second-tier provincial branches in 2000.

The nationwide back-office centralization started in 2002. Prior to that, each subsidiary had its own system. As a result, Ping An found it difficult to share customer information for efficient cross-selling. In an attempt to become more customer-centric with a leaner, more efficient organization, Ping An centralized all core back-office operations at the Integrated Operation Center (IOC) in Shanghai. The IOC was important to provide consistency and high-quality service, and it was also critical for information integrity. Before the IOC was set up, data entry had been done at the branch level, and the integrity of the data depended on the customer service staff's mastery of IT at the branch level, which made it difficult to enforce consistent standards.

Introduction of New Channels. The new millennium marked a new era for Ping An IT. In 2000, Ping An began experimenting with web technology, and it later launched the first version of its PA18.com portal, which provided existing and potential customers with online access to the most up-to-date insurance and financial planning services. This new channel enabled Ping An to start strategic partnerships with rising Internet ventures. For example, a strategic pact with SOHU.com (a leading Chinese search engine company) in 2001 allowed Ping An to leverage SOHU.com's user base of 12.5 million and more than 90 million daily page views, an enormous branding opportunity reaching a highly targetable population of well-educated middle-class urban youths.

Later the same year, Ping An built its first national 24-hour customer service call center in Suzhou, a first for China's insurance industry. The initial purpose of Ping An's telephone hotline (which could be reached by dialing 95511) was to provide basic customer services, answering inquiries, processing orders, and handling complaints. In line with its proactive, customer-centric sales goal, Ping An wanted to improve the scope and quality of its services in order to generate profit through telemarketing and outbound telesales. The effect was to turn the customer call service center from a cost center into a profit center.

The Path to Growth

The Beijing Summer Olympics in 2008 symbolized the emergence of China as a player on the world stage and the resurgence of national pride and patriotism. In 2006, with only two years to go, preparations were under way to construct world-class infrastructure and spectacular venues for the athletes and visitors. It was a unique opportunity to present the best of China to the world.

At the same time, Ping An was busy working on its own Olympian project for 2008. Its goal was to transform Ping An into a leading integrated worldwide financial services provider, as well as to make it truly customer-centric with integrated systems linking processes from customer service to sales support to back-office operations for each of its product lines and channels.

In its early years, Ping An had generated more than 70 percent of its revenue from one product: life insurance. Ma wanted to change the mix to two products contributing 70 percent of revenue by 2008, and to three or more products contributing 80 percent by 2014. To reach its new target, Ping An had acquired several existing banks, including the Fujian Asia Bank, in 2004. But working toward the target was not always easy, especially in 2005. Richard Jackson, the head of Ping An's financial businesses, explained, "Foreign interest in Chinese banks had risen in recent years, pushing the price multiple for these banks to unprecedented levels."

As a result, foreign banks began bidding for and buying stakes in Chinese banks. In 2005, Ping An failed in a bid to acquire a stake in the second-tier Chinese Industrial Bank. Around the same time, Citigroup agreed to quadruple its stake in the Shanghai Pudong Development Bank for about $878 million. In June of that year, Bank of America paid $3 billion for a 9 percent stake in the China Construction Bank. Two months later, HSBC paid approximately $1.75 billion for a 19.9 percent stake in the Communications Bank of China. The acquisition spree reached its peak in 2006, which began with a blockbuster bid for the Guangdong Development Bank, a provincial bank with 26 branches. Citigroup raised its bid to just over $3 billion for an 85 percent stake in the bank, exceeding Ping An's RMB 22.6 billion bid. At this price, Citigroup would be paying more than twice the bank's book value for a stake of less than 50 percent, with Citigroup's local partners owning the rest.

This was a second setback for Ping An after its failed bid for the Chinese Industrial Bank. Ping An pondered whether it was wise to continue looking for acquisition targets. There were arguments on the side of looking for existing banks. As Richard Jackson noted, "Acquiring an existing bank will give us the licenses to sell the financial products with the physical branch distribution network and existing customer base that would take years to build up."

Ma, however, was concerned about potential problems in a post-merger integration. Would Ping An have the capabilities—business knowledge and IT platform—to integrate the acquired bank into the group smoothly? After all, the insurance industry is very different from the banking industry. More important, would the acquired bank embrace the Ping An culture that had brought the company to where it was today?

An alternative to acquiring a physical bank was to do direct banking along the lines of ING Direct, a subsidiary of ING Group. Since its inception in 1997, ING Direct had successfully applied the direct banking model, earning €617 million in 2005, a 41.8 percent increase from 2004. In addition to products related to saving, ING Direct cross-sold credit cards, adjustable-rate mortgages, and home-equity line products to its 15 million customers. This approach fit well with Ping An's customer-centric model, and it would enable Ping An to cross-sell its financial products without paying a high price for a brick-and-mortar bank. It would also avoid concerns about post-merger integration issues. But a direct banking license was also likely to be difficult to obtain given Ping An's relative lack of experience in the banking sector and the fact that the China Bank Regulatory Commission's primary focus was to ensure the sound growth of the banking industry in China.

The company also considered the option of continuing to focus on its core insurance businesses while strengthening Ping An's internal capabilities in financial services, as it had done with the creation of Ping An Asset Management and Ping An Annuity Company in 2005. However, Jackson worried that that strategy might be too slow. "The approach would simply take too long," he said. "It would take more than ten years just to get all the licenses required to offer all the financial services products we wanted to have. Banking was our insurance for the future, and we had to move quickly."

Entering the Troubled Waters of the Global Marketplace: Bidding for Fortis

The company's strategic framework was based on insurance, banking, and asset management. Insurance accounted for 77 percent of profit, overshadowing the 10 percent produced by banking and the 13 percent coming from asset management. It would take significant time and effort and internal growth for the banking and asset management businesses to become as profitable as the insurance unit. Management looked to acquisition, and especially foreign acquisition, as a necessary shortcut.

WHY FORTIS?

The European bank Fortis appeared to be the most promising target. Fortis had similar business lines of insurance, banking, and asset management, as well as a generous dividend policy. Every six months, Fortis paid out roughly 45 percent of its profits as dividends, and the company honored this policy even after the dot-com bubble burst. Investing in Fortis would allow Ping An to learn from Fortis, boost its two weak units, and enjoy stable financial gains.

A report by Goldman Sachs argued that Ping An would benefit in three areas by buying Fortis' asset management unit, Fortis Investments. First, Ping An's capital management scale and products would improve, particularly by enhancing asset management experience for third-party customers. Second, Ping An would obtain skills in product design, investment management, research, IT, and marketing. Third, Ping An's joint venture was likely to give the company a competitive advantage over domestic competitors in areas of overseas investment and overseas investment products. The reasons were so compelling that Ping An moved swiftly to acquire a stake in Fortis.

Fortis was a familiar competitor that had been expanding its business in China for a decade. In 2001, Fortis had acquired a 24.9

percent stake in Pacific Life. In 2003, the company had formed an asset management company with Haitong Securities, taking a 49 percent stake. In 2007, Fortis had put up €24 billion as its part of the RBS (Royal Bank of Scotland) consortium bid for ABN Amro. Fortis was managing total assets of about €133 billion at the time. Adding ABN Amro's business would increase that to €245 billion. Fortis issued stock options, convertible debts, and asset securitization products in order to raise cash for the purchase. No-core assets were also sold. When the financial crisis hit in late 2007, the company had to write off billions of euros to cover its subprime-related assets. Under pressure to raise cash for the acquisition of ABN Amro, Fortis took on debt in a weak fixed-income market. The company became vulnerable to a ratings downgrade.

THE TAKEOVER

Ping An made its initial investment in Fortis in October 2007. By the end of November, Ping An had bought 95.01 million shares in Fortis. By January 2008, Ping An had raised its holdings to 110 million shares, raising its total stake in Fortis to 4.99 percent. The investment was valued at €2.11 billion. Ping An became Fortis's largest single shareholder.

On March 19, 2008, Ping An and Fortis jointly announced the signing of a memorandum of understanding establishing a global asset management partnership. Ping An acquired a 50 percent stake in Fortis Investments, the global asset management unit of Fortis, for €2.15 billion in cash. Fortis Investments was rebranded "Fortis Ping An Investments." Ma announced:

> The creation of Fortis Ping An Investments is a win-win collaboration for both sides, and it carries significant and strategic rationale and value to Ping An. With this partnership,

Ping An will immediately establish a global asset management business platform that covers various major financial markets in the world through competitive distribution networks from both institutions. With joint efforts from Ping An and Fortis, Fortis Ping An Investments will enter a new era of solid growth, and firmly establish itself as a leading global asset management company.

Through this partnership, Ping An would significantly move forward to establish a global asset management business. Fortis would benefit from Ping An's presence in China and a new channel to attract Chinese capital. However, the agreement was contingent on the pending deal between Fortis and ABN Amro. Besides, the agreement also had to be approved by regulators.

RESULTS OF THE INVESTMENT

The subprime crisis and continuing market uncertainty depressed Fortis's shares to the point that the governments of Belgium, Holland, and Luxembourg were forced to bail out the company. In October 2008, Ping An announced that it was ending its efforts to purchase a 50 percent interest in Fortis Investments.

Although it had stopped purchasing shares in Fortis Investments, Ping An still took substantial losses as one of Fortis's biggest shareholders. Ping An's holdings in Fortis lost more than 90 percent of their value. In April 2009, Ping An reported a write-off of $3.34 billion on its stake in Fortis, resulting in a 99 percent drop in its 2008 net profit. The investment in Fortis effectively evaporated. Originally hailed as a success story, the investment had turned into one of the worst overseas investments by a Chinese company.

The Future

The disaster had a sobering effect on Peter Ma's ambitions to extend the company internationally, but he remained determined not to retreat from his original vision. Ping An remained committed to becoming a financially integrated international leader. Ping An had financial licenses in life, property, pension, banking, securities, and trust insurance. The banking unit sold credit cards to existing insurance clients at very low cost. The company intended to sell banking and investment services to its 50 million customers with a one-stop shopping model. It also expected its banking, asset management, and insurance operations to each contribute a third of its total profits within a decade.

Louis Cheung, the president of Ping An, said Ping An would succeed in bancassurance because it had developed each facet of the business. "Universal banking is dead," he said, "but we are different. We built each of our businesses from scratch, and we have a young client group that continuously expanded during the process."

Insights

China's service sector still accounts for only an estimated 43% (source: CIA World Fact Book for 2011) percent of China's GDP, far behind the world average of 63.2 percent as of 2010 (source: CIA World Factbook 2011). A number of factors promise to make the service industries the fastest growing sector in China's economy. The growth in services will accelerate with China's urbanization, and China's new middle class is likely to become a major consumer of services. With China's accelerated integration with the rest of the world, China will need to develop its skills in the areas of accounting, management consulting, and law in order to bring itself in line with international standards. The Chinese government has adopted a new strategic policy to drive China's economy by encouraging more domestic consumption and less investment. The manufacturing sector will continue to grow, but the service sector, especially finance, banking, and insurance, is likely to grow faster.

The bancassurance model, which has been abandoned in many countries, may still find a welcoming home in China. Chinese consumers were exposed to so many services in the early days of privatization that they were confused by the variety of choices. Ping An's one-stop shopping model simplified the process for clients, and cross-selling had the added benefit of maintaining economies of scale. In China's current phase of development, universal banking just might work.

Ping An's international ambitions suffered a setback with Fortis, but the company is sticking to its strategy of offering integrated financial services and extending itself internationally. As the company discovered, the best strategy can be affected by timing in a volatile market.

Han's Laser
Creating New Markets

The journey of a thousand miles begins with one step.   —Lao Tzu

GAO YUNFENG FOUNDED Han's Laser Technology Company, Ltd. in 1996. Gao was 29 years old at the time, and China's economic landscape was vastly different from what it is today. Then, there were only 10,000 privately owned industrial enterprises in the entire country. While private enterprises were very much on their own, the more than 80,000 state-owned companies not only received generous government funding but also had close connections to provincial politicians, many of whom depended on the state-owned industries to provide employment for their constituents. These bureaucrats naturally tended to be suspicious about the approaching transition to a "socialist market economy." In this climate, private entrepreneurs were dealing with odds that were heavily stacked against them.

From outside China, it looked as though Deng Xiaoping had given an official green light to private enterprise during his famous 1992 trip to Shenzhen, when he delivered the famous line "To get rich is glorious." But the truth is that Deng's strategy was still far from accepted by everyone. His trip to southern China had actually been a public relations maneuver intended to undercut budding opposition to his economic reforms. True, at the top and the bottom echelons of Chinese society, there was pressure to move forward and to liberalize the economy. But at the middle levels, especially in provincial bureaucracies, vested interests remained resistant to change.

From the entrepreneur's perspective, bureaucratic difficulties were only part of the problem. The real challenge was access to start-up capital. China, emerging from a centralized economy, had almost none of the options for financing commonly available in the West. State-owned banks tended to deal with state-owned companies. Anyone outside the loop was left to scrounge for funds elsewhere. Deng had tried to open China to the outside world, but the Cultural Revolution of the 1960s had closed many of the country's schools, dispatched intellectuals to the countryside, and jailed people for knowing how to speak English. The social and economic inertia that needed to be overcome in order to achieve Deng's vision was enormous. The entrepreneurs who took on Deng's challenge and eventually changed the shape and the direction of China's economy were in every sense of the word pioneers in a new environment that still needed to be defined.

Gao's Early Life and Background

Gao Yunfeng was born during the Cultural Revolution on February 1, 1967, in Jilin Province. He was the fifth of eight children. His two older brothers were forced to do farm work in the fields in order to support their younger brothers and sisters in school.

When the Cultural Revolution ended and China seriously turned its attention back to education, Gao placed 79th in the county-wide exam to enter senior high school. Gao recalls that when he was in high school, his family would give him 12 buns and tell him that they had to last him for a week.

In senior high school, Gao quickly rose to the top of his class, and his academic achievements in high school earned him a place in Beijing's prestigious University of Aeronautics and Astronautics, where he majored in aircraft design and the application of mechanics. After graduation in 1989, he secured a teaching position at Nanjing's University of Aeronautics and Astronautics. Gao and his family were so poor that when he decided to get married, none of his family members were able to attend the wedding because they did not have enough money to pay for a train ticket to Nanjing. As time went on, however, Gao eventually managed to help all of his siblings attend university. Two obtained doctorates.

Laser Marking Machines

In 1992, Gao landed a job in Hong Kong to work as a technician on laser marking machines. Laser markers, which cost around $80,000, use laser beams to emboss patterns and logos on a variety of different products ranging from ordinary buttons to shoes, bags, and accessories. Although laser markers were beginning to be used on assembly lines in the West, there were fewer than ten machines in all of China. In Hong Kong, where laser markers were in wider use, it was widely acknowledged that they added value to the manufacturing process, but the downside was that they often broke down. Trying to get a manufacturer to repair one was a nightmare. The average wait for a technician was around eight weeks, and while the machine was down, the entire assembly line ground to a halt. Breakdowns were not only inevitable; it was also virtually impossible to run one of the machines for 24 hours without having it malfunction.

Gao went to work analyzing the frequent breakdowns and concluded that minor variations in the electric current were at the root of the problem. He designed a circuit board to automatically maintain a level voltage in the machine despite line voltage fluctuations. Gao's enhancements cut the work stoppages dramatically.

In 1995, one of the Hong Kong company's clients, who had been impressed by Gao's ingenuity, contemplated buying a new machine from Germany. Gao told the client that he thought he could build the same machine for a third of the price. In addition, Gao offered to sweeten the deal by promising the client a substantial holding in the new company that he intended to start with the capital that he would put together from the payment for the new machine. Gao also offered to refund the full amount if his machine failed to work properly.

To Gao's surprise, the client—who was considerably older than him—offered to pay Gao the full purchase price for the machine and also to let Gao keep all the shares in his new company. The client added that if Gao's machine failed, he would be under no obligation to refund the purchase price. Gao was so impressed by the man's generosity that he worked around the clock to finish the machine in three months. It worked perfectly and Gao collected $80,000, which he used to officially register Han's Laser as a company in Shenzhen in 1996. Gao had officially become one of China's 10,000 private entrepreneurs who promised to make dramatic changes in the future direction of China's economy.

Han's Laser Begins

Getting a license was one thing. Managing to sell a highly sophisticated machine in China's primitive environment was something else. Deng Xiaoping had realized early on that the key to moving China toward private entrepreneurship was to encourage light industry based on simple machinery. Most entrepreneurs, operating on razor-thin margins, simply did not have the capital to spend on expensive equipment, especially if it was not clear how it would add value.

When Gao started Han's Laser, hardly anyone in China even knew what a laser marker was or why anyone would need it. The major hurdle was price. By the time a laser marker reached China, it was likely to cost around $100,000. It would have to operate under primitive conditions, and servicing it was likely to be extremely difficult.

TARGETING STATE-OWNED ENTERPRISES

Gao's first idea was to hit the large state-owned enterprises, which at least had easy access to financing. He was enough of a realist to know that he would need connections to well-placed senior government officials. He didn't have these kinds of connections, but he did have some former classmates who were now working for a massive state-owned automobile conglomerate, the China FAW Group, which happened to be based in his hometown in Jilin Province. Gao called his friends, who found a small hotel for him to stay in while he tried to contact the company's management.

The executives at FAW told him to wait for an appointment. At the end of a week, Gao realized that nearly everyone in the hotel was waiting for a similar appointment. Some had been waiting for months. The state-owned companies, he concluded, were not likely to be interested in a small start-up with no track record. He realized that he had picked the wrong target. Changing direction, Gao decided to focus on small entrepreneurs like himself. He picked Wenzhou in Zhejiang Province as the place to start.

FOCUSING ON THE ENTREPRENEURS OF WENZHOU

During China's transition to a market economy, Wenzhou had virtually cornered the market for manufacturing buttons, shoes, and electrical parts, all of which were prime candidates for laser marking. Even better, Wenzhou was exporting globally to a wide range of clients who would be more likely to understand the utility of laser marking than the average manufacturer in China.

Gao also felt a certain sense of identification with the business mentality in Wenzhou. The city was bursting with small to medium-size enterprises, and the companies seemed to have that entrepreneurial spark that made them open to new ideas. As it turned out, Gao's analysis was only partly correct. Everyone in Wenzhou loved the idea of a laser marker, but none of the entrepreneurs he contacted had the cash to spend $80,000 on an untried concept. Most of Wenzhou's businesses were simply too small to take the risk. Laser markers, Gao realized, faced a Chinese version of Catch-22. No one knew about laser markers because there was no market for them, and a market was unlikely to develop because the machines were too expensive to buy without first seeing a demonstration of their value. To do that, Gao needed to establish a market.

Gao spent six months combing the region and passing out fliers explaining the idea. The response was zero. Then Gao realized that the answer was to create the market himself. He needed to make the entrepreneurs of Wenzhou actually earn money with a machine so that they could see the machine's true value.

Gao ordered a laser marking machine shipped to Wenzhou, and he began producing a broad array of sample designs on buttons, shoes, bags, lighters, and just about anything else that would take a laser imprint. Realizing that most of the entrepreneurs were only semiliterate and that hardly any of them knew English, Gao also began drafting sales pitches in English, explaining the added value of laser marking to potential overseas customers. Gao realized that he would have to create a market for laser markers by demonstrating to the Wenzhou entrepreneurs that the machine would make their products more exportable.

Nine months later, the first tentative overseas order for a shipment of laser marked products from one of Wenzhou's entrepreneurs came in. It brought with it a new dilemma. The prospective client who had received the order wanted to buy one of Gao's machines, but he also wanted Gao to promise not to sell machines to anyone else in Wenzhou. Since Gao's ultimate objective was to create a market for the machines, the offer was a nonstarter. It was also a sobering moment. Han's Laser was already on the verge of bankruptcy, but if he agreed to the deal, he was pretty certain that future bankruptcy would be virtually guaranteed. Gao told the client thanks, but no thanks. He decided to hold his ground.

Not long after that, another prospective client received an overseas order, and this time the client was ready to buy one of Gao's machines with no strings attached. Gao delivered the machine and within two months, his client had recouped the original purchase price of the laser marker. The man's friends and relatives now clamored to buy machines, too. Gao was suddenly in business. Within a few years, the industrial marking by Han's Laser would be credited with having helped to generate more than nearly $40 million in sales for the cloth button industry alone.

Sustaining the Business

For Gao, however, launching the business was only the beginning. Sustaining it in China's rapidly changing economic environment was a different prospect altogether. Gao realized quickly that cost and maintenance were key issues in building a market. He began reducing costs by determining which parts could be manufactured locally. By using local manufacturing for all but the core components, he managed to stake out a competitive advantage over machines manufactured outside China. Eventually, he was able to start producing the key core components in China as well. An important element in Gao's strategy was to streamline the machine's design to the smallest number of components actually needed to accomplish a specific job. If additional capabilities were needed, they could be added later. Eventually, Gao succeeded in reducing the sales price for his laser markers to $30,000 to $40,000. The competition from Han's Laser eventually forced foreign manufacturers to cut their prices by 20 to 30 percent in the Chinese market. Even with the cost reductions, Han's Laser managed to maintain gross margins at around 50 percent.

Most companies dealing in a new technology need to invest heavily in R&D, and it can take 18 months or more to develop a marketable product. Gao felt that he didn't have the financial resources or the time to invest in that kind of development, so he designed the best machine that he could with the information and experience that he had. Then, he assigned a technician to follow and adapt each machine for six months after it had been sold. The technician filed daily reports to headquarters on the machine's operations, and adjustments were made until it worked satisfactorily.

On the surface, this looked to the customer like a generous offer of personalized attention, but in fact it constituted a slimmed-down, learn-as-you-go form of R&D that enabled the company to make substantial savings. Instead of trying to foresee all of the potential things that might possibly go wrong, Gao had the company do its research on the fly and correct problems as they developed in real time. The small R&D team at headquarters was able to focus on the specific problems that actually arose on a working assembly line. By the time all of the adjustments had been made, each machine was perfectly designed for the special needs of the customer who had bought it. This made Han's Laser marking machines a more practical choice for customers. The fact that the machines had also been cheaper to produce was a bonus.

As Han's Laser acquired more experience, its machines improved substantially from the R&D that emerged from the field. Between 1996 and 1999, Han's Laser introduced 3,000 improvements to its machines, while each machine seemed uncannily designed to fit each customer's specific needs. The strategy sounded simple enough, but it was actually the direct application of an important principle of Gao's basic philosophy. Gao was determined from the start to make technology responsive to actual market conditions, rather than to push a product out and expect the market to adapt to a design that had been thought up by engineers operating in a vacuum.

Gao remembered the frustrations of his days as a technician in Hong Kong, when most companies took eight weeks or more to respond to a failure in their machines. Gao did not care how remote a client's location was. If a machine broke down, he had a technician on the spot almost immediately. Han's Laser eventually established 150 sales and service centers throughout China. While most foreign manufacturers provided standardized software, Han's Laser generated its own software that could easily be adapted on the spot to a customer's needs. As a result, Han's Laser machines appeared to be more flexible and better adapted to the specific work at hand.

The ultimate benefit of creating its own software came when the company finally broke through the barrier that had kept machines confined to an operating run that was less than 24 hours. By fine-tuning the software and adjusting the motion sensors and photonics, Han's Laser was able to eliminate the small glitches that had led to the machine's inevitable malfunction after only a few hours. The breakthrough was so revolutionary that competitors initially accused Han's Laser of false advertising. A government inspector insisted on sitting next to one of the machines for more than 24 hours while it ran continuously. When the test was concluded, he was forced to admit that the machine had accomplished what had previously been considered to be impossible.

Gao realized that many of the people who would be using the machines were likely to have only a partial education. Han's Laser set up its own schools and training facilities and began publishing manuals on how to use both the machines and basic computers. The program was so successful that clients began sending their children to advance their education.

The International Market

Once Gao felt that the company had established itself in the domestic market, he began looking toward foreign buyers as well. Gao heard that a foreign-owned keyboard manufacturer whose factory was in China was about to sign a contract for a laser marking machine with a U.S. producer, and he dispatched his sales team to try to make a counteroffer. The keyboard manufacturer showed no interest. Undeterred, Gao approached one of the company's major shareholders. The selling point that Gao harped on was the delay that was virtually guaranteed if the company bought from a producer in the United States. The U.S. company, Gao argued, would need at least eight weeks to deliver its machine. Gao, who was well aware of the frustration that that kind of time lag could produce, convinced the shareholder to let Han's Laser offer its laser marking machine for free during the period that the American company would need to actually deliver its machine.

A hand-picked team was assigned to install the Han's Laser marker on the keyboard company's assembly line at night, and it finished installing the machine only minutes before the employees showed up for work in the morning. An emergency maintenance crew stood by in case anything went wrong. Eventually, the American machine arrived. The client decided that while the American machine produced slightly more polished results, the fact that Han's Laser was able to provide immediate high-quality service that fit his company's special needs was a deciding factor. The company's subsequent orders went to Han's Laser.

Gao's Management Approach

Apart from technological innovations, Han's Laser owed its success to Gao's management approach. In contrast to most other Chinese companies, at Han's Laser, Gao had ruled out nepotism from the start. Family members, friends, and close associates were banned from employment at Han's Laser. Gao liked to describe the employment structure as being shaped like a barbell, with the sales team at one end and the engineers at the other. The basic salaries were purposely kept below subsistence level but supplemented by bonuses for exceptional work. The basic salary for a salesperson was around $100 a month. For an engineer, the starting salary was $400 a month. At the sales end, the system acted according to a Darwinian elimination. There was no limit to how much a salesperson could earn in bonuses, but he or she had to make bonuses in order to survive. As a result, salespeople who couldn't sell were quickly eliminated and, gradually, the most successful ones rose to the top.

The same process was employed with engineers, only in this case the question was how many new innovations and applications the engineers could come up with and how much profit they would be likely to bring to the company. As Gao saw it, R&D was, in effect, a revenue-earning center.

The Need for Financing

In fact, Gao had created a nearly perfect business model. What he hadn't counted on was the time it would take for the business environment in China to catch up. China was moving from a state-controlled, centralized economy to a socialist free market model, but it hadn't yet managed to create the independent sources of credit needed to get private enterprise up and running. Gao's major problem was undercapitalization, which was even more dramatic in his case because of the high cost of the machines.

Gao had tried to get around the problem by taking a build-to-order approach. He depended on a 30 percent advance payment from clients to buy the necessary components. He would then assemble the machine and deliver it a few months later. If everything worked correctly, he would get the final payment once the machine was up and running. While this was an effective way of financing a new business in a developing economy, it also made the company vulnerable to a variety of risks. A client could refuse to pay, a machine might run into unexpected problems, or there could be a sudden surge in orders that required extra financing, not to mention a surge in the cost of components. Any of these factors could cause serious cash flow problems.

The year after Gao founded the company, he faced a crisis when he couldn't meet salaries in time for his employees' traditional trip home to celebrate the spring festival. Each employee expected to receive an extra $120.00. Gao was forced to pawn the company's van for $3,600. On another occasion, he had to pawn it for RMB 90,000 just to buy components. To make matters worse, Gao had used up all his available collateral. He had exhausted the possibility of taking out more loans. While his competitors were able to get substantial financing from state-owned industries, he risked being left behind. In desperation, he wrote hundreds of letters in search of a financial partner.

A state-owned company based in Shenzhen seemed like the ideal white knight. The company had specialized in working with SMEs, and it was interested in Han's Laser as an intriguing growth opportunity. Furthermore, it seemed to like Han's Laser's entrepreneurial spirit and the fact that Han's Laser had developed its own software. Four months of discussions followed, and the Shenzhen company made an offer. The only drawback was that it wanted a 51 percent controlling interest in Han's Laser. The argument was that unless the state-owned company gained a controlling share in Gao's company, it would appear to lose face.

Gao held out for five months, but the state-owned company refused to change its position. Gao finally realized that without an injection of cash, he was likely to go bankrupt. The one concession he managed to get was a provision in the deal that allowed him to buy back the Shenzhen company's shares if Han's Laser was able to increase its net asset value to $2.4 million within 18 months. Han's Laser's net assets were valued at just over $1 million at the signing, and the Shenzhen company thought it was highly unlikely that Gao would be able to meet the deadline.

As it turned out, the Shenzhen company had badly miscalculated. The injection of cash enabled Gao to leapfrog over the obstacles that had previously held back Han's Laser's growth. The connection to the state-owned company opened up a $3.5 million credit line, and Han's Laser could now borrow from state-owned banks. That cleared the way for Gao to break away from his build-to-order model and to keep an inventory of components, which dramatically reduced the lead time for new orders. In 1999, Han's Laser managed to sell 69 machines, compared to only ten the year before. Its original target had been to sell 50 machines. A year later, sales nearly quadrupled to 249 machines, and revenues hit $7.2 million. Han's Laser had become the dominant manufacturer of laser marking machines in China, with a 60 percent market share for all of China and a 90 percent market share in hyper-dynamic Guangdong Province.

The phenomenal growth was not without a price. The state-owned company from Shenzhen had insisted on placing its own man as chairman of the company, and in an unsettling departure from Gao's opposition to nepotism, the chairman had begun slipping his relatives into key positions. Since the Shenzhen company had controlling interest, there was little that Gao could do about it. Finally, when Han's Laser's cash flow was threatened after the chairman's brother-in-law misappropriated a large sum of money, Gao complained, and the scandal went public. The chairman retaliated by refusing to sign the company's tax statements.

Gao Tries to Get His Company Back

By October 2000, the 18 months were up, and Gao decided to exercise the clause allowing him to buy back the shares from the state-owned Shenzhen company. By then, Han's Laser was valued at more than $3.6 million—$1.2 million more than the amount required. The state-owned company was understandably reluctant to let Han's Laser go, but it finally agreed grudgingly to sell back its shares, amounting to 46 percent of the company, for RMB 17 million. Gao agreed to let the state-owned company hold on to 5 percent of the shares as a future investment. Gao used his own shares as collateral for a loan enabling him to make an advance payment of half the amount. In the meantime, Gao had to obtain signatures from a variety of government agencies in order to close the deal. The process dragged on toward the end of the year, and before it could be completed, Gao was informed that a new law had just been passed changing the rules of the game. Henceforth, any sale of shares in a state-owned company had to be submitted to a public auction, which would be handled by a different state-owned company, the Shenzhen Enterprise Ownership Exchange Center. The declared intention was to maximize profits to state-owned industries that were in the process of being privatized. For Gao, this meant that his agreement to buy back the shares for RMB 17 million was no longer valid. When he asked for his money back, he was told that there was a "cash flow" problem and the money was no longer available.

It looked like a classic scam intended to keep Gao from exercising his option to win back control of his company. In addition to losing his $1 million, the new rules required Gao to put up a deposit of $600,000 before being allowed to take part in the auction for his own company. Since it would be an open auction, the shares were certain to cost more than the $2 million originally agreed on. Gao was clearly being taken to the cleaners. To make matters worse, the Shenzhen Enterprise Ownership Exchange Center, which was organizing the sale, began aggressively recruiting Han's Laser's competition to compete in the bidding. If a competitor secured controlling interest, Han's Laser would very likely be sidelined or eliminated from the market. At best, the company's internal management problems would be likely to deteriorate even further. Gao had the option of taking the state-owned Shenzhen company to court, but since he was up against a state-owned company with political connections, he realized that the outcome was not likely to go in his favor.

Instead of surrendering to panic, Gao had a brilliant insight. He decided to present his dilemma to the lender who had supplied him with the original $1 million loan and was now holding Gao's personal shares in Han's Laser as collateral. If Gao lost the bidding, he reasoned, the company would disintegrate, and the lender's shares would no longer be worth anything. The lender would lose his $1 million along with Gao. On the other hand, if the lender bankrolled him further, he would be likely to increase his profit even more. The lender accepted Gao's logic and offered to bankroll him to the end.

The auction took place on April 4, 2001, and after hectic bidding, Gao finally won back control of the company. The cost was nearly $3 million instead of the original $2 million, but it soon turned out to be worth it. On June 15, Gao managed to put together a private group of investors who paid 3.8 times the net asset worth for shares in Han's Laser. Gao arranged the deal so that no single investor had more than a 10 percent share in the company. He was not going to make the same mistake twice. With the private placement, Gao succeeded in paying back the original loan along with RMB 4.3 million in interest.

Going Public

Back in control, Gao was now determined to take Han's Laser public. His chief competitors, Beijing Daheng and Huagong Tech, had already raised $54.4 million through IPOs in 2000, and Han's Laser still had cash flow problems. In 2002, the company had nearly $20 million in revenues with nearly $4 million in profits, but its accounts receivables were $7.9 million and its cash flow was $1.24 million in the red. Two years later, on June 11, 2004, the company went public on the Shenzhen Stock Exchange's Board of Small and Medium Enterprises. At $1.09 per share, the IPO raised $28.8 million. On the day it was listed, the stock opened at $4.83 a share and closed at $4.82. The shares represented 43.36 percent of the company. Gao's personal worth skyrocketed to more than $217 million. The IPO enabled Gao to reward key employees, especially his best engineers, with shares in the company.

The cash flow problems that had held Han's Laser back were now largely over. By 2006, Han's Laser, which had started out by servicing the cloth button industry in Wenzhou, had expanded its scope to more than 70 industries, and it was constantly adding new applications. The company had added laser cutting, engraving, surface treatment, labeling, PCB drilling, and laser welding to its specialties. Han's Laser was now the world's leading producer of laser markers, with an 80 percent share of the China market. The company had also emerged as the second leading producer of laser cutters in China, and it was the world's second largest producer of PCB laser drilling equipment. In 2007, sales reached RMB $196.3 million—more than four times the sales before the IPO. The company had begun to run out of factory space to fill orders.

In July 2008, Han's Laser made an SEO (seasoned equity offering), which raised nearly $146.4 million. The proceeds went into building the largest laser production site in the world.

Gao's Success and Future Prospects

In 2010, Gao Yunfeng—at the age of 43, when most people are just beginning to approach their prime—was listed by *Forbes* as the 366th wealthiest person in China, with a personal worth estimated at $200 million. It was a long way from the young high school student who had to ration 12 buns over a week's time to have something to eat.

Gao had taken incredible risks in his career, and they had paid off handsomely. Any other executive might have opted for early retirement and a life of ease. Instead, Gao continued to be concerned about the future of the company he had created. Gao was particularly concerned about the fact that the market for laser markers was very specialized and had a relatively small number of potential customers. "I feel that I am digging my own tomb," he once remarked. "Every machine I sell means that there is one less machine that anyone needs to buy."

Han's Laser had been growing at a compound annual growth rate of 50 to 60 percent, and it was continuing to add new industries and new products, but that kind of growth seemed unsustainable over the long haul. The company dominated the market, but Gao knew that sooner or later it would experience pressure at the top end of the market as well as from the bottom. Han's Laser's competitors had already shifted much of their manufacturing to China to cut costs, and competition would inevitably heat up in the China market. Gao's dilemma was that even without external competition, by improving his machines and making them last longer, he was effectively saturating the market that the company depended on to survive.

The worldwide financial crisis came as a wake-up call, affecting Han's Laser along with everyone else. In the case of Han's Laser, it meant that the growth rate decreased to a mere 15 percent over the previous year and that profits dropped by 39.37 percent. Any other company might be satisfied with that, but Gao saw it as a preview of dangers on the horizon. He was convinced that the company needed a new strategy to continue growing.

As Gao saw it, the options were mixed. Han's Laser could expand beyond lasers and offer its own total production solutions to selected industries, but that would require a substantial investment in R&D and in its production capacity. Han's Laser had already tried to replicate its business model in South Korea and had failed. The synergy available from operating in China was not there. Costs were too high, and the market was too far away and too different from the company's home territory.

Another option might be to expand beyond lasers and to look at the broader photonics industry. Han's Laser had started experimenting with LEDs (light-emitting diodes) in 2007, and growing concerns about climate change and energy conservation made LEDs look like a good bet. Solar energy was also emerging as a new interest. On the other hand, Han's Laser could move entirely out of its field of expertise and explore the service industry. The government had set a target of having more than 50 percent of China's GDP come from the service industry by 2020, and the mass migration from rural areas to the cities made real estate look promising as an investment.

The final option was to go global. This is what Gao had dreamed of doing all along. The brief foray into South Korea had failed, and the company had also briefly tried to set up a partnership with a foreign company in Singapore. The Singapore partner initially wanted Han's Laser to build a factory to produce components locally, but then it terminated the relationship and began building its own factory in order to compete directly with Han's Laser. The sudden switch came as a warning to Gao about the dangers of competing globally.

As Gao saw it, going global meant actually becoming global. Han's Laser had bought a 9.92 percent share in an Italian manufacturer, Prima Industrie Group, hoping to gain knowledge of high-powered lasers used in cutting. But Gao quickly realized that Western companies were constantly afraid that China would try to steal their technology, so the relationship tended to be awkward at best.

The solution, Gao finally decided, was to put together his own international R&D team and have it work for him. He had already contracted what he considered to be a world-class R&D team and installed it in Shenzhen in 2004. The team brought its own patents, redesigned Han's Laser's research process, and helped train the company's R&D staff. By the time the team left in 2005, Han's Laser had developed its own ultraviolet laser technology, which was considerably more advanced than the competition's. Gao later said that the lesson he had learned was that you needed to be very precise about what it is that you want to achieve.

By 2008, Han's Laser had more than 30,000 machines in operation around the world. The company had always expanded market share by offering free service, but now the maintenance services it was offering were eating up profits. Free maintenance, in fact, equaled 60 percent of the gross profits. The company found itself as at a crossroad, pondering whether to continue to seek greater and greater market share or shift its focus to maximizing profits.

Whichever way Han's Laser ultimately decided to go, Gao had clearly turned his creation into a major player on the world stage.

The challenges of launching a company in China's fast-changing and often turbulent economic landscape had taught him lessons that were likely to serve him and the company he had founded well in taking on world competition.

TEN

Cracking the American Retail Market
Who Is Haier?

First we observe and digest. Then we imitate. In the end, we understand it well enough to design it independently.
—Zhang Ruimin, CEO of the Haier Group

IT WAS NOT EXACTLY a boardroom panic, but there was no question that the top management of Whirlpool, one of America's leading household appliance manufacturers, was beginning to see a looming threat on the horizon. Whirlpool's senior executives had just learned that the company's troubled rival, Maytag, was up for sale and that it might well become the property of a Chinese competitor, Haier. If the sale went through, Haier would be able to market its products under a well-known American brand name, and that promised to turn Haier into an even more formidable competitor.

Although American consumers tended to look at Haier as a manufacturer of cheap refrigerators and air conditioners, Whirlpool already had a deeper knowledge of the company. Whirlpool had tried to break into the China market years earlier through a joint venture with Haier's leading competitor, Guangdong Kelon. Kelon's strategy had looked good enough on paper, but the company had fared badly in a head-on competition with Haier. Worse, Whirlpool had lost millions of dollars when it made the unwise decision to try to dump refrigerators using Freon as a coolant on the Chinese market. The joint venture's executives had reasoned that the Chinese buying public was unlikely to be aware of the fact that the use of Freon, which damages the ozone layer, was already prohibited in many more developed markets. They had guessed wrong. The Chinese knew about Freon, and they shunned Whirlpool and Kelon's product line. Now—faced with the possibility of having to compete with a Chinese dragon armed with an American brand name—Whirlpool felt that it needed to outbid Haier, and in the end it paid a substantial price to protect its home turf.

Haier's first foray into the U.S. market had seemed innocuous enough. The company had started in a niche market, selling inexpensive mini-fridges for student dorm rooms. Haier executives soon realized that college students were short of space, so the mini-fridges were designed to double as computer desks, which students liked. Meanwhile, the major players like Whirlpool looked on with amusement. The cheap fridges seemed to confirm the stereotype that the Chinese were not up to competing at the high end of the market. As it turned out, Haier was following the carefully thought-out strategy of its founder, Zhang Ruimin, who was convinced that the most effective way to enter a developed market is to focus on sectors that the major players consider too insignificant to bother with.

Having conquered the market for America's college dorms, Haier introduced a refrigerator designed to act as a wine cooler. Normally, only passionate collectors bother to keep wine at an electronically regulated, precise temperature, and usually the equipment to meet their standards was inordinately expensive. But Haier's coolers sold for around $200, allowing young urban professionals to experiment with the privileged lifestyle of a connoisseur. Before long, Haier dominated the market in wine coolers. What Haier was after, however, was not just profits but acceptance by the leading American discount chain stores. It had taken Haier a year just for its sales department to arrange a meeting with Walmart. Haier's niche products were the wedge needed to get in the door. By the time Haier's U.S. competitors realized what was happening, it was already too late.

Already a Giant in China

The man responsible for Haier's success, Zhang Ruimin, had entered the U.S. market with a strategy that relied on stealth. Zhang's tactic was to identify an overlooked segment of the market, test the waters, and then spread out progressively to more competitive sectors.

While many Americans thought of Haier as just another low-cost producer of inexpensive appliances, Haier was, in fact, already a giant. It had long ago become the leading appliance producer in China, where its products regularly sold at a premium of 15 to 20 percent above market price. Given the choice between expanding market share by price-cutting or improving quality, Haier had always gone for quality. Haier was a winner not because it was cheaper but because it was better than its competition. It was also better organized. The *Wall Street Journal* called Haier the best-managed company in China. In expanding its reach to international markets, it was certainly one of the most successful. The Haier

Group's companies were listed on both the Hong Kong and Shenzhen Stock Exchanges.

Haier's astonishing rise was due in large part to the foresight of Zhang Ruimin, an avid reader of books on modern business strategy. The saga that led to the creation of Haier had begun in 1984, just five years after China's first tentative steps toward a market-driven economy. A still relatively small band of private entrepreneurs were struggling to stay afloat, but it was already apparent that China's economy was going to experience dramatic changes. Support for state-owned enterprises was shrinking, and in the private sector, fortunes were being made.

At the time, Zhang had what appeared to be a stable civil service job as vice-general manager of the home appliance division of the municipal administration of the city of Qingdao. The factories in Qingdao were turning out refrigerators that were so shoddily constructed that they barely worked, yet demand was so high that customers were lining up to buy them as fast as they came off the assembly line.

Despite the heated market demand, the Qingdao General Refrigerator Factory was nearly bankrupt. It had been forced to borrow from neighboring municipalities to pay its employees. The factory was a collective enterprise, which meant that the workers owned its assets. The municipality levied taxes and could influence senior management choices and major business decisions, but the lack of clarity about who was really in charge had virtually eliminated any effort at quality control. The Qingdao municipality wanted Zhang to cast aside his "iron rice bowl" (guaranteed job, income, and benefits) and take over the nearly bankrupt enterprise. Zhang accepted the challenge.

Zhang's critical insight was to realize that in the long run, quality would be more of a determining factor than price. Zhang reasoned that the Chinese public, like everyone else, would be willing to pay a premium for a product that worked as promised and could be easily serviced if it failed to function correctly.

China had roughly 300 companies manufacturing refrigerators when Zhang took on the failing Qingdao factory. Nearly all of the factories were producing mediocre products. To get a different perspective, Zhang went to Germany and made a quick comparison between European appliances and those being produced in China. The Germans were not necessarily smarter than the Chinese, Zhang reasoned, so why couldn't Chinese products be just as good as those of the Germans? Zhang defined his strategy: "First we observe and digest," he said. "Then we imitate. In the end, we understand it well enough to design it independently."

Zhang began by licensing the latest technology from Germany's premium refrigerator manufacturer, Liebherr. Back in China, he marketed the factory's revamped production line under the brand Qingdao-Liebherr. He later imported production lines from Sanyo and a Danish company, Derby, and he signed joint ventures with Mitsubishi and Italy's Merloni. In 1991, the company's name was changed to Qingdao-Haier. The word *Haier* was a transliteration of the Chinese characters for "herr" in *Liebherr.* In 1992, "Qingdao" was dropped, and the company became known simply as the Haier Group.

Quality Matters

While upgrading the factory's technology, Zhang also realized that he needed to change the mentality of its workers. The crucial turning point arrived when a customer returned a defective refrigerator to the factory and asked for a replacement. Zhang looked at the refrigerators coming off the assembly line and discovered that 20 percent of them didn't work. In a less than subtle gesture, he had 76 defective refrigerators pulled out of the line and smashed to bits in front of the workers.

The message was clear: A new baseline for quality had been set in Qingdao. To ram the point home, Zhang had a pair of yellow footprints painted on the factory floor. Anyone whose performance was considered not up to standard had to stand on the spot and explain his or her errors to his or her fellow workers. The tactic had a shock effect in China, where face is considered extremely important. Zhang was, in fact, leveraging Chinese culture to make certain that no one missed the point that he was trying to make. Eventually, when Zhang opened factories in the United States, he would adopt some of the same principles. Workers who performed well would stand in front of a blue line, and those who performed badly would have to stand behind a red line. Peer pressure enforced the new standards more than any management directive could hope to achieve. In addition, in contrast to the lack of individual accountability that resulted from collective ownership and guaranteed employment, Haier also introduced the Western notion of a management "bake-off." The company set a policy that the company's top 10 managers would be publicly commended for their work, while the bottom 10 would either be fired or demoted. (In January 2009, the company demoted six vice presidents because of poor sales in its TV and personal computer divisions.)

In its second year of operation, Zhang's rejuvenated company made more than $11 million profit. In 1988, the company won a gold medal in a national refrigerator competition. By 1989, oversupply was beginning to swamp the Chinese market and many of the manufacturers were engaged in a price war, which inevitably led to reduced profits and lower quality. Zhang decided to take the opposite approach and raise his quality standards even higher. Haier began commanding a 15 percent premium in the market, despite the price war.

Diversification Through Acquisition

By the beginning of the 1990s, Haier had begun to diversify and branched into air conditioners and freezers. Its strategy was to identify market demand and then to look for companies that were producing products that were in demand but were failing because of ineffective management. Haier's first two candidates were the Qingdao Air Conditioner Factory and the Qingdao General Freezer Factory. Haier took over the debt of both factories and kept most of the workers. Within a year, both factories were making a profit.

The company had changed its name to the Haier Group in order to reflect its diversification. Just as everything seemed to be coming together, however, it faced a potential disaster. To consolidate its expanded business, Haier bought 500 acres in an industrial park for roughly $9.5 million. Its annual profits in 1992 were just under $6 million, and construction costs were estimated at nearly $12 million. Haier had been promised a bank loan to cover the amount, but less than a month after the deal had been signed, the government tightened credit in a move intended to stop real estate speculation.

As often happens, an impending catastrophe that could have driven the company into bankruptcy eventually served to accelerate its growth even faster. With no other option for raising capital, Haier decided to launch an IPO on the Shanghai Stock Exchange, offering up 43 percent of its refrigerator division. It was a risky gamble, but in the end the IPO produced more than twice as much cash as the company had been planning to borrow through its now defunct bank loan. The additional funding enabled the company to expand even more rapidly.

Haier had always focused on quality and resisted overly rapid expansion, but it now found that its successes had effectively turned it into an angel of salvation in the eyes of local politicians. In 1995, the Qingdao municipality turned to Haier to save its nearly bankrupt Red Star Washing Machine Company. Haier was expected to keep the factory's employees and take on its accumulated debt of more than $15 million, which was again roughly equal to Haier's annual profits. Within a year and a half, Red Star was ranked as the best washing machine manufacturer in China. By 1997, Haier had taken over 15 companies, producing products ranging from washing machines to television sets and telecommunications equipment.

Increasing Competition in Its Domestic Market

By 1998, Haier had a third of the Chinese market for washing machines, refrigerators, and air conditioners. As retail sales in the major markets began to taper off, Haier looked toward China's rural markets, and it had begun to consolidate its sales, service, and finance operations into group-wide divisions.

But Haier now faced new challenges. Refrigerator manufacturers in China were locked in a Darwinian struggle. By the end of the 1990s, there were only 20 major producers, and ten of them accounted for 80 percent of sales. Three of these accounted for 60 percent of the market. Estimates were that a manufacturer had to produce and sell at least a million refrigerators a year to remain profitable. The large companies also had to compete with small enterprises that were often focused on one or two products. These companies often failed to sustain themselves on their own, but they were kept in business by local municipalities that were more interested in maintaining employment than in making a profit.

Haier faced competition from another refrigerator manufacturer, Guangdong Kelon, which had merged with an air conditioner manufacturer and then listed itself on the Hong Kong Stock Exchange. Kelon had signed a deal to manufacture washing machines in China for Whirlpool, and in contrast to Haier, it followed a multi-brand strategy. It sold its high-end products under the Kelon brand and then targeted the middle- and lower-market layers with cheaper products manufactured on independent assembly lines. The different product lines made it difficult for Kelon to maintain economies of scale, and it regularly posted losses. At the same time, Kelon realized that the greatest growth was likely to come from the second- and third-tier markets in rural areas, and that put it into competition with Haier. The struggle for these markets intensified when China entered the World Trade Organization in 2001, and the way was opened for multinationals to compete with Chinese brands inside China. Some of the foreign competition had already entered China under joint venture deals in the early 1990s.

The multinationals aimed for the high-end market in China's major cities and then for the market in rural areas. Now that China had opened its doors to sophisticated Western manufacturing, most of the multinationals expected the stiffest competition to come from other multinationals. In fact, they quickly discovered that the technology being offered by Haier and Kelon was often just as good, only less costly and better designed to match Chinese tastes. The multinationals for their part had made the mistake of looking at China as a monolith. They failed to grasp the diversity of the population and the differences in taste that distinguished one region from another. China was simply too vast for most foreigners to understand, and the multinationals tended to take a "one model fits everyone" approach. The multinationals also tried to get away with selling technology that was already becoming unfashionable in the West. Then, thinking that the Chinese public would not notice the difference, Whirlpool attempted to sell refrigerators that still used Freon as a coolant. This was despite the fact that most developed countries were already moving toward a technology that was safer for the environment. The Chinese public proved just as savvy as buyers in the West, and Whirlpool racked up heavy losses.

Innovative Ideas and Creative Management

Far from resting on its laurels, Haier invested 5 to 7 percent of its revenues in R&D on a yearly basis and boasted that its products were being rendered obsolete by its own new products coming on line rather than by the products of its competitors.

But Haier's biggest achievement appeared to be its ability to keep improving on management while maintaining its sensitivity to the Chinese market. It established a system of basic platforms that could be equipped with different combinations of standardized modules to fit any customer's requirements. In the end, the company produced 96 product categories with 15,100 specifications. If customers wanted a special compartment in their refrigerators to store pungent Korean kimche, Haier could produce it. The ability to do this didn't cost much, and the customers loved Haier's adapting products to their needs.

The ultimate example of the Haier approach occurred when a rural farmer in Sichuan complained that his washing machine kept breaking down. A Haier repair technician noticed that the machine was filled with mud. It turned out that the farmer had been using it to wash sweet potatoes. Instead of correcting the farmer, Haier reconfigured the washing machines and launched an advertising campaign boasting that Haier's machines were ideal for washing clothes, sweet potatoes, and peanuts. In Shanghai, known for its summer heat waves, Haier introduced a tiny washing machine just big enough for a single change of clothes. In Shanghai's tiny apartments, the machine became an instant hit. Haier followed up with a washing machine that cleaned clothes without detergent and another that washed and dried clothes in the same machine.

Most of these appliances, tightly targeted to meet local tastes, were made possible through the ingenious combination of standard modules and subsystems configured to meet local requirements on standard frames. "Periodically, we add some new features," Zhang explained, "but the basic model is there. We don't change randomly."

Haier's most innovative thinking, however, was incorporated into its creative management. In 1990, Haier introduced a computerized tracking system that enabled its newly established service system to track tens of thousands of customers. After-sales service was a rarity in China at the time, and even high-end foreign appliance brands had difficulty providing service throughout the country. By 2004, Haier had established a network of 5,500 independent contractors to provide after-sales service throughout the country. Customers could call a nationwide hotline to arrange for house calls. If the appliance had to be sent to a workshop for repair, Haier provided a replacement.

Haier also became a leader in just-in-time purchasing of raw materials. A distribution network serving the entire country operated out of 42 centers and employed 300 transport companies with 16,000 vehicles. Haier moved an average of 100,000 pieces of merchandise a day. By creating a single operation to service all its needs, Haier was able to achieve impressive economies of scale. Foreign companies contracted Chinese transport companies as well, but they often found it difficult to establish a reliable network that covered the entire country, and their costs were invariably higher.

Haier Goes Global

Despite Haier's success, the company's executives were cautious about the future. In the fast-changing global environment, they were constantly expecting that competition from both foreign and domestic companies would eventually catch up. In 1997, Zhang Ruimin announced a goal of having Haier produce and sell a third of its goods in China, produce a third in China to sell in foreign countries, and both produce and sell the remaining third in foreign countries.

Throughout the 1990s, Haier had been experimenting with a number of joint ventures, all of which helped build experience in international operations. But 1997 marked a turning point. Haier refrigerators had been selling very well in Germany, where Liebherr marketed them under the Blue Line brand. In a blind quality test run by a German magazine, eight of Haier's refrigerator models beat out seven of those manufactured by Liebherr. Haier decided it was time to begin selling in Germany under its own brand name. It also introduced the Haier brand to Asian regional markets, selling refrigerators, washing machines, and other appliances manufactured in the Philippines.

Zhang made it clear that while most Chinese companies exported to earn foreign capital, Haier had a more fundamental objective. "Our purpose in exporting," he said, "is to establish brand recognition overseas." In keeping with that philosophy, Zhang decided to focus the company on building sales in the developed markets rather than go after the less demanding emerging markets. Zhang reasoned that if Haier could succeed in the markets where the competition was the strongest and regulations were the most demanding, it would have no trouble competing in the easier markets afterward. Once Haier had established its brand in Europe and the United States, it could enter the developing markets at the same level as well-known brands like GE, Matsushita, and Philips.

Through the Backdoor

Zhang concluded that the best tactic would be to focus on a few niche products in each market to test the reaction, while staying out of the way of potential competitors. Despite the strategy, Haier still met with challenges. To succeed, the company had to win over the major discount chain stores, which proved harder than expected. Haier's initial entry into the American market was on a small scale at first. The opportunity to break into the U.S. market presented itself in 1994, when Michael Jemel, a partner in a New York import company, showed interest in Haier's compact refrigerators. Only three of Haier's compact models met U.S. energy and safety standards, but Jemel bought 150,000 of them and managed to sell all of them within a year, under the Welbilt brand.

In 1999, Jemel and Haier launched Haier America as a joint venture. With the exception of the venture's accountant, who came from Qingdao, the Haier America staff were nearly all Americans. Zhang recognized that salaries were far higher than in China, but since he planned to sell the products at a premium, he figured that Haier could afford the cost.

Jemel concentrated on getting the big retail chains as customers. It took him a year just to get an interview with Walmart, but the strategy worked. Within three years, Haier had captured 30 percent of the compact refrigerator market in the United States. When other companies tried to copy the concept, Haier resorted to innovative design ideas that kept its products a step ahead of the competition. Haier built a $40 million industrial park and refrigerator factory in South Carolina. By 2002, Haier was selling 80,000 full-size refrigerators in the United States, accounting for 2 percent of the total market. Walmart, which hadn't wanted to listen to Haier in the beginning, bought 400,000 compact refrigerators, washing machines, and air conditioners from Haier in 2002. Haier found it had to begin importing refrigerators from China to satisfy the growing U.S. demand. By 2005, Walmart was selling 44 Haier product lines, mostly to college students. The Haier brand was still relatively unknown, but the company was investing 10 percent of its revenues on global branding and marketing.

Maytag Enters the Picture

While Haier's prospects were expanding dramatically, those of Maytag, one of its major American competitors, were declining at an unnerving rate. The company, which began in Newton, Iowa, in 1893, was named for its founder, F. L. Maytag, and had initially manufactured farm tools. In 1907, it developed one of the first successful washing machines, which consisted of a hand-cranked mechanism attached to a wooden tub. The company branched into refrigerators and stoves in 1946. Maytag had a solid reputation in the United States, but it had failed to keep up with changes in the global economy. It was trailing in third place behind Whirlpool and General Electric, and it was losing $9 million a year on sales of $4.7 billion. Whirlpool, in contrast, made profits of $406 million a year on sales of $13.2 billion.

Maytag had based its sales network on some 10,000 independent appliance dealers that were gradually being driven into bankruptcy by giant discount retailers like Walmart and Best Buy. Competition from foreign manufacturers, such as LG, Daewoo, Samsung, and Haier, drove prices down, reducing the company's profit margin even further. The foreign brands also competed for floor space in the larger appliance stores. Already in debt, Maytag was looking at an even more dismal future.

On April 22, 2005, Maytag's stock price dropped 28 percent after it failed to make its first quarterly earnings target. Maytag's board of directors turned to the investment bank Lazard Ltd., to see if there might be an interested buyer. The board fairly quickly arrived at an arrangement to sell the company to a private equity group, Ripplewood Holdings, for $1.13 billion. The sale represented roughly $14 a share.

Haier suddenly saw Maytag as an opportunity to obtain instant brand recognition in the United States, and it made a subsequent offer of $16 a share. The offer added up to $1.28 billion. Haier did not have enough cash to cover that amount on its own, so it enlisted two financial partners, Bain Capital and the Blackstone Group. The impromptu alliance attracted the attention of the top U.S. appliance manufacturer, Whirlpool.

In contrast to Maytag, which had focused primarily on sales in North America, Whirlpool had already gone multinational years earlier. At least 40 percent of its sales were outside the United States. More than a third of its production was based in developing countries including Brazil, China, India, and Mexico. From its global viewpoint, Whirlpool saw Haier as a competitor not only in the American market but in the emerging markets as well. Besides that, buying Maytag appeared to Whirlpool to be an effective way to leverage its low-cost manufacturing in the United States and to increase its clout with the major chain stores.

Whirlpool offered $17 a share, or a 21 percent premium over the initial offer from Ripplewood. Maytag would have to pay Ripplewood a $40 million cancellation fee, but it would still come out substantially ahead. Whirlpool's purchase of Maytag promised to make it the world's largest appliance manufacturer. There were some concerns about it becoming a monopoly in the United States, but the company countered that there was already so much competition from Asia that the prospect of a monopoly was no longer a danger.

The offer from Haier was complicated by the fact that it had been made just as CNOOC—China's National Offshore Oil Corporation—was attempting to buy the U.S. company Unocal. (This case is discussed in detail in Chapter 2.) The CNOOC offer had sparked a wave of jingoistic nationalism in conservative circles in Congress, and both Haier and CNOOC now faced a rising wave of suspicion about China's long-term goals. As temperatures rose in

Washington, CNOOC quietly dropped the plan to buy Unocal, and Haier also withdrew its offer to buy Maytag.

With Haier out of the way, Whirlpool was able to close the deal, but, according to Market Watch, it cost Whirlpool $2.3 billion in stock, cash, and assuming Maytag's debts. Almost immediately, questions were raised as to whether Whirlpool had been tricked into spending far more for Maytag than it was actually worth. It subsequently emerged, according to a report in the *New York Times*, that Maytag had contacted more than 30 potential buyers before signing its initial deal with Ripplewood. None of the other buyers contacted had shown much interest. That added to the impression Haier had succeeded in bluffing Whirlpool into making an unnecessarily expensive purchase.

Haier had lost the bidding war to Whirlpool, but the company had achieved its ultimate objective, which was to make its brand a major player in the American appliance market. The fact that Zhang had accomplished this without having to spend Haier's capital only made the situation sweeter.

Not long after the bidding war for Maytag, a full-page ad appeared in a glossy women's fashion magazine. It displayed a stylishly gleaming new refrigerator in a brilliant designer orange. The color looked stunning, but it was the caption that caught the readers' attention: "The most eco-friendly refrigerator in the world." The message was not hard to miss. The refrigerator was simply better than the competition. The name on the refrigerator door was "Haier," exactly the way Zhang Ruimin had wanted it all along.

Haier and Whirlpool Emerge as the World's Two Leading Giants

In 2005, while Haier and Whirlpool were sparring with each other over the purchase of Maytag, Whirlpool's annual sales were around

$13 billion. By 2009, Haier was registering annual sales of roughly $18 billion. Whirlpool's gross revenues were still greater than Haier's, but Haier had emerged as the world's largest manufacturer of refrigerators and washing machines in terms of units produced, and it was selling its products in 60 countries. In 2009, according to AP–Dow Jones, Haier's sales in the United States increased by roughly 9 percent. Haier had 29 factories and eight R&D centers overseas and some 50,000 employees worldwide. Zhang Ruimin was quoted in China Daily Information's Business Daily Update as saying somewhat modestly, "The International market is the best classroom for us to learn the basic rules of doing business overseas."

In China, Haier benefitted from a government program to subsidize appliance purchases in rural areas. The subsidies were open to foreign companies as well as Chinese ones, but Haier nevertheless managed to capture 32 percent of that market. Haier's sales to Chinese rural areas in 2009 increased by around 30 percent.

In 2010, Haier mulled over buying the appliance arm of General Electric and in the end decided that it didn't need what GE had to offer despite the fact that the appliance division was one of GE's biggest moneymakers. Haier's reason for dropping the sale was twofold. First, it felt that the price had been set too high, and Zhang was not about to repeat Whirlpool's extravagant purchase of Maytag and, second, the company was beginning to look closely at the difficulty of blending Chinese management styles with the executives inherited from recently purchased Western companies. Chinese companies were learning that it was easier to teach young Chinese students Western business techniques than it was to get Western senior executives to understand China. In January 2011, Haier did sign a memorandum of understanding with Honeywell, but as in its beginning arrangement with Liebherr, the deal involved access to technology. It covered Honeywell's support to Haier's research and development of "smart" home appliances, with an emphasis on low-emission, high-efficiency solutions. Honeywell declared that more than 50 percent of its energy-saving materials, intelligent building techniques, and industry control were in keeping with Haier's global brand strategy and environmental protection policies.

As for its business strategy, by 2011, roughly half of the Haier Group's sales were overseas, and Zhang still planned to boost that to two-thirds of the company's total. The plan was to emphasize three areas for growth: the United States, Japan, and Southeast Asia. The United States is the world's second most important consumer of household appliances, surpassed only by China. Japan is the third largest consumer, and Southeast Asia is growing fast. The Haier strategy called for establishing production and distribution networks and doubling its research and manufacturing capacities for each of these regions.

Haier was aiming for a 10 percent increase in sales in Japan, along with the launch of 50 new products aimed at the Japanese market. In 2009, after only eight years in Japan, Haier already controlled 40 percent of the market for small refrigerators and washing machines, and it now planned to conquer the market for larger machines.

Among all the Chinese companies trying to expand into the global marketplace, Haier ranked as one of the most successful. Under Zhang Ruimin's stewardship, it had come a long way from the nearly bankrupt refrigerator factory that had been forced to borrow from neighboring villages to meet its payroll. More important, it was fast on its way to becoming one of China's best-known brands abroad, earning high marks for quality and excellence, and it had achieved that relying on its own name.

ELEVEN

China Moves Ahead on Clean Energy

Several countries in Europe, most notably Germany, have been the solar industries' most stalwart supporters. It is no surprise that 66 percent of our revenues were gen-erated from shipments to European customers. . . .

—Dr. Zhengrong Shi, founder, chairman, and CEO of Suntech, China's largest producer of photovoltaic solar panels

THE CIRCUMSTANCES SURROUNDING Zhengrong Shi's birth looked less than promising. Shi was born in 1963 on Yangzhong Island in a small farming community where the conditions were desperate in the wake of what came to be known as China's Great Famine, the catastrophic follow-up to the Great Leap Forward. In the three years leading up to Shi's birth, more than 20 million peo-ple had starved to death, and that figure may have been an under-statement. Some experts put the actual death toll closer to 40 million. Shi's parents already had two children whom they could barely support, and the prospect of another mouth to feed threat-ened the entire family with disaster. To make matters worse, it had been a twin birth. Shi's parents did not see how they could keep both babies. As it turned out, another family had just lost their baby, who was stillborn. That tragedy offered a solution, and Shi's biological parents suggested that the other family raise Shi in place of their lost child. The spur-of-the-moment adoption may have saved Shi's life. It certainly saved his future.

Under the careful eye of his new parents, Shi proved himself to be a brilliant student. At 16, he left home to attend university in Manchuria, then transferred to Shanghai University for a master's degree in laser physics. In 1988, he managed to get an exit visa and gain admission to the University of New South Wales in Australia.

Martin Green, the executive research director of the university's ARC (Australian Research Council) Photovoltaics Centre of Excellence, recalled in an interview in *Time* magazine that Shi had come into his office a year after arriving in Australia and asked if he could apply for a full-time job. Green, a keen eye for talent, rejected Shi's request on the spot. Instead, he arranged a scholarship for Shi to obtain a PhD focusing on photovoltaic cells. Six years later, Shi became deputy research director of the Photovoltaics Centre. His mandate was to research the next generation of solar technology.

Suntech Is Born

In 2001, Shi—who had by then become an Australian citizen—returned to China to open a factory to produce solar cells in the city of Wuxi. Within four years, Shi had managed to organize a buyout of the factory's other Chinese investors. A few months after that, he succeeded in getting the company he had founded, Suntech, to become the first private Chinese corporation listed on the New York Stock Exchange.

In 2006, just a year later, *Forbes* listed Shi as 350th of the 500 wealthiest people in the world. By then, Shi had assets worth more than $2 billion, and he was briefly classified by *Forbes* as the richest man in Mainland China. Shi was unquestionably brilliant, but he was only one among an increasing number of stars in China to make their fortune by envisioning the future of energy.

The Possibilities of Energy

Energy is the key to economic power, and it is economic power that places nations in a dominant position on the international stage. If the late 20th century made oil king, it is still too early to tell what form of energy will finally dominate the 21st century.

For the Chinese, it is obvious that the American economic model, which relies on exploiting roughly a fourth of the world's energy to satisfy the consumer appetites of less than 6 percent of the world's population, is clearly not an option. The West, with its elaborate infrastructure already in place, is understandably reluctant to think about what will happen when the oil runs out, but China is building an infrastructure for the future, and it is coming to the industrial scene relatively late in the game. While China makes it clear that it is going to have to depend on fossil fuels as well as nuclear power for the foreseeable future, it is already looking for alternatives, and it is counting on people like Shi to show the way. The fact that the West continues to dither about the economic viability of alternative energy only serves to give the Chinese a head start at mastering the energy technology of the future, if only to escape from the deadly pollution that is already resulting from its overreliance on coal-fired power plants.

Until recently, wind and solar power appeared unrealistically expensive when compared to electricity produced by nuclear power. The March 2011 earthquake and tsunami in Japan, which caused a number of accidents at a nuclear power plant, showed just how expensive nuclear power can be when it goes wrong. That—combined with oil costing more than $100 a barrel—is beginning to make alternatives like wind power, solar power, and biomass fuels look much more attractive. Booming sales of hybrid cars (which can switch between gasoline and electric systems) and cars with flex-fuel engines (which can use alternative fuels like ethanol) show that the public is increasingly ready to try something new. The Chinese estimate that renewable energy could account for 15 percent of their total energy needs in the next ten years or so. That may not sound like much, but in a country the size of China, it can make a huge difference.

Early in his presidency, Barack Obama gave a passing acknowledgment to the importance of developing renewable energy technology, but the aftermath of the financial crisis and the growing obsession of the conservative Tea Party movement with cutting as much government spending as possible put the U.S. commitment into question. Financial problems in the Eurozone have also put a crimp into competitive efforts to develop renewable energy in Europe.

In contrast, China is starting out relatively fresh, and it has plenty of motivation to move quickly. What is more, it has the cash to buy or develop the technology. When the Obama administration announced in July 2010 that it was committing $2 billion in stimulus spending to solar energy, it seemed like a significant gesture. But Bloomberg New Energy Finance reported that the China Development Bank approved $19 billion in credit facilities to all aspects of solar energy in just the last half of 2010. The U.S. investment seems paltry in comparison.

Chinese Efforts in Solar Power

While competition among suppliers may look slightly chaotic in China today, there is a method to the madness. Instead of rushing into production of solar cells for China itself, the government in Beijing appears to be backing as many Chinese companies as possible to strive for foreign market share rather than domestic sales.

Zhengrong Shi, CEO of Suntech, notes that two-thirds of his company's sales are to the European market. The success of clean energy depends on some level of government subsidy, but the Chinese have been holding back on deploying solar power in China itself until they can analyze Europe's experience. They are anxious to avoid the speculation that has appeared as collateral fallout in European efforts to pick up part of the tab for solar deployment.

While China's own purchases of solar panels accounted for less than 3 percent of the 18.5-gigawatt capacity of the solar panels sold in 2010, the ultimate plan is to eventually expand China's own solar installations by more than 6,000 percent to produce 20 gigawatts of electric power. By then, the manufacturing process will have matured, and China's aggressive campaign for market share and competition among suppliers will have driven the price of solar panels down to a level that is likely to prove far more affordable. In addition, by then, the Chinese companies will have priced most of their competition in the West out of business. When and if China does finally commit, Suntech, China's largest producer of high-quality solar panels, is likely to be well positioned to set standards for the rest of the world. For Zhengrong Shi, already one of the world's wealthiest individuals, it may be only the beginning.

Chinese Efforts in Wind Power

For the moment, however, the most advanced deployment of new clean energy technology in China, not counting hydroelectric power, is from wind turbines. Once again, China has managed to take the lead.

As far back as 2005, China appeared to have only a negligible presence on the clean energy scene, but by 2011, China was already dominant in the market. At least seven of the top 15 producers of wind power today are Chinese companies. Financial analyst Frost & Sullivan noted that the global market for wind power, which was worth nearly $9 billion in 2009, is likely to be worth $52 billion by 2016. *(?)*

In 2007, only 20 companies in China were involved in wind-generated electricity. By 2010, that number had risen to 80, and price competition was intense. According to the Global Wind Energy Council, China had 42.3 gigawatts of installed capacity in 80 wind farms. It had just managed to surpass the United States, which had 40.2 gigawatts of installed capacity.

The most productive wind-producing areas in China were Inner Mongolia, which had more than 5,000 gigawatts of installed capacity, and the southeastern coast, where much of China's manufacturing capacity is located. China's meteorologists predicted that China could eventually produce 150 gigawatts of electricity from wind power alone by 2020. According to a report by Credit Suisse, the China Electricity Council reported in December 2010 that apart from hydroelectric power, wind accounted for 99 percent of China's installed capacity of renewable energy. The World Wind Energy Institute reported that the United States had increased its wind capacity by only 1.5 gigawatts in 2010. In contrast, China was increasing its capacity by 13 to 14 gigawatts a year, and it was striving for a rate of increase by 16 gigawatts a year. While the United States accounted for nearly half the wind power market in 2010, and Asia accounted for another fourth, analysts were predicting that China alone could account for nearly half the world's wind power within the next few years. World capacity stood at 194.4 gigawatts in 2010 but was projected to exceed 450 gigawatts by 2015.

While most of the manufacturing of wind turbines and gearboxes in China had previously consisted mainly of assembling components bought from Europe and the United States, that situation seemed likely to change. The financial crisis had slowed wind development in the United States, and the European market was beginning to appear saturated. Manufacturers in Europe and the United

States were consequently less likely to get the kind of investment that China was positioned to offer its own manufacturers, and in any case, the Western companies would have a hard time competing with the Chinese on price.

The saturation problem in Europe was only partly a question of where to put the turbines. A more important issue was the need to reconfigure Europe's electrical grid to handle power on a continent-wide basis rather than on a country-by-country basis. Most European countries had configured their power grids to serve their own domestic needs. While there were estimates that Europe could produce up to 100 gigawatts from wind farms in the North Sea and solar installations in the south, the European grid could take in only around 20 gigawatts. With most Europeans questioning the future of the euro and their own employment prospects, investment in a major undertaking such as reconfiguring the continent's electric power grid seemed difficult to imagine.

With the European market temporarily reaching saturation, future production appeared likely to go to China, where costs were lower and future market needs were clearly greater. Despite its rapid growth, the installed wind capacity in China stood at only around 3 percent of China's total installed capacity of 962 gigawatts in 2010. That compared with 19 percent in Germany, 19 percent in Spain, and 4 percent in the United States. China clearly had room to grow, and it was very likely that by growing in wind power, as with solar power, China would be positioning itself to set future standards and pricing for the foreseeable future.

TWELVE

All Roads Lead
to Innovation

*Students need to strengthen their theoretical knowledge. It is the foundation of
their future work.*

—Guan Tongxian, former CEO of
Zhenhua Port Machinery Company

UNTIL RECENTLY, THE UNITED States took the lead when it came
to promoting the virtues of capitalism and a worldwide free market
economy. Today, Chinese business is both taking advantage of and
profiting from the philosophy that Americans supported for so long.
Most people in the West still believe in free trade, but they are also
beginning to see the disadvantages when another country suddenly
proves equally competitive. The United States is still the world's
leading national economy, and despite its financial difficulties,
Europe is also a regional powerhouse that cannot be taken lightly.
How long the United States and Europe stay on top, however,
depends to a large extent on how they can cope with the fact that

China

products manufactured in China are not only less expensive but also often just as good or better than those being produced in the West.

Both China and India are not so much emerging economies as they are reemerging economies. In the early half of the 19th century, the economies of China and India accounted for more than half the world's wealth, while Europe accounted for less than 40 percent. Meanwhile, input from the United States was only beginning to be taken seriously. The failure of China and India to adjust to critical changes in modern technology and the way the global economy was actually working led to both countries succumbing to the surging force of colonialism coming from the West, resulting in their eventual destruction. It is a historical fact that the Chinese have not forgotten.

The reemergence of China and India is once again creating a sudden change in both the landscape and the rules of the game for global business. In this rapidly evolving environment, staying on top requires intelligence, speed, flexibility, and most of all innovation.

Approaching the New Economic Landscape

This increasingly fluid environment works against those large, established corporations that tend to be prone to inertia and whose management finds it difficult to recognize and readapt to new market situations. If China has one great advantage, it is the fact that the Chinese approach this new economic landscape with a fresh vision. In contrast to the West, which sees its share of the pie diminishing, the Chinese look at the future as opportunity, and they have much less to lose.

While the giant Western multinationals tend to have a macro vision of the world, the Chinese still maintain a micro vision of business. In practice, the Chinese remain intensely focused on the needs of their individual customers. In contrast, many Western executives have tended to focus on cost cutting and eliminating those aspects of their business that fall short of maximum profits. Customer support is increasingly handed over to the circular hell of automated answering machines or farmed out to call centers in India or the Philippines. CEOs know that their individual customers are upset, but they don't care. What counts is the bottom line.

The Chinese, who have intimate knowledge of the pain that comes from poverty, are hungry for advancement. In the new breed of Chinese companies, if an executive is trying to break into a new market and the machine he has just sold doesn't work, he will go the extra distance to find out why. It may take a multinational several months to get around to responding to the same complaint. In essence, then, the Chinese advantage is people. Having humans do the work is more affordable in China, and even a relatively uneducated human being is likely to be smarter than a machine or an automated answering machine.

In this new climate, the Chinese know that they are coming from behind and that there is a lot of catching up to do. That is why China is putting enormous resources into education and into subsidizing its industrial development. The money to do this has largely been supplied by the readiness of the West to take advantage of cheap labor in China. There is nothing wrong with this. It is the way free market capitalism is supposed to work. The irony, however, is that while China races to catch up, the West is slashing its own education budgets, starving its R&D funding, and hollowing out the social safety net that ought to enable it to remain competitive with the East.

Innovation: The Key to Staying on Top

Ultimately, the key to staying on top is innovation, both in ideas for new products that solve new problems and in the way business is done. Different companies and products have succeeded or maintained success in recent years for different reasons. As discussed in

Chapter 10/Whirlpool survived because it armed itself to respond to the growing globalization of the world economy and to the rising importance of discount stores like Walmart and Costco. Maytag failed to sense the changes in the air, and it was eventually driven out of the marketplace. China manufactures more than a billion watches a year, but many Chinese are obsessed with buying watches from Switzerland, which in fact dominates the world market in terms of value. Apple sells more in terms of value in China than any Chinese computer manufacturer, despite the fact that Chinese computers are less expensive. In short, products that hold their place in the market need to be unique, either in terms of ingenuity or in getting the job done faster, better, and at less expense than anyone else's products. The key to achieving that is innovation. In a sense, innovation can be summed up by the tag line from the old *Star Trek* television series: ". . . To boldly go where no man has gone before."

While it often comes from the young, innovation is not really tied to an executive's age but more to his or her intellectual ability to understand the different challenges and to come up with intelligent solutions for the brave new world that is taking shape around him or her. Courage to take risks and to try to accomplish the impossible counts more than anything else. Guan Tongxian is a case in point.

Guan Tongxian and the Zhenhua Port Machinery Company

At 59, Guan was ready to step down after a difficult career as a government bureaucrat. Instead of retiring, though, he agreed to set up a private company to manufacture equipment for the port of Shanghai. China, facing a manufacturing boom, needed cranes to handle the increased flow of maritime traffic resulting from its enormous economic expansion. Guan had spent his life around cranes and was all too aware that the ones being manufactured in China were so shoddy that the major ports were being forced to import from Europe. With a small group of colleagues, Guan created the Zhenhua Port Machinery Company (ZPMC), a subsidiary of the China Central Communications Company. ZPMC had never actually manufactured a crane on its own, but the charismatic Guan was so persuasive that the Port of Vancouver in Canada agreed to an advance purchase in 1991, before the company had actually been put together. ZPMC was officially launched a short while later in 1992.

The parts that go into the cranes used to handle container traffic are generally too large to be transported over land. ZPMC had the advantage of access to a large amount of waterfront property on Changxing Island at the mouth of the Yangtze River, about an hour from Shanghai. The company set up a huge construction area along two miles of waterfront and an industrial terminal with a dock that extended one mile.

Guan insisted both on quality and on building the ZPMC brand, and the company's cranes quickly saturated the market in China. Guan was selling cranes to Chinese ports and to ports outside China, but he soon realized that he was going to have to put an added emphasis on expanding internationally if he wanted to keep growing. He targeted the ports on the receiving end of the shipping lanes used to transport Chinese manufactured goods.

Guan faced a dilemma, though. The fully assembled cranes appeared too huge to ship by sea, yet ZPMC's cranes were more affordable than those of foreign competitors precisely because labor costs for the company's 45,000 Chinese workers were low. Training a European or U.S. labor force to assemble the cranes in a foreign port would take too long and would in any case be prohibitively expensive. Sending a Chinese labor force to do the job in Europe or the United States would wipe out any cost advantage as well. Guan realized that he would also have to pay stiff fees simply to stockpile the different parts of the cranes until they could be assembled. The project looked like a nightmare to everyone except Guan, who announced that he would fully assemble the cranes in China and then ship them to the acquiring port. The idea sounded ludicrous to Guan's competitors. It had never been done before. The cranes were so tall and heavy, it was reasoned, that the weight would capsize any ship carrying them.

As Guan was to demonstrate, though, the current climate in China encourages thinking big. Guan had a ship retrofitted to take on the cranes and managed to handle the shipment and installation successfully according to plan. With most Chinese ports already equipped with ZPMC's cranes, the company followed up its initial contract with Vancouver with contracts to build cranes for Miami, Florida, and then Antwerp, Belgium, and finally Hamburg, Germany. The German sale was considered crucial because until ZPMC's appearance on the scene, Germany had dominated the market for high-quality cranes.

In the end, ZPMC's cranes were not only as good as or better than the German models, but they were also considerably less expensive. By the time that Guan finally accepted retirement in his mid-70s in 2010, ZPMC—which had by then changed its name to Zhenhua Heavy Industries Group—controlled more than 60 percent of the world market for large harbor cranes.

Not content to simply copy Western-style cranes, the company also made major advances in R&D. For example, it launched an ocean-going crane capable of lifting 4,000 tons, and no sooner had the new giant proved its effectiveness than the indefatigable Guan announced that he would build an even bigger one capable of lifting 7,000 tons. While most water-borne cranes are too top-heavy to risk going far from land, the ZPMC design enabled the crane to rotate and align its boom with the ship's deck, thus making it more seaworthy. Another company initiative was to design the first dockside crane capable of lifting two 40-foot cargo containers at the same time.

In 1995, the company established its own shipping company with 24 vessels to carry cranes around the world. A decade later, it had sold cranes to at least 73 countries. A video running on YouTube showed a ZPMC ship carrying six cranes.

From building cranes, ZPMC expanded into steel girders and other types of structural materials for major architectural projects. ZPMC's ultimate coup was the contract it won to replace key parts of San Francisco's Bay Bridge, which had been damaged in a 1989 earthquake. ZPMC's part in the reconstruction involved 450,000 tons of steel. According to the *New York Times*, California state officials turned down federal funding for the project precisely because it would have demanded that the steel parts be produced in the United States at considerably higher cost. The officials were pleasantly surprised by the quality of ZPMC's work, but even more, they estimated that the state had saved $400 million by turning to the Chinese to do the work.

Price played an important part, but the real reasons behind Guan Tongxian's success were a readiness to think big, a willingness to try the impossible, and the courage to follow through on an idea. Before he retired, Guan had ZPMC sign an agreement with Shanghai's Maritime University. The company and the university would collaborate on training, scientific cooperation, and the sharing of resources. In addition, ZPMC agreed to pay full salaries for selected employees to do postgraduate work for a year. "Students need to strengthen their theoretical knowledge," Guan announced when the deal was signed. "It is the foundation of their future work."

Innovation and R&D

Not all Chinese companies are as innovative as ZPMC. As pointed out in Chapter 4, the giant Chinese television manufacturer TCL relied on efficient management rather than its own R&D to turn around floundering companies with otherwise interesting products. As long as the existing technology remained unchanged, TCL's formula worked.

The lack of R&D, however, meant that TCL was taken by surprise when flat screen TVs suddenly entered the market. Without their own flatscreen technology, TCL was condemned to remain six months behind the market curve. In contrast, Huawei (discussed in Chapter 3) invested heavily in R&D and managed to stay ahead of its competition. It was not surprised by market changes because it was in a sense helping to define the market thanks to its R&D. When some countries, notably the United States, balked at giving a Chinese company access to their sensitive communications systems, the pressure to let Huawei into the market was intense, not just because Huawei was cheaper and more flexible but also because its extensive R&D began producing technology that do more than the competition.

Most Chinese companies fall somewhere between these two extremes of not doing any R&D and doing a great deal. Many companies understand the importance of innovation but lack the finances and the depth to provide the kind of massive R&D facilities available to large American corporations.

The solution in China, where manpower and technical expertise are less expensive than in the West, is to develop a lean, progressive R&D component that is often supported by a technician on the site. Han's Laser, for instance—as discussed in Chapter 9—assigned a technician with each of its laser marking machines to file daily reports and fix problems as they arose. The strategy meant that

Han's Laser could eliminate a great deal of expensive factory testing and could also offer a basic model that could be gradually adapted to the customer's true needs. The end result was a machine that was gradually tailor-made to better suit each specific situation. It turned out to be a more effective approach than a one-size-fits-all design that would have only partially met each customer's requirements.

As Han's Laser progressively adapted its machines, it was able to improve its basic design. Between 1996 and 1999, the company made more than 3,000 improvements to its original machine. Delivery to customers was faster. Cash flow was substantially improved. Service was immediate. Customer satisfaction and loyalty reflected the fact that having a technician on the scene increased brand loyalty and a sense that the company actually cared about each individual client.

Other Ways to Innovate

Not all innovation is in the product. Occasionally, tweaking the business model can lead to a dramatic change. In the early 1990s, China International Marine Containers (CIMC) imported its production line of 10,000 containers a year from Germany. Over the next five years, CIMC began producing its own containers, and its technicians began applying technology borrowed from the auto industry. By 1996, the company had increased production by 2000 percent, making CIMC the world's largest producer of shipping containers. In fact, by 1996, CIMC was producing one out of every five new shipping containers in use around the world. It progressed far enough to establish its own R&D center in 1997. One of its first innovations was to replace the expensive aluminum used in refrigerated containers with a specially treated steel at a substantial cost savings. The development, done in partnership with Germany (which licensed the steel treatment technology to CIMC), resulted in a substantial increase in the cost-effectiveness of the containers. CIMC had evolved from copying the West to working in collaboration as an equal partner with Western companies.

Solar panels emerged as another area where an innovative approach paid off. A major Chinese solar panel producer managed to avoid the expensive turn-key cost of setting up a solar production plant by carefully identifying which key components and assemblies could be produced more cost-effectively by foreign suppliers. It then streamlined less critical production by local suppliers or its own in-house equipment. As a result, the company was able to cut its capital expenditure by more than 60 percent. This hybrid approach, aimed at obtaining the maximum effectiveness from limited investment resources, is increasingly common for Chinese companies in the private sector.

A third approach to innovation is to emphasize rapid response to problems in the field and quickly adapt products to new local requirements. In a sense, it is an application in business of the old Chinese adage that change presents opportunity. An illustration (discussed in Chapter 10) is Haier's response to rural washing machine buyers whose machines had become clogged with mud when they used the machines to clean potatoes and peanuts. While a typical technical representative might have scolded the peasants and told them that the machine couldn't handle mud, Haier saw a new sales opportunity. It quickly adjusted its machines and began advertising their new capacity to wash vegetables as well as clothes. The choice between buying Haier or a competing brand was soon obvious to most rural buyers.

When Chinese mobile phone manufacturers realized that Chinese youth often like to use their phones as portable televisions and music players in noisy places, Chinese companies responded to the new market immediately by equipping their phones with six to eight speakers. This gave them an advantage that immediately snatched the market lead from foreign-made phones that many Chinese youth found too limited for their contemporary culture.

Ultimately, however, Chinese entrepreneurs count heavily on speed and rapid product innovation. In the year before the 2008 Olympics in Beijing, the Chinese mobile phone company Tianyu produced no less than 100 new models, including one fashioned to reflect the "Bird's Nest" and "Water Cube" Olympic sites.

In the final analysis, the reason Chinese companies are innovative is that they need to be in order to survive. To stay ahead of the competition in the fast, highly competitive Chinese market, they are driven to develop lean and ultra-dynamic strategies. For the most part, the market in China is so chaotic that they do not have to worry about protecting an established brand identity, so they are free to let the customer do the product testing. If it doesn't work, they simply sell a different product under a different name. Some products are winners. Others are losers. Eventually, the best ones emerge, establish themselves, and become more sustainable. While the method may seem haphazard, it is actually very cost-effective. In a sense, it is a Darwinian approach to low-cost product development. And that goes for the companies that produce the products as well as sell them.

The downside is that as Chinese companies are increasingly forced to expand globally in search of new markets and to climb the value chain, they will eventually need to think in terms of developing recognized brands. If they want to secure the kind of innovation that has made companies like Apple, Google, Boeing, and others world leaders, they will need to invest in a deeper kind of R&D. That is already happening. China is placing an enormous emphasis on education.

Like everyone else, the Chinese are going to find that they also need to change the way they do business in order to respond to the evolving global environment. R&D at a more complex level will inevitably lead the Chinese, like everyone else, to want to protect their intellectual property. That is, in fact, already beginning to happen in some industries. The old days of widespread piracy are gradually fading now that China is on the point of surpassing the United States in patent applications, but China still has a long way to go when it comes to protecting intellectual property.

The Case of the Internet

Ironically, the area in which China is already outpacing the United States, at least in terms of market size, is the Internet. In the United States, roughly 240 million people were connected to the Internet in 2010. In China, the figure was more than 420 million, and it increased to 457 million over a six-month period. Because of relative size, penetration in China is still only about half what it is in the United States—34.3 percent in China, compared to 77.3 percent in the United States—but the potential for expansion in China is also much greater, which gives Chinese programmers an incentive to innovate, leapfrogging on the technology already developed in the West.

The two leading Chinese Internet companies, Tencent and Baidu, have market capitalizations considerably smaller than the leading U.S. brands. Tencent had $39.7 billion compared to $190.8 billion for Google, and Baidu had $25.7 billion compared to $81.2 billion for Amazon. But the profit margins in China are much greater than they are in the United States. Baidu had a profit margin of 47.5 percent compared to only 29.21 percent for Google, and Tencent had a net profit margin of 40.99 percent compared to 19.69 percent for eBay.

In 2003, eBay entered the Chinese market and bought a share of the Chinese auction site EachNet. eBay controlled 79 percent of China's online retail market at the time. By 2005, eBay's share had dropped to 29 percent of the market. In 2009, Google's market share in China peaked at 43 percent, compared to 56 percent for

Baidu, and in 2010, Google closed down its mainland operations and channeled its search traffic through Hong Kong.

Like everyone else, Chinese companies face a piracy problem over the Internet, but again, Chinese companies have turned to innovative solutions to the problem.

Convincing Chinese Users to Pay Online

When it turned out that many Chinese were skeptical about using credit cards online, Chinese companies responded by distributing prepaid cards for use on the Internet for sale by local merchants. The prepaid cards can be bought by teenagers and used to participate in online games. Mobile phone companies also set up systems for online bill payment with an easy-to-use single itemized bill at the end of the month. Alipay, an escrow facility, has provided a number of formulas for its 550 million registered users, who now engage in some 8.5 million online transactions a day. These tactics made it even harder for foreign companies to compete in the Chinese Internet market.

To overcome the reluctance to pay for Internet content, Tencent in 2003 instituted its QQ show, a free virtual game in which customers participate via their online avatars. Each avatar gets access to 100 basic sets of clothing. To get more stylish clothing, players need to invest $1.50 a month to join the "Red Diamond Club," which gives them access to 50,000 outfits, hairstyles, and accessories. Several million people have signed up for the service so far.

The market for virtual goods was developed even further in The Legend of Mir, an online multiplayer game produced by the Chinese company Shanda Interactive Entertainment. In the game, players can obtain virtual weapons and equipment either by scoring points through the game or buying them online. More than 40 different swords featured in Kung Fu movies are available. Customers don't have to pay, but eventually, they want to.

At least 42.6 percent of China's Internet users, nearly 195 million people, use the Internet to read literature, mostly over smartphones on their way to or from work. Shanda Literature—a Chinese online publisher that is part of Shanda Interactive Entertainment—lets readers download original fiction at the rate of 100,000 words for 30 to 50 cents. Anyone who wants to write can contribute to Shanda Literature's website. If a work attracts a large number of readers, Shanda offers to buy the copyright and publish the work on its VIP site, which offers a few chapters of a novel for free and then requests payment for the entire novel. Profits are split equally between the company and the writer. The success of Shanda and similar sites has led to a renaissance in publishing in China. As publisher Tim O'Reilly puts it, "The enemy of the author is not piracy, but obscurity."

The Story of Hali-Power

Of course, the eventual goal of every company manager is to compete at the high end of the value chain. Most of the components of today's iPad are manufactured in China, but the idea behind the machine was born in the United States. China will feel that it has arrived only when the original concepts as well as the finished products actually originate in China.

As the case of battery maker Hali-power demonstrates, that day may not be far off. Mobile phones constitute the single most ubiquitous element of technology in China. In 2003, a Chinese entrepreneur, Harry Zhu, realized that the heart of China's mobile phones—the crucial piece that makes the phone actually work, or stop working—is not its integrated circuit but the battery. At the time, 90 percent of the mobile phone batteries in the world were manufactured in Japan. Zhu decided to get into the business and launch Hali-power.

Mobile phone batteries do not involve complicated technology, and the cost of entering the market is relatively low. Hali-power started with around 100 employees, only a half-dozen of whom had any technical training. Zhu, however, was obsessed with producing high-quality batteries. The market in China was chaotic when it came to quality control, so Zhu decided to focus on Italy and Norway. His goal was to sell backup batteries for Nokia and other phones. Buyers were more likely to take a chance on a less expensive backup, since it was intended only as a secondary precaution in case the manufacturer's original battery accidentally ran down.

Within a year, Hali-power had racked up sales of $1.5 million, but the company was barely staying afloat. Zhu realized that his problem was the lack of a recognizable brand and the fact that his batteries were indistinguishable from those of any other manufacturer. The development of battery-dependent digital cameras gave the company another boost, but Zhu realized that what he really needed was brand recognition. He invested in a costly distribution network and in advertising, but the company was still having trouble taking off. When a potential customer offered a large order on the condition that he could use his own brand instead of Hali-power's, Zhu turned him down. He reasoned that if he built a new factory to handle the order, the customer would have him at its mercy for the next order, since he wouldn't be able to leave the factory idle.

The introduction of Apple's iPod, iPhone, and iPad was the break that Hali-power needed. Zhu had resolutely insisted on maintaining high production standards, which made him attractive to Apple. When he approached Apple about producing components, Apple accepted his offer. Even before Apple gave its final approval, Zhu invested RMB 300,000 in R&D to meet Apple's requirements and hired graphic and industrial designers. Each new project meant that Hali-power had to spend between RMB 500,000 and RMB 1 million in R&D. But by then, Harry was employing 500 people, with 90 assigned to R&D. The company had already registered 67 patents. The company's breakthrough invention, marketed under its brand MiLi, was its Power Pico Projector, which was essentially a battery that not only served as an extended protective case for the iPhone but also contained a miniature laser projector that enabled the iPhone to project films and sales presentations on a wall. The product slogan is "Show your life anytime and anywhere."

Zhu's key insight was that although battery technology is relatively simple, it is the distinctive benefit that comes from the design and user interface that provides an advantage. It is a philosophy that Apple's Steve Jobs had espoused all along. The longer reaching lesson in Hali-power's case is that innovation, accompanied by brand development, is essential if a company wants to distinguish itself from the competition, especially when it is dealing with a consumer product that is easy to copy. As Hali-power discovered, building a brand does not come cheap, and it requires determination and a long-term vision by a company's CEO to stick to the course. Quality was an essential element in Hali-power's connection to Apple, but it was really Hali-power's unique design and original thinking that went into extending the batteries' capabilities beyond the ordinary that made the company a winner. That also did not come cheap, and it also required foresight and vision from the company's CEO.

In producing its unique design, Hali-power achieved the status of having one of America's leading consumer technology companies treat it as a respected partner. In a sense, Hali-power had crossed a threshold and achieved maturity in doing so.

Not all Chinese companies have managed to accomplish that, but it is clear that China, and more importantly Chinese companies, have managed to make astonishing progress in an amazingly short period of time. They have learned an enormous amount along the way. While some Western companies have allowed themselves to become complacent with respect both to markets and the customers that they ultimately depend on, the Chinese are lean, hungry, and ready to step into the breach, and they do so with verve and imagination. According to the rules of capitalism—at least those preached in the West—that is the way it should be. China, in a sense, represents today's dynamic force for renewal. Competition is what the game is about, and in a world increasingly defined by technology, that means investing in people and knowledge. We are all going to have to act and think smarter if we do not want to fall by the wayside.

T H I R T E E N

The Implications for China and the Rest of the World

E Pluribus Unum ("Out of many, one")
—Motto on the Great Seal of the United States and on most U.S. coins

GM and the Volt: A Deal with China?

EXECUTIVES AT General Motors, the U.S. automobile giant, faced a dilemma. After skirting bankruptcy in the financial crisis and being forced to accept a U.S. government bailout, the company seemed on its way to full recovery. GM had been slow to develop a clean energy vehicle, but it now had the Chevrolet Volt, a nifty plug-in hybrid that relied on both batteries and a small gasoline-powered electric generator to extend its range to around 350 miles. GM was counting on the Volt to regain territory lost to Toyota's pioneering hybrid Prius.

One of the Volt's major drawbacks was that it cost more than $40,000. Even with buyers receiving a federal tax credit of $7,000, the price was high enough to make many Americans pause before purchasing a car that depended on a relatively new technology—especially with the U.S. economy showing unprecedented volatility and Wall Street analysts pondering the likelihood of a double-dip recession. GM was initially hoping to sell up to 10,000 Volts in the U.S. market. To any realist in the automobile business, though, the real market to aim for was China, where enthusiastic drivers had purchased 17 million cars in 2010.

The China market looked even more attractive to GM because the Chinese government, anxious to wean itself from imported oil, was offering subsidies of up to $19,300 for each new electric vehicle, which promised to cut the Volt's selling price in half. The dilemma that GM faced, however, was that the Chinese government was demanding something in exchange before the Volt could qualify for the subsidy. It wanted GM to transfer information on one of the Volt's three main technologies to a joint venture with a Chinese company. Without access to GM's technology, there would be no subsidy and no deal.

STRONG COMPETITION FOR GM

GM executives were understandably upset, but they were also concerned about possible competition from Ford and other automobile companies entering the market. Daimler AG, manufacturer of the venerable Mercedes-Benz, had created a joint venture, called Beijing Benz Automotive Co., Ltd., with a new cutting-edge factory capable of turning out 100,000 new cars a year. In addition, Sweden's high-end luxury car company, Volvo, was courting Chinese investors in desperate hopes of avoiding bankruptcy.

The final straw may have been Toyota's announcement in 2011 that it would soon begin manufacturing parts in China for its new Prius Plug-in, a car designed to compete with the Volt.

A HARD BARGAIN AND A DIFFICULT DECISION

Although GM was clearly rankled by Chinese demands and tempted to reject the Chinese offer regarding the Volt out of hand, there were, in fact, powerful arguments for agreeing to it. To begin with, the market in China was so huge that it promised to help sales of the Volt reach a critical mass almost immediately. A sudden rush in orders from China would not only establish the car as a winner but would enable economies of scale that could drive down the price for cars sold in the U.S. and Western European markets. In addition, GM planned to produce the Volt in Michigan, which would create a badly needed boost in employment there.

If GM refused the deal, the likelihood was that the Chinese would be able to get the technology they wanted anyway. Given China's engineering and manufacturing expertise, it would be relatively easy to reverse-engineer the Volt and obtain its secrets without GM's help.

If GM went along with the Chinese and made a success in the China market on the Volt, the car stood a good chance of emerging as a winner. If not, the Volt risked becoming a once promising contender that never quite made it, and a year or so down the line, its breakthrough technology would begin to look dated.

The most profitable course for GM was to take advantage of the immediate market opportunity with China and then put all its energy into innovating faster than anyone else. If GM could offer better value and design than anyone else, it stood a good chance of maintaining a leading position, even if others tried to copy its technology. (An example was the Swiss watch industry, which continued to sell extremely expensive watches in China despite the fact that local manufacturers had flooded the market with cheap watches that were often just as accurate at telling time.)

The hardball tactics of the Chinese with GM are another sign of a much larger shift in economic reality that is taking place thanks to globalization. As wealth and influence shift to the emerging economies, it is natural that shrewd businesspeople will leverage their assets to get the maximum advantage possible. For the Chinese, an entry pass into China's internal market is a privilege that is not to be given away lightly and that can be traded for something of value—in this case, access to technology.

The Chinese feel that there are plenty of examples in history in which the West forced China to accept conditions that were largely to the West's advantage. What has changed now is the relationship between wealthy countries and the developing world. The term *developing* used to be a euphemism for "undeveloped" or "underdeveloped" but, in fact, China and India—which used to be lumped in with the world's poorest nations—have made substantial progress and no longer completely qualify as undeveloped. China actually fits into both camps, as part of the developing and developed sectors. Parts of China's interior provinces remain extremely poor and still need substantial help, but the booming industrial cities along the coast are beginning to look like many cities in Europe or the United States (and in some cases, better). China might have seemed backward in the past, but these days, the country is sending thousands of students to some of the best universities and business schools in the world. And when it comes to strategy, the Chinese are showing both sophistication and an uncanny aptitude for business that can be quite sobering.

The Train Is Leaving the Station

Only a few of the Chinese companies described in this book can be described as unqualified successes at the time of this writing. Huawei Technologies has emerged as the world's second largest producer of telecommunications equipment. Most of the world's leading telecommunications companies use its equipment, and it has been courted by AT&T and Sprint Nextel. If it had not been for objections from the Pentagon and the U.S. National Security Agency (discussed in Chapter 3), Huawei might have been involved in designing the next generation of communications equipment in the United States. Another company discussed in this book, Haier, is now one of the world's top manufacturers of home appliances and one of the few Chinese companies besides Lenovo that has managed to successfully establish its own brand. Lenovo itself has had its ups and down, but it is generally acknowledged as one of the leading producers of powerful, high-quality laptop computers for much of the world, especially developing countries. Meanwhile, after its initial failed attempt to buy Unocal, CNOOC has emerged as a solid player in the world energy market. Most of the other companies discussed in this book are potential players, and it remains to be seen how they will stand the test of time.

While not every Chinese company can claim success yet, China is clearly on a roll. As one Western executive noted, "The train has left the station. There is still time to climb on board, but that won't be the case for long."

Despite scare talk of China taking over the world economy, the Chinese realize themselves that they still have a long way to go. "We will probably be copying for the next decade," a Chinese executive said candidly in a recent seminar. "It may take 50 years before a new generation can break free from its parents and think on its own."

Fears of China's impact on the U.S. economy also tend to be exaggerated. A recent study by the Federal Reserve Bank of San Francisco pointed out that 55 cents out of every dollar spent in the United States on imports from China goes to an American company. The Chinese share of that dollar is only 45 cents. In addition, the profits in the United States from doing business with China are much greater than they are from business with any other country. The San Francisco study points out that American companies retain only an average of 36 cents on the dollar for goods imported from other foreign countries. The study also points out that only about 13.9 percent of U.S. consumer spending is devoted to exports, and of that, only 1.9 percent is Chinese.

While low-cost labor in China has managed to stave off inflation in the West, the increased buying power of China's burgeoning new middle class is also managing to inject new life into various aspects of Western economies. Middle-class Chinese tourists have flooded into major Western cities, anxious to buy luxury goods, and the fascination with Western brands has given new energy to some companies that risked fading into obscurity. Purchases by Chinese tourists in France, much of it in Paris, added up to $890 million in 2010—more than double the expenditure in 2009. According to Kelvin Chan, writing in the *New York Times,* China could become the second largest market for luxury goods this year. And the rush by Chinese tourists to buy expensive real estate in New York and major European cities has reinvigorated the market.

The need to construct and update nearly every aspect of China's infrastructure has led to a similar surge of orders for resources and technical skills from many Western companies ranging from cement and steel to telecommunications, data management, and traffic control.

Lessons to Be Learned by China

While it's easy to be dazzled by China's amazing economic growth, Chinese business remains vulnerable on a number of scores. Sudden success can lead to a certain arrogance, which can undercut the very qualities that have made some entrepreneurs so successful. Many of China's self-made millionaires were self-taught. They were opportunistic, operated on instinct, and took enormous risks. That kind of risk taking is easy when there is nothing to lose; it can be dangerous when a company reaches the size needed to become multinational. Running an international company is also much more complex than operating in a familiar market. To succeed on a global scale, Chinese companies will need to institute systems that enable management to have an accurate vision over all aspects of production and distribution, but which are still flexible enough to allow them to remain creative and innovative.

To compete effectively on a global basis, these companies need to develop global human resources able to work effectively in different cultures and geographic regions. A genuine understanding of foreign markets usually requires employing executives from different nationalities and getting the entire, diverse organization to work as a team. Until now, Chinese companies have had considerable difficulty trying to get that kind of synergy to work. Many Chinese managers find it difficult to function in a non-Chinese cultural environment, and in contrast to most leading multinationals these days, few Chinese companies hire foreign executives for senior *Note* management positions.

Speed is essential to competing effectively in China, and Chinese mangers clearly score well in this regard, but the accelerating pace of business in China also means that there is less time to think and reflect. This poses a significant danger to both the personal development of China's managers and to the Chinese economy itself. When there is little time to think, it is difficult to know whether success is the result of leadership ability and business acumen or whether it is from luck and fortunate market conditions. The distinction has important implications when it comes to what one learns from experience and how the validity of a business strategy is evaluated. Managers may become convinced that their strategies are invincible, when in fact their success resulted only from a combination of favorable market factors that may change unexpectedly, with serious consequences for their companies. Arrogance is particularly dangerous in China's case because competitors are likely to think that China's impressive growth has come at their expense. The antidotes for arrogance are reflection and introspection, both of which require taking the time to think and to objectively analyze the factors affecting a company's growth. Reflection, introspection, and time are also necessary to develop a long-term strategy for the future.

An objective assessment of the long-term costs of short-term profits is also needed, especially when it comes to providing an overall direction to China's economy and quality of life. Much of the industry that is feeding China's accelerated growth produces toxic waste and social disruption. For example, ordinary people are uprooted to make way for urban modernization projects. Real estate speculation results in towns being built and then virtually abandoned because no one can afford to live in them. Rural farmers find their land poisoned by pollution from nearby coal mines or factories. Provincial authorities often look the other way because industrial development has been given a priority over the rights of individual peasants. Petitioners who want to express grievances against local officials are denied access to government offices or are beaten until they withdraw their complaints. All of this contributes to social unrest and promises problems in the future.

Those Chinese who can afford it often end up buying property outside China as a precaution or simply to have somewhere else to go where the quality of life is more secure, less polluted, and more bearable.

Structurally, China remains very much a hierarchical society, with a top-down centralized authority that still believes in imposing its vision of the future and in controlling information that clashes with that vision. China's old guard has only limited tolerance for dissent. This is at a time when most global companies realize that the world economy is changing so fast that the old-fashioned form of top-down management simply can't react fast enough to keep pace with new developments.

The free flow of information is essential to the kind of financial infrastructure needed to support sustainable growth, yet authorities continue to regard economic information as a state secret that needs to be tightly controlled for reasons of national security.

To be truly competitive, businesses need to be innovative and to be constantly questioning themselves. In short, they need the kind of executives who can think independently outside the box. Censorship and the punishment of dissidents, no matter how outrageously the dissidents may behave, hardly encourages deviation from the accepted norm. The result is that creativity is defined by the lowest common denominator.

What the West Has to Learn

It does not take much imagination to see that sooner or later, China will inevitably emerge as a leading world power. The question is whether the West will be able to keep up. From a business perspective, it is clear that CEOs in the West need to reevaluate how they see Asia. Many multinationals are doing that now, and the best have created divisions that focus solely on China.

The early mistake made by most multinationals was to see other Western multinationals as their primary competition. In the process, they underestimated just how fast China was developing. For Western companies, China was seen as a place to dump products no longer considered cutting-edge enough to make it in Western markets. Whirlpool's joint venture with Guangdong Kelon (discussed in Chapter 10) tried to sell refrigerators that still used ozone-damaging Freon as a coolant, thinking that the Chinese wouldn't know the difference. The mistake damaged the joint venture and cost millions. In another case, Kodak thought that it could continue to sell photographic film in China while the rest of the world went digital. It seriously misjudged the market and took significant losses as a result.

If the Chinese have trouble understanding Western culture, Western companies have just as much trouble understanding China. Western sales campaigns that are merely translated into Chinese rarely work because the cultural values and aspirations are often different, whether the product is a washing machine being sold in a rural area or life insurance. Locally manufactured Chinese products tend to sell in China, even if they are less sophisticated than Western ones, simply because the Chinese companies speak the language and understand the culture better. Chinese companies take the time to develop credibility in rural areas, and then they approach the major cities. Most Western multinationals, in contrast, rarely make it out of the major cities into the countryside. These multinationals need to rethink their value proposition and strategy. Customer needs and the market environment are fundamentally different in China. Blindly basing a sales and distribution strategy on what is done in Europe or America is not likely to work. It is difficult to see the world through the eyes of local customers, but that is exactly what is needed to compete in local markets.

That said, there is no reason why Western companies cannot compete and obtain a significant position in China's market. The best strategy for the multinationals is not only to aim at the top tier of the market but also to hit the middle tier where pricing counts, margins are lower, and the competition from local Chinese companies is likely to be the fiercest. The enterprise may be costly at first, but taking the leap is the fastest and best way to learn how Chinese companies compete in this segment. The mid-tier segment in China is huge. Leveraging economy of scale in mid-tier segments helps multinational companies to compete in China as well as globally. Companies in the middle segment of the China market are evolving quickly, and the market is changing rapidly. Multinational companies often underestimate how rapidly these local competitors develop and how quickly they are able to challenge market leaders. The high-end niches make it easy to fall victim to pride and complacency. Experience shows that most companies need to move faster than they initially thought necessary, and even then, the chances are that they will not be fast enough.

Over time, local markets merge with the higher tiers both in technology and price. The "China price" soon becomes the "global price." Local markets are the breeding ground for the future global competitors.

Just as China will inevitably be forced to go through structural changes in order to be able to compete internationally, the West is going to have to change structurally and to reeducate itself about global competition. The West, and especially the United States, argued forcefully for a global free market economy. Now that they have one, the key to future success for any company will be its ability to innovate and to produce products that are universally considered to be good value for the money. Apple is a prime example. What kept Apple from being just another computer company was its capacity to keep coming up with new products and new ideas. If it were not for the iPod, the iPad, and the iPhone, and the fact that the company brought superior design and aesthetics to otherwise average products, Apple would probably not be in business today. Apple products have never been cheap, but nevertheless, when Steve Jobs died, the Chinese erected shrines in his memory. Apple's sales in China were worth more than the sales of all China's other computers combined.

Creative thinking comes from societies in which education and new ideas are a priority, and in which people feel secure enough about the future to take chances with their careers and try new ideas. As more wealth is transferred from the rich countries to emerging economies, the natural trend is for companies to make up for the lost revenue at home by cutting costs. Inevitably, cuts in education and the social safety net follow. When the public is anxious about its future, it tends to hunker down and be less willing to take chances. As a result, the society becomes less competitive in the global marketplace. For the West to remain competitive, it needs to reverse both trends.

East and West

In the end, China's growing status as a major power could produce a return to the kind of superpower rivalry that characterized the Cold War. On the other hand, we could see a gradual evolution to a more integrated world, in which China's economic growth actually produces new opportunities for everyone.

For the moment, we seem on course for the latter option. China's economic future is already heavily intertwined with that of the West. An economic crisis in the West is likely to have serious repercussions in China, and likewise, disruption in China would have serious effects for most Western businesses that now depend on the global supply chain. In a sense, the world economy is already inextricably linked together.

China clearly sees the West's future affecting its own. In the first half of 2010, at least 30 percent of China's $64 billion investment in Europe was directed to countries where the euro was under threat. This included Greece, Spain, Portugal, and Italy.

The fact is that the more China buys into the rest of the world, the more China's fate is linked to that part of the world in which it has invested, and the more its interests are likely to be aligned with the common good. In the end, like it or not, we are all in it together.

The result is likely to be a more equal playing field. From now on, the company that succeeds will be the one that establishes the most credible brand, senses most clearly what the customer wants, and offers the best value for the money, which is the way it should be.

As China's companies increasingly compete in the global economy, it is natural that the shifting balance of power will generate fear in those groups concerned that China's gain will be their loss. But fear or no fear, like it or not, the globalization of China's companies is already becoming a reality. In a frequently repeated metaphor (used already in this chapter), the train has left the station. It is only beginning to pick up speed. It is still possible to catch it, but it won't be for long. Its destination should be clear to anyone objectively assessing the flow of events in the global marketplace. One can either climb on board the train and face the new reality, taking advantage of the opportunities it presents, or one can stand idly on the station platform, pondering where the train is going and what to do next. By the time the last group of passengers wakes up, the train and the possibilities it offers will be long gone. There are three types of people: those who make things happen, those who watch things happen, and those who have no idea what happened. The choice is yours. Don't miss the train.

INDEX

ABOUT THE AUTHORS

WINTER NIE

For the last two decades, Winter Nie has researched and consulted with many of the world's leading multinational corporations in Asia, Europe, and the United States. She is a leading expert on contemporary Chinese enterprises, and is currently a professor at IMD, one of Europe's leading international business schools, located in Lausanne, Switzerland, where she regularly teaches classes attended by senior Chinese executives.

Born and raised in China, she did her graduate studies in the United States, and received her Ph.D. from the University of Utah. Her extensive experience working with the executives of the world's most successful multinationals as well as China's most dynamic companies gives her unique insights into the cultural differences that are shaping the aspirations and the reality of the new global economy.

Her previous book, *Made in China: Secrets of China's Dynamic Entrepreneurs*, demystified the success of China's newly created privately owned enterprises, and explained how they changed China's economy and produced today's economic miracle.

WILLIAM DOWELL

During a career spanning more than thirty years, William Dowell has reported on news events in nearly every corner of the globe, including nearly eight years spent in Asia. After stints reporting for

ABC News and NBC, he worked as a correspondent for *TIME* magazine for more than a decade, and ran *TIME*'s Hong Kong bureau shortly before the former colony's return to China's control. He is currently based in Geneva, Switzerland, where he continues to write on international affairs.

Abraham Lu provided research for *In the Shadow of the Dragon*, while based in Lausanne, as a research fellow at IMD. He currently lives and works in China.

P129 - Pay - $L63 to $125/week (½ of West pay)

Foxconn - many suicide (200 Mile wild peff ?city).-

Largest human migration in history)

P246 - Shr (turned out great

— Worth $2 billion (Revised by step-parent)

* [Blacks so much more to be killed in auto accident
than by Police (Fox)]

Kadlaw
a thr Letter